A TALE OF TWO CITIES

A TALE OF

This exhibition and catalogue were made possible by major grants from the National Endowment for the Humanities, the New York State Council on the Arts, and the Joe and Emily Lowe Foundation, Inc., as well as generous support from individual donors, the Peter Cats Foundation and the Estate of Jacob Perlow.

TWO CITIES

Jewish Life in Frankfurt and Istanbul 1750–1870

BY VIVIAN B. MANN

WITH ESSAYS BY
Robert Liberles and Joseph Hacker

WITH ENTRIES BY
Vivian B. Mann, Emily D. Bilski,
Martin S. Cohen, and Joseph Hacker

The Jewish Museum/NEW YORK

PHOTO CREDITS:
Color photography by Malcolm Varon
Black and white photography by Graydon Wood
COVER PHOTOGRAPHS
top: From the collection of historic
photographs of the Harvard Semitic Museum
bottom: **The Frankfurt Stadtarchiv**

Catalog designed by Peter Oldenburg
Prepared and Produced by Layla Productions
Inc., New York
Edited by Estelle Whelan
Typography by Precision Typographers, Inc.
Exhibition Designed by Leone Design, Inc., New York

Copyright © 1982 by
The Jewish Museum,
1109 Fifth Avenue, New York, New York 10028,
under the auspices of
The Jewish Theological Seminary of America.

Manufactured in the U.S.A.

ISBN: 0-87334-016-7

Library of Congress Cataloging in Publication Data

Main entry under title:
A Tale of two cities.
Bibliography: p. 167
1. Jews—Turkey—Istanbul—Exhibitions.
2. Jews—Germany—Frankfurt-am-Main—Exhibitions.
3. Istanbul (Turkey)—Social life and customs—Exhibitions. 4. Frankfurt-am-Main (Germany)—Social life
and customs—Exhibitions. I. Mann, Vivian B.
DS135.T8T34 1982   943'.41   82-17950

TABLE OF CONTENTS

Director's Forward

Attempting to convey the full range of ideas and experience that define Jewish culture poses simultaneously an opportunity and a challenge for The Jewish Museum. It is virtually impossible at any one time to offer to the visitor a single comprehensive view, yet the structure of the Museum and its rich collection do allow for consideration of a broad range of ideas within the context of individual exhibitions.

In *A Tale of Two Cities* the interaction of the Jewish people of the Diaspora with the cultural *milieux* of Frankfurt and Istanbul within a period of 120 years is examined. Artifacts, both borrowed and drawn from the Museum's collection, are assembled in order to illuminate the contrasting religious, artistic, and social perspectives of the Ashkenazi and Sephardi communities; together they reveal a complex tale of survival, continuity, and achievement.

In preparing the exhibition, the catalogue, and related educational programs, we have turned to several institutions, funding sources, and individuals, and we are grateful for the enthusiasm with which they have responded. Special thanks are due to The National Endowment for the Humanities, which provided the initial financial support, to the New York State Council on the Arts, and to the Joe and Emily Lowe Foundation, which furnished a generous matching grant. We are most thankful for further contributions from members of Congregation Shearith Israel, New York, as well as for the encouragement and generosity of the Peter Cats Foundation, Edith and Nash Aussenberg, Ruth Blumberg, Juliette Halouia, Mr. and Mrs. Leon Levy, and Ivan and Leila Schick. Additional thanks for support go to the Estate of Jacob Perlow, Mr. and Mrs. Fred Alcott, Mrs. Gladys Benbasat, Mr. and Mrs. Maurice Dana, Mr. and Mrs. Isaac El-Hassid, Louis N. Levy, Mr. and Mrs. Peter Neustadter, Fortuna and Felix Roth, Judge and Mrs. Abraham Sofaer, and Mr. and Mrs. Paul Yanowicz. The exhibition has provided an opportunity for the Museum to make closer contact with the Sephardi community of New York, and its response has been both stimulating and productive. Sephardic House at Shearith Israel has cooperated with the Museum in sponsoring joint events related to this exhibition in the upcoming program year. We hope this occasion marks the beginning of many more, similar ventures.

The success of an exhibition as ambitious as *A Tale of Two Cities* and of the activities surrounding it necessarily depends upon the generosity and expertise of individuals both within and outside the Museum. Particular credit goes to Vivian Mann, Curator of Judaica, who conceived the exhibition and whose knowledge and understanding of the objects have enabled her to interweave effectively many aesthetic, religious, and historical threads. She has been ably assisted by the staff of the Judaica Department, interns, and consultants. Foremost among them are Assistant Curator Emily Bilski, whose scholarly research and participation in all aspects of the exhibition have been invaluable; Exhibition Coordinator Karen Wilson, whose unstinting scholarly and organizational work did much to guarantee its success; and Administrative Assistant Sharon Makover, who contributed extraordinary dedication, good humor, and hard work. Intern Keren Whitman and Slide Librarian Reba Fishman generously gave time to the organizational aspects of the exhibition, and volunteer Research Associates Ruth Blumberg, Elizabeth Cats, and Naomi Strumpf, did important work in gathering information for the exhibition. To all of them we express our warmest gratitude.

The following colleagues contributed essays, advice, and information: Marc Angel, Esin Atil, Chaya Benjamin, Berthold Bilski, Richard Cohen, Walter Denny, Mark Epstein, Shifra Epstein, Solomon Gaon, Joseph Hacker, Rosemary Hoffmann, Esther Juhasz, Miriam Katz, Barbara Kirschenblatt-Gimblett, Robert S. Liberles, Abraham M. Mann, Michael Meyer, Alan W. Miller, Ismar Schorsch, Shlomo Spitzer, Norman Stillman, Yedida Stillman, Pilar Viladis, and Paul Walker. The kindness and enthusiasm with which they offered their expertise are deeply appreciated.

Without the generosity of the Library of The Jewish Theological Seminary of America, which lent many works, this exhibition would not have been possible. Particular thanks are due to Menachem Schmelzer, Librarian, for his continual guidance, and to Martin S. Cohen, Assistant to the Librarian, for writing catalogue entries. We also wish to thank Nadia Kahan, Manuscript Librarian, and Edith Degani, Administrative Librarian, for their help.

The Leo Baeck Institute, New York, provided invaluable access to archives and collection material related to the Frankfurt community. Fred Grubel, Director of the Institute, has been particularly helpful not only in lending materials but also in providing advice and cosponsorship of public programs. We especially thank Sybil Milton, and also Diane Spielmann, Jonathan Sperber, and Alene Pritchard of the Institute for their time and assistance.

Bringing forth rarely seen objects from the Museum's own storerooms requires the skill and work of many people. Special gratitude is owing to the Museum's volunteer textile staff: Ellen Abramson, Bernice Aisenson, Clara Mermelstein, Shlomith Goldberg, Linda Brainson, and Edith Ratner, who also helped with research on Frankfurt materials. These women have been ably supervised by the Museum's consultant on textile conservation, Judith Eisenberg. Conservator/Curator Norman Kleeblatt also consulted and helped prepare paintings and works on paper shown in the exhibition. We are particularly happy to acknowledge the important work of Virginia Strull, Julie Zeftel, Carol Weisz and Scott Spector in fund raising, of Margo Bloom in developing public programs, of Judith Siegal and Phyllis Greenspan in preparing school programs, of Rita Feigenbaum and her assistant Anne Driesse in facilitating loans, and of Ruth Dolkart, Philip Goldman, and the operations staff of the Museum in expediting the actual mounting of the exhibition.

We also extend special thanks to exhibition designer Lucian Leone and his assistant Dan Kershaw; Peter Oldenberg, who designed the catalogue, and Lori Stein, who produced it; photographers Malcolm Varon and Graydon Wood; Estelle Whelan, who served as both consultant and editor; and Syrl Silberman, Sid Darion, and Milton Krents, who helped produced television material related to the exhibition.

The separate histories of the Jewish communities of Frankfurt and Istanbul are brought to life through the objects that have been assembled in this exhibition. We offer a final word of thanks to all the lenders who have been willing to share their collections and thus to afford both the Museum staff and the public the pleasure of learning from them and enjoying their beauty.

Joan H. Rosenbaum
Director

8

Color Plates

No. 123 (right): *Havdalah* Candle and Spice Holder, Frankfurt, Jeremias Zobel, before 1731; No. 74 (center): Spice Box, Frankfurt (?), c. 1550, repairs and additions, 1641; No. 122: (left) Spice Box, Frankfurt, Rötger Herfurth, 1748–1776.

No. 57: Torah Curtain, probably Frankfurt, 1752–1753.

No. 116: Hanging Lamp for
Sabbath and Festivals,
Frankfurt, Johann Valentin
Schuler, 1680–1720.

No. 29: Scroll of Esther, Frankfurt, Jacob b. Bezalel, 1806–1807.

No. 196: Torah Curtain, Istanbul, c. 1735.

No. 163: Cushion Cover, Istanbul, late 17th or early 18th century.

No. 201: Torah Mantle, Turkey, 19th century; No. 202: Torah Shield, Turkey, 1863–1864; No. 203: *Rimmon* (right) Turkey, late 19th century; No. 204: *Rimmon* (left) Turkey, late 19th century.

No. 161: Ewer and Basin Used on Passover, Istanbul, early 19th century.

Introduction

BY Vivian B. Mann

One of the more paradoxical yet wonderful aspects of Jewish history is the fact that, though Jews have been scattered across many countries for more than 2,000 years, they have nevertheless felt bound to one another. Despite the diversity of cultures into which Jews have integrated themselves, they retain a sense of interconnectedness with Jews from elsewhere. The statement from the prayer for the New Moon that "All Israel [is] knit together" is literally true![1] Yet how different are the histories, the appearances, the homes, the customs, the mores of Jews settled in one area of the world from those of Jews settled elsewhere.

Today there are two major Jewish ethnic groups, the Ashkenazim and the Sephardim, in addition to other, smaller communities. Ashkenazim are called after the Hebrew word for Germany (ashkenaz). Individual Jews lived among Germans even in Roman times, though continuous Jewish settlement in northern France and the Rhineland dates back only to the ninth century. From this center Ashkenazim later migrated in great numbers to eastern Europe; in the nineteenth century many thousands came to the United States to form the largest group in the American Jewish community.

At nearly the same time that some Jews were founding communities on the banks of the Rhine, others were settling in Spain (sepharad in Hebrew). They and their descendants developed a rich culture, a synthesis of Judaism and aspects of Muslim and Christian Spanish culture. The expulsion of the Jews from Spain in 1492 and from Portugal in 1497 scattered the Sephardim to other areas of Europe, to the Near East, to North Africa, and, in smaller numbers, to the New World, where in 1654 they founded the first Jewish settlement in North America at Nieuw Amsterdam, later New York.

The events of World War II and its aftermath caused major upheavals in the patterns and history of Jewish life all over the world. Such prominent centers of Ashkenazi life as Frankfurt, Berlin, Vilna, and Warsaw, where Jews had lived for more than 1,000 years, were all destroyed. Today the Jewish communities of those cities either no longer survive or are minuscule, devoid of the creative vigor that characterized them in the past. A parallel disruption in the history of Sephardi Jewish life occurred after the founding of the state of Israel in 1948. Jews in Islamic lands became the focus of increased hostility and repressive measures. As a result, most left their homes and migrated to Israel or to the United States.

There have consequently been significant demographic changes in the American Jewish community, as well as concomitantly greater interest in Sephardi culture in the United States. The Jewish Museum of New York has therefore mounted the exhibition *A Tale of Two Cities,* in recognition of the pluralistic nature of the American Jewish community and in order that the viewer may understand both the ties that bind all Jews together and the religious and cultural differences that distinguish among them. Additionally, the Jewish Museum is mounting *A Tale of Two Cities* because it believes in the power of objects, of works of art, to speak to the viewer. From works of Jewish ceremonial art one can learn of the individual's devotion to his faith and how he expressed that dedication; from a group of synagogue furnishings, one can understand the life of a community. And, in the varied range of ceremonial objects used by Ashkenazim and Sephardim, one can see reflected that paradoxical combination of unity and diversity that characterizes the Jewish people as a whole.

An examination of the range of ceremonial objects created over the centuries for use by Jews in the practice of their religion reveals that some types of objects have long histories and are mentioned in early texts, whereas others are relative newcomers and became popular only in the last few hundred years.[2] Furthermore, although some Jewish ceremonial objects are topics of lengthy discussions by the rabbis in the Mishnah, in the Talmud, and in later halakhic literature, others, which are today taken for granted and whose use is considered essential to the celebration of holidays or of events in the life cycle are discussed briefly or not at all.[3] In many instances halakhic discussions of "newcomers" was a consequence of their use by the general Jewish population and not the result of divine commands for their incorporation into Jewish ritual.[4] The requirements established by *halakhah* for Jewish ceremonial objects are thus not uniform but varying.

The forms of only a few objects are completely specified in Jewish law: the Torah, the scroll of the *mezuzah,* and *tefillin.*[5] All three must be written on the skins of *kosher* animals that have been finished and coated. Lines are drawn on the parchment to ensure the evenness and beauty of the script, which can be written only by a scribe using a quill and special ink. These and other requirements have ensured the consistent appearance of the *torot, mezuzot,* and *tefillin* used by Jews of different cultural affiliations.

All the remaining works of Jewish ceremonial art may be classified in three groups: those whose forms are determined to some extent by *halakhah,* those whose functions are required but whose forms are not specified, and those that have developed from the Jew's desire to perform his religious acts in the handsomest way (*hiddur mitzvah*).[6] A Hanukkah lamp is an example of a ceremonial object in the first group. It must consist of eight lights, one for each day of the festival; these lights must be set on the same level and must burn for a minimum period of time.[7] Sabbath lights, too, must be at least two in number and must burn for a specified period, their flames fed by one among a list of acceptable fuels; but the shapes of the lamps and their appearance were not established by the rabbis.[8] Over the centuries Sabbath lights have been clay or glass lamps, candlesticks, candelabra and hanging lamps, all varying in material and sumptuousness.

There is also a large group of Jewish ceremonial objects whose functions are mandated by law but whose forms and appearances are at the discretion of the individual. For example, one of the means by which the Sabbath is set apart from the working week is the recitation of *kiddush* (the sanctification over wine). Though *kiddush* is a ceremony that occurs often in Jewish life, not only at the onset of Sabbath and festivals but also during the holy days, at their close, and at certain events in the life cycle, the rabbis specified the minimum measure of wine to be sanctified but not the form of its container.[9] Similarly, the sanctity of primary objects used in Jewish worship led to the creation of Judaica intended to safeguard the form or *kedushah* (holiness) of other objects. *Tefillin*, for example, are considered ritually fit only if the boxes housing the parchment scrolls are neither nicked, or otherwise damaged; an *etrog* for Sukkot is considered *kosher* only if its stem is unbroken. Both objects require protective covers whose shape and appearance are not specified in Jewish law (nos. 12, 13, 21, 22). And the Torah, the most revered object in Judaism, has inspired the creation of several types of Judaica intended to safeguard its sanctity (for example, the binder, the pointer, the mantle, the ark, nos. 62–4, 72, 199–201, 207) or to enhance its appearance (for example, crowns and *rimmonim*, nos. 69–70, 203–6). The halakhic requirements governing these last works are a function of their relation to the Torah.

The most free from all legal strictures are ceremonial objects commissioned or made by Jews out of piety and enthusiasm to enhance the beauty of a religious event or place. Carefully embroidered, woven, or painted hangings for the synagogue (e.g., no. 6), beautifully embroidered pillows for carrying infants to circumcision (no. 163), special ewers and basins for ceremonial ablutions (no. 126)—these and many other ceremonial objects are the most open to outside influences on form and decoration by virtue of their freedom from legal requirements. It is in such objects that we can expect to see the greatest impact of local culture on the ceremonial art of a community and the greatest diversity among examples from different communities. For example, the Sephardim living in Turkey emulated the Ottoman taste for rich embroideries and adapted it to Jewish ritual. Judaism requires a bride to immerse herself in a ritual bath before marriage; in Turkey the decorated bath sheet became part of a Jewish bride's dowry (no. 194). Richly embroidered cloths were also used to cover the walls of the *sukkah*. In contrast, these forms are unknown among the Ashkenazim.

Although these are instances of entirely new forms of Judaica created under local cultural influences, even the traditional objects used by Jews show the impact of local culture in inverse proportion to the strictness of Jewish laws governing their fabrication. *Rimmonim* (finials for the Torah scrolls) are an example. These objects were generally created out of respect for the Torah and out of a desire to enhance its appearance, but they are without ritual function. Ashkenazi examples most often assume the form of a tower, echoing familiar architecture of the medieval, baroque, and later periods (no. 69). The *rimmonim* of Turkey, however, are shaped like fruit, reflecting the emphasis on vegetal forms in Ottoman decorative arts and perhaps more closely adhering to the spherical shape of the earliest removable *rimmonim,* which may have developed out of the simple knobs on rods for classical scrolls (nos. 203–6)[10]. The Torah curtain is a second example; a ritual object known from the period of the earliest synagogues, whose later manifestations reflect local forms. The portal frame enclosing a central mirror is a standard Ashkenazi type that may be linked to the Renaissance use of *aediculae* as frames both for sculpture and for the title pages of books (no. 57).[11] Arches on Ottoman objects generally enclose lamps, reflecting the composition of prayer niches and prayer rugs used in the mosque. Such Ottoman rugs were obviously the direct inspiration for Ottoman Torah curtains and reader's desk covers woven as carpets (nos. 197–8).

What is striking about these examples of local stylistic influence on Judaica is the underlying similarity of usage and form in different parts of the world. Future excavation of ancient synagogues may reveal early examples of other ceremonial forms still in use today, which, supplemented by textual information, may further our understanding of the common fund of Judaica known before the Jews' migration from their ancient homeland.[12] If not attributable to common sources, then the concurrence of ceremonial forms among Jews of different cultural origins may reflect cross-cultural influences that were facilitated by values commonly held. For example, the continuous and deep commitment to Eretz Israel as the Jewish homeland, which is part of everyday prayer, found a common form of artistic expression in special plaques for the synagogues and homes of both Ashkenazim and Sephardim (nos. 4, 6, 168).

On the other hand, the most striking difference between the Judaica used by the Jews of Frankfurt and Istanbul respectively is in the attitudes manifested toward representation of the human figure. The great works of Frankfurt Judaica, even synagogue objects, incorporate three-dimensional human figures (nos. 59, 116, 123). This lenient interpretation of the Second Commandment reached an extreme in the use by one Ashkenazi family of a *seder* tablecloth incorporating representations of God (no. 111). That Judaism was never monolithic in its attitude toward representational art is now amply demonstrated by numerous archaeological finds and by the writings of rabbis during the Middle Ages and later. Surrounded by a Christian culture that espoused the use of images as educational tools in the service of religion, many traditional Jews did not abjure the use of images, though, in every age, there were fundamentalist groups that took an iconoclastic view.[13] The prohibition against images in religious art was always more strictly observed by Muslims than by Christians and Jews. As a result, Jews living under Muslim government did not incorporate the human form into ceremonial art but focused instead on abstract, vegetal, animal, or architectural forms.

Another major difference is the role played by Jews in the creation of ceremonial objects. In Germany Jews were generally excluded from membership in guilds until the nineteenth century.[14] Consequently, if a Jew wished to own a fine piece of Judaica other than a textile, he was forced to commission it from a Christian. The Jew functioned as patron but not as craftsman, and his artistic input was therefore limited. Still, the beautiful silver Judaica extant from the sixteenth century onward are evidence of fruitful collaboration between the Jews of Frankfurt and the leading silversmiths of that city.[15] For Jews living in the Ottoman Empire the situation was different. Although subject to some restrictions, they were able to practice a far broader range of occupations, and a high proportion of them were artisans.[16] Eastern Jews could exercise greater creativity than was possible in Germany before the Emancipation, though to what extent they did so is impossible to tell because of the anonymous character of Ottoman Judaica.

In the late nineteenth century Jews in both the East and the West adopted a new attitude toward their ceremonial art: Some of them became collectors and historians. The Judaica from Turkey and from Frankfurt in the Jewish Museum represent the two different ways in which great collections were formed: by private initiative and by public effort. Hadji Ephraim Benguiat, born in Izmir, was the son and grandson of dealers in antiquities who gradually, out of a love of beautiful objects, amassed a broad collection of his own. Among them were 400 works of Jewish ceremonial art, which Benguiat and his son Mordecai considered to be of special value because of their role in the history of the Jewish people.

Reflecting their sensitivity the Benguiats collected widely, not limiting their purchases to Sephardi objects but acquiring outstanding examples of Ashkenazi ceremonial art as well. Still, because of their personal history, the

21

Benguiat collection included many fine examples of Ottoman Judaica. In 1888 Hadji Ephraim brought the collection to Boston, where it was exhibited at the Museum of Fine Arts. Four years later Dr. Cyrus Adler persuaded the Benguiats to lend the collection to the United States National Museum (now the Smithsonian Institution), where it remained for thirty-two years. During that period Dr. Adler became Chancellor of The Jewish Theological Seminary of America and thereafter instigated efforts to purchase the collection for the Seminary museum. In 1924 the H. Ephraim and Mordecai Benguiat Family Collection of Jewish Antiquities became part of the holdings of the Seminary Library, forerunner of The Jewish Museum.

In contrast, the core of the collection of Frankfurt Judaica now in the Jewish Museum was formed through the awareness of a single museum director, who first recognized the lack of any scholarly research on Jewish ceremonial art. Dr. Heinrich Frauberger's interest in Judaica was aroused by an inquiry about Jewish motifs that had been addressed to his office at the Düsseldorf Kunstgewerbe Museum. His efforts resulted in the formation of one of the first societies devoted to the study of Judaica, the *Gesellschaft zur Erforschung Jüdischer Denkmäler* and of its publications the *Mitteilungen* and the *Notizblatt* which served as forums for studies by such noted scholars as Hermann Gundersheimer, Rudolf Hallo, Ida Posen, and Guido Schoenberger. The creation of the Frankfurt Jewish Museum followed. Fortunately, many of its treasures were saved and brought to the United States in 1952 through the Jewish Cultural Reconstruction, an organization founded to recover works confiscated from their Jewish owners. Dr. Guido Schoenberger, who had worked for the Frankfurt Jewish Museum, continued his research at The Jewish Museum, New York, after World War II.

In presenting *A Tale of Two Cities* we pay tribute to the collectors and scholars who first had the vision to create a public museum of Jewish ceremonial art designed to exhibit the material heritage of the Jewish people. Two thousand years ago, Rabbi Elazar wrote in the name of Rabbi Ḥanina "Scholars increase peace throughout the world for it is said 'All your children shall be taught of the Lord, and great shall be the peace of your children.' Read not . . . your children but your builders." (Babylonian Talmud Berakhot 64a). It is the sincerest hope of the staff at The Jewish Museum that by building on the work of our teachers and predecessors in creating this exhibition, we shall afford the public a view of the common Jewish values that lie behind the visible differences and the means for understanding the varying customs and practices of Ashkenazim and Sephardim. In the words of R. Elazar, may these efforts "increase peace" and also mutual understanding.

NOTES

1. *Daily Prayer Book* (trans., by P. Birnbaum) (New York: 1949), p. 382.

2. The *kiddush* cup and Sabbath lights are examples of ceremonial objects discussed in the Mishnah and the Talmud. (Babylonian Talmud, *Pesahim* 108b; *Berakhot* 51a–b; Mishnah, *Shabbat* 2:1–4.) However, the Torah shield is first mentioned by R. Israel b. Pethahia Isserlein (1390–1460). (*Terumat ha-Deshen*, no. 225) and plaques for the synogogue inscribed with the Decalogue occur from the 17th century on. (J. Gutmann, "How Traditional are our Traditions?" *Beauty in Holiness*, p. 418)

3. For example, although the *havdalah* ceremony with spices is mentioned in the Mishnah (*Berakhot* 8:5–8), there is no mention of a box to hold spices until the 12th century (M. Narkiss, "Origins of the Spice Box," *Journal of Jewish Art* 8 (1981), p. 36.) The cushions used during circumcision ceremonies by both Sephardim and Ashkenazim are an example of an object used in a life-cycle ritual which is not required by Jewish law. (See no. 163 and *Fabric of Jewish Life*, no. 138.)

4. Early discussions of Torah shields and crowns are instances of this phenomenon. The first mention of a shield is in the *responsum* of R. Israel b. Pethahia Isserlein cited above in which the author remarks that the plaques placed on the Torah scroll to indicate the reading to which the Torah scroll was turned were functional devices which were not mean to beautify of the Torah (see above n.2). By the mid-sixteenth century, Torah shields were made of silver as the earliest extant examples and documentary sources demonstrate, thus obviating R. Israel's objections. (See H. Lazar, "De nouveau dans l'art sacre juif," *L'Oeil*, 288–9 (1979), pp. 62–63; H. Gundersheimer and G. Schoenberger, "Frankfurter Chanukahleuchter aus Silber und Zinn," *Notizblatt* 34 (1937), p. 10.) One of the earliest writers to mention silver Torah crowns is R. Abraham of Lunel who discussed the practice of placing women's jewelry on the Torah during services on *Simhat Torah* (ca. 1204), an issue which had also been discussed two centuries earlier by the Hai Gaon. (F. Landsberger, "The Origin of European Torah Decorations," *Beauty in Holiness*, pp. 94–96.) R. Abraham's solution was to suggest making a silver crown. (Ibid., p. 96.)

5. *Shulhan Arukh, Yoreh De'ah*, ch. 271 ff.

6. For the sources which discuss the concept of *hiddur mitzvah* see M. Berlin and J. Zevin eds., *Talmudic Encyclopedia* vol. VIII (Jerusalem: 1957), pp. 271–284 (Hebrew).

7. A brief summary of the laws relating to Hanukkah lamps is in S. Ganzfried, *Code of Jewish Law* (trans. by H. Golden) (New York: 1963), ch. 139:5–10.

8. Mishnah, *Shabbat* 2:1–4; *Code of Jewish Law*, ch. 75:2–3.

9. Babylonian Talmud, *Pesahim* 108b; *Berakhot* 51a.

10. F. Landsberger, "The Origin of European Torah Decorations," *Beauty in Holiness*, pp. 88–89.

11. F. Landsberger linked the portal design to book frontispieces. ("Old-Time Torah Curtains," *Beauty in Holiness*, p. 151.)

12. In 1981, excavations of the synagogue in Nabratein yielded fragments of a Torah ark decorated with two rampant confronted lions executed in relief. (E. M. Meyers, J. F. Strange, and C. L. Meyers, "The Ark of Nabratein—A First Glance," *Biblical Archaeologist*, 44 (Fall, 1981), pp. 237–243.) Other ceremonial objects recovered from ancient synagogues are lavers and basins, *bimot*, chairs for dignitaries and *menorot*. (L. I. Levine, ed. *Ancient Synagogues Revealed* (Jerusalem and Detroit: 1982), pp. 91, 116–117, 123 ff., 134–135, 181.)

13. Roth, *Jewish Art*, pp. 11–17.

14. Moses, p. 137; J. Gutmann discusses German-Jewish participation in crafts other than silversmithing (*Jewish Ceremonial Art* (New York and London: 1964), pp. 12–13). R. Hallo cites one exception, a Fürth silversmith, J. Rimonim active in the first half of the 18th century (*Notizblatt*, XXIV (1929), p. 10, n. 39).

15. The Frankfurt silversmith's register contains lists of objects made for Jewish patrons. (H. Gundersheimer and G. Schoenberger, "Frankfurter Chanukahleuchter aus Silber und Zinn," *Notizblatt* 34 (1937), p. 10.) Court records involving disputed commissions reveal that Jewish patrons made specific requests regarding the design of Jewish ceremonial objects (W. K. Zülch, *Alt Frankfurt* (Frankfurt a. M.: 1929), p. 61).

16. See below pp. 44–45.

The Jews of Frankfurt: 1750–1870

Robert S. Liberles

THE GHETTO OF FRANKFURT, best known for the financial power that was seeded within its walls and easily recognizable from the maps and pictures in which it is portrayed, has come to symbolize the closed doors and locked gates that German Jews strove to open from the period of the Enlightenment to the attaining of emancipation. Frankfurt Jewry was confined behind ghetto walls until the end of the eighteenth century, when the walls were demolished by the French during the course of battle.[1]

The exit of more than 3,000 Frankfurt Jews from the ghetto did not entail a demographic change: Jews continued to live in the vicinity for decades to come. Rather, the exit from the ghetto involved processes of educational achievement, economic improvement, and often frustrated social striving, which are the focus of this essay.[2]

Heinrich Heine gave poignant expression to some of the hopes of Jews who sought to move up and out of the confines of their past. His later recollections began with the Napoleonic period:

> At first it was the splendor of the Empire that dazzled my mother, and when the daughter of a hardware manufacturer of our neighborhood, a friend of my mother's, became a duchess and told her that her husband had won many battles and would shortly be promoted to kingship—ah, then my mother dreamed for me of the most golden of epaulettes or the most elaborately embroidered office at the Emperor's Court, to whose service she designed to devote me.[3]

The fall of the Empire demolished the hopes that had been built by Jews in many parts of Germany—especially, as we shall see, in Frankfurt. Heine's mother formulated new plans:

> The house of Rothschild, with whose head my father was acquainted, had already at that time entered upon its fabulous prosperity; and other princes of banking and industry had arisen in our neighborhood, and my mother declared that the hour had come when a man of brains could attain an incredible height in business, and could raise himself to the loftiest pinnacle of temporal power.

But economic fortunes rise and fall, and although the Rothschilds did not exactly suffer, Heine's father did.

> She now thought I must by all means study the law. She had noticed that in England for a long while, but in France also and in constitutional Germany, lawyers were all-powerful, and in particular, by reason of their habit of public speaking, advocates played principal roles of loquacity and thereby rose to the highest offices of state.

These plans for Heine's success and advancement had been focused successively on government, finance, and one of the educated professions. In the end, Heine took his own path, but his mother's choices reflect, in one individual sequence, some of the paths broached by Frankfurt Jews in their own endeavors to attain a securer economic, social, and legal position.

Education was the cornerstone of efforts by Frankfurt Jews to improve their lot. They had always excelled in educational accomplishments, and they continued to do so, but the values and orientation of Jewish education changed greatly during the eighteenth and nineteenth centuries.

From the late sixteenth century through the early 1800's the *yeshivah* of Frankfurt was known for its high level of rabbinic learning. Younger children were instructed by private teachers, supervised by a community commission headed by the *Rosh Yeshivah.* As late as 1780, between 120 and 130 boys were studying in the *yeshivah.* The strength of the school depended on the support of the community to finance the institution and to accommodate the students. In the late eighteenth century this support began to decrease. Simultaneously, the interests of young people became more diverse. In 1793 the *yeshivah* had only sixty students. Nevertheless, years later—long after the community had shifted its primary support to secular studies—students were still coming to Frankfurt to study rabbinics.[4]

Toward the end of the eighteenth century the desire for secular education began to increase. Among adults much of this learning was autodidactic. Medical doctors, however, were among the few who had obtained formal secular education, and they formed the nuclei of several reading circles established at the turn of the century. Of three such groups in existence by 1801, one claimed 100 members in 1804. Even earlier, parents took the initiative in providing general education for their children. Wealthier parents could and did engage private tutors, but, in addition, they made the first attempts to establish a Jewish school for secular instruction. This project, proposed in 1794, failed because of stiff opposition from the rabbinate and communal leadship, as did a second attempt in 1801.[5]

Meanwhile, other sources of secular instruction were found. The most popular solution was to send the children to local non-Jewish schools. Between 1800 and 1803, twenty-nine Jewish boys attended the local Gymnasium; only six had attended in the decade between 1789 and 1799. When the Model School was established in 1803, twenty-two students, one fourth of the total number, were Jewish. Other parents sent their children out of the city. Between 1804 and 1807, thirteen boys from Frankfurt attended the school run by Israel Jacobsen in Westphalia. Girls were also sent to non-Jewish schools during this period, though in smaller numbers than the boys. Of the thirty girls attending the Model School in 1803–1804, again one fourth were Jewish.[6]

It was during those early years of the nineteenth century that a group of Frankfurt Jews established the Philanthropin School, with the purpose of providing progressive secular and religious education for the poorer children of the city. Concern about the economic diversification and occupational training of Jews was widespread at this time. Economic matters had been the major focus of Emperor Joseph II's Edict of Toleration in Austria (1782) and in the subsequent legislation enacted in Russia (1804) and Prussia (1812). Economic complaints against the Jews in nearby Alsace were also brought frequently to the attention of Napoleon's counselors and ministers during this same period. Even earlier than in Frankfurt, Jews in other cities had founded a number of schools to provide occupational training, especially for poorer children. Such schools were founded in Berlin in 1778, Breslau in 1791, Seesen and Dessau in 1801, and in Frankfurt itself in 1804. A similar school for girls was opened in Frankfurt in 1810; sixty-one pupils were enrolled by the end of the first year.[7]

Despite its philanthropic origins, the Philanthropin gradually evolved into a middle-class institution. From the outset it accepted paying students to help with finances, and after the first two years tuition-paying students predominated. Even in the early period of 1804–1812, there were only forty-three free students, compared with 170 who paid. In 1822 the Philanthropin, renamed the Bürger und Realschule, became the official school of the Jewish community. By that time its emphasis had changed from training in manual skills to commercial education.[8]

Alternative institutions were established to achieve the original philanthropic objectives. In 1813–1814, the Volksschule was founded for poorer children, and again greater emphasis was placed on manual skills. This school grew in the early years, reaching an enrollment of sixty pupils in the lower of two classes, but a decline occurred during the 1840's, and in 1854 the Volksschule was closed down. Schools like the Philanthropin and the Volksschule did not always suit the needs of poorer families, who may have sought more traditional religious education on one hand, and may have required a more immediate source of financial assistance on the other. Perhaps more helpful to such families were the efforts of a society for promoting training in skilled labor, which financed periods of apprenticeship for Jewish boys. Founded around 1825, the society reported in 1839 that it had assisted some 439 lads, the vast majority of whom came from the surrounding areas of Hesse but forty-seven of whom were from Frankfurt. Those supported in this way included, among others, one architect, eleven bakers, fifteen bookbinders, three book printers, twenty lathe turners, two painters, seven glaziers, and two tanners.[9]

Still, it was the Philanthropin (Realschule) that more accurately represented the aspirations of the Frankfurt Jewish community. Some limited statistics are available on the occupations of its early graduates through 1812. Of the free students, four became craftsmen (a baker, a bookbinder, a tailor, and a carpenter), two became teachers, and a number opened shops of various kinds. Among the paying students the variety of subsequent occupations was greater: There were eight skilled workers, a musician, an architect, three lawyers, five doctors, and an astronomer. Two men received Ph.D. degrees, and a number opened firms, including several banks, bookstores, and large shops. The Frankfurt Jewish community certainly did not abandon the field of finance, but it was coming to place greater trust in education and commerce.[10]

Legally, Frankfurt Jewry in the early nineteenth century was still governed by a set of ordinances, dating back to 1616, that severely restricted rights of occupation, domicile, and freedom of movement within the city. New ideas on the proper position of Jews in society had been circulating in Germany since at least the early 1780's, when Christian Dohm's classic work, *On the Civil Improvement of the Jews,* appeared almost simultaneously with Joseph II's Edicts of Toleration of the Jews of the Austrian Empire. In later discussions of the Jewish situation in Germany Frankfurt was frequently cited as a blatant example of restrictions still imposed on Jews.

Napoleon's armies brought this question to the forefront. The ghetto walls were battered during various battles in the 1790s, and the question of their renovation led naturally to more basic discussions of the position of the Jews. Diplomatic maneuvers by the community brought a sympathetic response from other German states, but the powerfully organized merchants and artisans of Frankfurt, fearful of economic competition, successfully resisted efforts at change.[11]

Napoleonic hegemony in Germany led to the first changes in the legal status of the Jews of Frankfurt. Policies toward Jews differed among the various German states, depending on local conditions and on relations with the regime in Paris. Areas that had been annexed to France, like Hamburg, actually extended only limited forms of emancipation to Jews, in accordance with the restrictions of the Napoleonic decrees of 1808. Ironically, the more independent province of Westphalia, ruled by Napoleon's brother Jérôme, instituted a policy of complete emancipation coupled with aggressive intervention in Jewish community life under the auspices of the Westphalian Consistoire headed by Israel Jacobson. Within the Confederation of the Rhine, the variations were greater and more dependent on local conditions. When Carl von Dalberg was appointed Prince Primate in Frankfurt, he found strong local opposition to improving conditions for the Jews. He soon removed restrictions on Jews' entering public parks and ordered a moderate change in the Jewish oath, but major changes did not follow. A revised ordinance issued in 1807 emphasized religious and educational reform but still restricted trade. A modified ghetto without walls and gates was to be maintained. In 1810, however, Frankfurt became the seat of a duchy, and Dalberg was promoted to duke. The French political model was then followed more closely, and in 1811 an agreement was reached with the Jewish community in which equality was provided in return for a substantial payment.[12]

With the fall of Napoleon, most of these legal improvements were revoked. It may seem that the Napoleonic legacy to German Jewry amounted to no more than a memory and still unfulfilled expectations, but certain underlying changes were more lasting. The regimes installed by the French had accelerated the process of educational and religious reform and had reorganized the communal structure. Community leaders had been replaced where necessary by men more sympathetic to French objectives. After the departure of the French, the successor governments continued to encourage educational progress, and in Frankfurt the new community leadership remained in power. The legal status of the Jews deteriorated once again as many of the previous restrictions were restored in Frankfurt. As a conse-

29

quence, Frankfurt Jewry brought its case before the Congress of Vienna in 1815, where it received little immediate satisfaction.[13]

In the first years after 1815 a number of polemics on the plight of Frankfurt Jewry appeared, and the historian Isaac Mayer Jost even described Frankfurt as "the cradle of the struggle for emancipation." The Berlin community preceded Frankfurt in these efforts, however, and Berlin and Hamburg respectively produced more formidable spokesmen in David Friedlaender and the later Gabriel Riesser. Ludwig Börne wrote the best known of the Frankfurt emancipation polemics, but he quickly abandoned the struggle and converted to Christianity. On the whole, in Frankfurt it was the community board, or the few who spoke in its name (especially Börne's father, Jacob Baruch), who spearheaded efforts toward emancipation, rather than celebrated individuals acting independently of the community.[14]

While the local population strongly resisted an improvement in the Jewish position, considerable pressure was applied by other German states to bring Frankfurt into line with the civil advances achieved elsewhere. Prussia and Austria both supported the Jewish cause. Jewish influence on those states had grown remarkably, and the local authorities now found it impossible to propose legislation without consultation with the Jews. The influence of the Rothschilds contributed significantly to the sympathetic attention that Frankfurt Jews were receiving, but the historian of the community, Isadore Kracauer, also credited the local Jewish leaders, who spoke out strongly in pursuit of their goal. For example, they declared in a memorandum to the German Confederation in 1819:

> All states in the German Confederation have found it more or less appropriate to the spirit of the times to elevate their protected Jews to citizens of the state. Why should only in Frankfurt the Jewish citizens be degraded once again to the status of protected Jews? Have not the Jews of the city fought along with the other citizens for the liberation of Germany? Have they not borne collective war-taxes and contributions for the freedom of their native city? Were they to accept their disparagement before the eyes of the world willingly, so would they openly become unworthy of the title of citizen.[15]

Aside from the influence of the Rothschilds and the concerted efforts of the Frankfurt community, the intervention by the major German powers must have reflected their own conviction that improvements would succeed in breaking down the barrier between Jews and Christians only if they were undertaken throughout Germany. Others feared the migratory movements that could result from disparities in Jewish rights.[16] The combination of all these factors finally resulted, in 1824, in the passage of a new comprehensive Jewry Law.

The 1824 law improved the civil status of the Jews of Frankfurt, who were no longer designated as "protected Jews" but as "israelitische Bürger." In most areas of social and economic contact, they were to be treated as equal citizens. Among the remaining restrictions were the number of marriages allowed per year, some restrictions in forms of trade, and on entry into commerce.[17] The major deficiency in the Jewish legal position had thus become a political one. Jews could still not be elected to public office. The efforts to correct that deficiency came only later in the nineteenth century.

Whatever financial success Jews may have derived from educational reforms and improvement in legal status, social rewards were not forthcoming. Until recently the significance of the pursuit of social acceptance as a driving force in German Jewish history has been overlooked. It was Jacob Katz's book *Jews and Freemasons in Europe* that first focused attention on this question, and Frankfurt Jewry is at the very center of the story. A group of Frankfurt Jews struggled for decades to gain admission to local Freemasonic lodges. They even founded their own lodge, the Morgenröthe, in the expectation that membership would entitle them to visiting privileges in those older and established Frankfurt lodges that had rejected them as members. They were doubly disappointed. German mother lodges refused to recognize the Morgenröthe, which had to look abroad for official sponsorship, and Jewish members were still denied visiting rights at other lodges. The problem of admission was not resolved until 1848.[18]

These efforts toward social integration in Frankfurt had a definite impact on Jewish communal life. Katz has demonstrated that from 1817 to 1832 virtually the entire lay leadership of the community, including the members of the community board and both the lay and professional officials of the Philanthropin School, were members of the Morgenröthe lodge.[19] They had turned to the Freemasons in hopes that such formal affiliations would provide an appropriate beginning toward the social integration of Frankfurt residents who had until quite recently been enclosed behind ghetto walls.

With the passing of decades it became clear that social barriers would not fall easily, and formal restrictions proved no easier to combat than casual exclusion. An attempt by Jews in 1839 to gain admission into the Lesegesellschaft was outvoted by a membership consisting largely of doctors and lawyers. Members of the Morgenröthe lodge are reported to have been active in this effort as well. An exclusive club, the Casino, also rejected Jewish applicants, even prominent ones, though the Rothschilds were accepted.[20] It was becoming clear that a change in Jewish social circumstances depended on a further change in the legal status of Jews.

Renewed activity by the community board, Rabbi Leopold Stein, and others resulted in elimination of various disabilities during the 1840s. The restrictions on marriage were lifted in 1846, and the special oath required of Jewish witnesses was discontinued in 1847. In Frankfurt, as in most German states, complete emancipation was granted during the revolutionary period of 1848–1849, but as elsewhere the *status quo ante* was restored during the subsequent reactionary period. A lasting advance was achieved in 1853, however, when Jews first became eligible for some public offices and for membership in the Legislative Assembly, though the number of Jewish representatives was restricted. Jews were still excluded from election to the Senate and from appointment to judgeships and some of other public positions. All remaining disabilities were finally removed in 1864, two years before Prussian annexation of Frankfurt.[21]

In the late 1830's religious conflict led to division within the Frankfurt Jewish community. The seeds of this dissension had lain dormant since Napoleonic times, when the Reform party, which actually controlled the community institutions under government sanction, had begun to confine its religious activities to services conducted under the auspices of the Philanthropin School. With the increasingly liberal atmosphere in Europe, however, the Reformers, primarily merchants, professional men, and bankers, urged the introduction of religious innovations in the community synagogue. The dispute centered on two motifs frequent in such controversies: construction of a new building and appointment of a new rabbi. The rabbinate was still in the staunchly traditionalist hands of eighty-year-old Solomon Trier and his associates, who moved to block construction of a new synagogue, fearing that increased pressure for religious innovations would quickly follow. The Rothschild family negotiated a compromise in 1843, offering to pay for a new building in return for guarantees that traditional values would continue to be honored in the synagogue. The board's appointment of Leopold Stein as deputy rabbi seemed to violate that agreement, however, and Trier resigned as community rabbi. The Reformers were now in full control of the communal institutions. They had also demonstrated through free elections that they had the allegiance of two thirds of the community members.[22]

Frankfurt had become a focal point of Jewish religious controversy and activity in Germany, and it remained so until the end of the community. The various streams of religious opinion from radical Reform to staunch Orthodoxy all found a place in the Frankfurt community, and both extreme camps established Frankfurt as their center.

In the early 1840's a group of intellectuals and merchants—about twenty in number—organized a radical pressure group known as the Society of

Friends of Reform (Verein der Reformfreunde). The Reformverein, as it was known, succeeded in bringing controversial religious issues to the attention of the general public. Its efforts were well publicized in the general press and frequently denounced in the Jewish newspapers of the day, especially the liberal Jewish press. A concise statement of their creed included rejection of the divine authority of the Talmud and of belief in a messianic return to the Promised Land. There was also an active attempt to eliminate circumcision as a legal obligation for members of the Jewish community.[23]

The Reformverein itself lasted no more than three years, but its influence was felt for a much longer time in Frankfurt and throughout Germany. Similar groups were established in Breslau and in Berlin, and the Berlin society established a Reform congregation known for its independent and radical approach. The Frankfurt organization had succeeded in shaking the Reform moderates, including the rabbis, who, sensing the threat of lay impatience, initiated a series of three conferences to deal with the questions of Reform. The second of these rabbinical conferences was held in Frankfurt in 1845.

As one of these Reform rabbis, Leopold Stein served the Frankfurt community for nearly twenty years. His main interests were liturgy and the arts, and his editions of the *Siddur* include original hymns and translations of Hebrew prayers. Best known was his rendition in German of the Friday-night hymn *Lechoh Dodi.* Stein, a close friend of the Frankfurt painter Moritz Oppenheim, also wrote the commentary accompanying the series of Oppenheim's paintings entitled *Family Scenes from Jewish Life of Former Days* (see nos. 99 and 130 in the exhibition).

Much of Stein's rabbinical work was devoted to development of a new Reform liturgy for the synagogue, and liturgical matters dominated the 1845 rabbinical conference, over which he presided. Furthermore, in the 1850's Stein convened three little-known conferences of the Reform-minded rabbis of southern Germany; these dealt almost exclusively with the composition of a new prayer book specifically intended for use in the Frankfurt synagogue. Stein also published a newspaper, *Israelitische Volkslehrer*, during the 1850's, generally a difficult period for Reform; most other Reform newspapers, except for Ludwig Philippson's powerful *Allgemeine Zeitung des Judenthums*, closed down.[24]

Tensions within the Reform camp, first brought to the fore by the Reformverein, remained high. Stein's attempts to play an appropriate role within the community school were rebuffed by the lay leadership. Apparently the radicals had gained a dominant influence in the 1850's, and the community and the rabbi were locked in a struggle over the parameters of rabbinical power. In 1862, after eighteen years of conflict, Stein finally resigned and was replaced by the dean of the Reform rabbinate, Abraham Geiger, a native of Frankfurt. Geiger's years in Frankfurt coincided with Prussian annexation, but they were otherwise uneventful. He seemed bored and isolated, and in 1870 he moved to Berlin, where he headed the new Reform rabbinical seminary, an appropriate position for one of the dominant personalities in German-Jewish historical scholarship. Frankfurt continued to attract prominent liberal figures to the local rabbinate. They included Nehemias Bruell (1870–1891), Rudolf Plaut (1883–1903), and Caesar Seligmann (1903–1932).[25] Frankfurt became even more renowned, however, as the leading center of European Orthodoxy.

During the late 1830's and the 1840's, the Reformers enjoyed the support of the Senate, which ruled Frankfurt. In a number of disputes, including those over circumcision and Stein's appointment as deputy rabbi, the Senate refused to assist the Orthodox party. After 1848, however, a group of Orthodox leaders obtained Senate support for organization of the *Israelitische Religionsgesellschaft,* an autonomous congregation that soon became known as the "model community" of modern Orthodoxy. The I.R.G. was well supported by the Frankfurt Rothschilds and other wealthy members of the community. In 1851 it attracted to Frankfurt Samson Raphael Hirsch, then State Rabbi of Moravia. Hirsch served the Orthodox community in Frankfurt until his death in 1888.[26] Under his leadership and with readily available financial means, the I.R.G. was able to provide its members and the larger community with the institutions needed for a full religious life. It soon opened a school that combined religious and secular education. As in the Philanthropin, the emphasis in the secular curriculum was on subjects related to commerce. The synagogue service was conducted under the auspices of a cantor with the accompaniment of an all-male choir, and original music for the service was composed by the choir director, I. M. Japhet.[27]

By the time of emancipation in 1864, membership in the I.R.G had grown to about 300 families, all of whom paid full membership dues both to the I.R.G and to the officially recognized Jewish community. During the 1850s and 1860s, the I.R.G had frequently petitioned the Frankfurt Senate to restructure the Jewish community so that the I.R.G. would become a full and equal component. Similar arrangements, providing for parallel Reform and Orthodox congregations, had been made in Breslau and Hamburg, but the Jewish community board in Frankfurt resisted all attempts to reach a compromise.

Only in 1876, when Jews had already received full political rights and Frankfurt had become part of the German Reich, did a new Prussian law allow Jews to withdraw from membership in the Jewish community while retaining their legal identity as Jews. In the aftermath of bitter controversies within the I.R.G. itself, within the larger Jewish community, and between Hirsch and Seligmann Baer Bamberger, rabbi of Würzburg, a complex religious realignment appeared in Frankfurt. In order to preserve communal unity, the board agreed to establish a separate and equal Orthodox congregation within the community structure. Frankfurt thus had two Orthodox congregations, the independent I.R.G. and a new second congregation, functioning within the framework of the Jewish community.[28] Both groups were subsequently served by prominent spokesmen for German Orthodoxy; the I.R.G. by Solomon Breuer (1890–1926) and the communal Orthodox by Markus Horowitz (1878–1910), followed by Nehemia Nobel (1911–1922).[29]

Economic importance and religious activity were the major characteristics of Frankfurt Jewry during the period of emancipation. Few local Jews attained prominence in the cultural sphere, and those who did—the writer Ludwig Börne and the rabbi Abraham Geiger—did not stay in Frankfurt. In fact, aside from bankers, it was only the rabbis, who were attracted by the dynamic Jewish life of the community, who achieved significant recognition outside Frankfurt's borders.

Prussian annexation of Frankfurt in 1866 led to an impulse to broaden the horizons of the citizens, including of course, the Jews. The population increased rapidly, though the Jewish proportion remained constant:[30]

Year	Number of Jews	Percentage of Total Population
1867	8,238	10.0
1871	10,009	11.0
1875	11,887	11.5
1880	13,856	10.1
1890	17,426	9.7
1900	21,874	7.5

Jews increasingly found new and broader spheres of activity. They had never been particularly active in local politics, but with Frankfurt's incorporation into Prussia, they came to play a leading role in representing their city in Prussian forums. Mayer Carl Rothschild was Frankfurt's first deputy to the North German Reichstag, and he was succeeded by Leopold Sonnemann, editor of the liberal *Frankfurter Zeitung*.[31] The opening of Goethe University in Frankfurt in 1914 paved the way for the cultural leadership for which Frankfurt Jewry was known in its final decades. But our period, 1750–1870, is best characterized as the period in which Frankfurt Jews moved out of the ghetto.

In a sense not only had Frankfurt's Jews lived in a ghetto; there was also something ghetto-like about old Frankfurt itself: autonomous, particularistic, functioning as financier of the German states. The walls of the Jewish ghetto were torn down by the French, the walls of Frankfurt by the Prussians. Behind those double walls had been settled an old, distinguished, and vibrant Jewish community, one that well reflected the combination of traditionalism and modernity that characterized nineteenth-century Germany and that stimulated German Jews in their struggle for acceptance and identity.

NOTES

1. The walls were severely damaged during battles in 1796, and from that date on there were Jews living outside the ghetto. As late as 1810, however, even the French were considering a plan to require Jewish residence in the ghetto. The classic work on the history of Frankfurt Jewry is I. Kracauer, *Geschichte der Juden in Frankfurt a.M. (1150–1824)* (2 vols.; Frankfurt: 1927). An English version both condenses the German material and extends through a later period: A. Freimann and F. Kracauer, Frankfort Jewish Community Series (Philadelphia: 1929). Whenever possible, the English edition is referred to here; on the last phases of life in the ghetto, see pp. 180–182, 190–191, 207–208, 212.
2. A. Dietz, *Stammbuch der Frankfurter Juden* (Frankfurt: 1907), p. 433. On the social history of this period in general, see the important study by J. Katz, *Out of the Ghetto* (Cambridge, Mass.: 1973).
3. H. Heine, *A Biographical Anthology* (Philadelphia: 1956). The passages quoted here occur on pp. 44–47.
4. On the *yeshivah*, see S. Adler, "Die Entwicklung des Schulwesens der Juden zu Frankfurt am Main bis zur Emanzipation," *Jahrbuch der Jüdisch-Literarischen Gesellschaft*, XVIII (1927), pp. 143–173; and M. Eliav, *Jewish Education in Germany in the Period of Enlightenment and Emancipation* (in Hebrew; Jerusalem: 1960), pp. 149–150. Testimonies to the existence of advanced Talmudic studies in Frankfurt as late as the 1830s can be found in A. Weill, *Ma jeunesse* (Paris: 1870), pp. 199–211; and C. Seligmann, *Erinnerungen* (Frankfurt: 1975), p. 36.
5. Adler, "Die Entwicklung des Schulwesens der Juden zu Frankfurt am Main bis zur Emanzipation—II," *Jahrbuch der Jüdisch-Literarischen Gesellschaft*, XIX (1928), pp. 250–252; and H. Baerwald, *Geschichte der Realschule der israelitischen Gemeinde* (Frankfurt: 1904), p. 5.
6. Baerwald, *op. cit.*, pp. 6, 31.
7. *Ibid.*, pp. 7–16, 31–33.
8. *Ibid.*, pp. 37, 42.
9. *Ibid.*, p. 42; *Allgemeine Zeitung des Judenthums* III (1839), p. 37; and *Israelitische Annalen*, I (1839) pp. 52–53. These various efforts to increase Jewish participation in the manual occupations were late in coming, as Western society was already well advanced toward industrialization. On this point, see J. Toury, *Prolegomena to the Entrance of Jews into German Citizenry* (in Hebrew, Tel Aviv: 1972), pp. 102–106.
10. Baerwald, *op. cit.*, pp. 42–43.
11. Freimann and Kracauer, *op. cit.*, pp. 185–192. See also the fuller discussion in Kracauer, *op. cit.*, II, pp. 338–354.
12. B. Mevorach, *Napoleon U'Tekufato*, in Hebrew; Jerusalem: 1968), pp. 135–140; and Freimann and Kracauer, *op. cit.*, pp. 194–213.

13. For an overview of reactionary changes in the legal status of Jews, see I. M. Jost, *Neuere Geschichte der Israeliten*, vol. I (3 vols.; Berlin: 1846–1847). On the efforts of Frankfurt Jews at the Congress of Vienna, see M. J. Kohler, "Jewish Rights at the Congresses of Vienna and Aix-la-Chapelle," *Publications of the American Jewish Historical Society*, XXVI, pp. 33–125.

14. Jost, *op. cit.*, p. 23. Ludwig Borne's work was published anonymously under the title *Actenmässige Darstellung des Bürgerrachtes des Israeliten zu Frankfurt am Main* (Rödelheim: 1816).

15. Kracauer, *Geschichte*, II, p. 496.

16. Kohler, *op. cit.*, pp. 42, 80–81, 104.

17. Kracauer, *Geschichte*, II, pp. 513–517.

18. J. Katz, *Jews and Freemasons in Europe* (Cambridge, Mass.: 1970).

19. *Ibid.*, pp. 93–95.

20. On the attempt to enter the Lesegesellschaft, see *Orient* I (1844), p. 6; and *Allgemeine Zeitung des Judenthums*, IV (1840), 74. On exclusion from the Casino, see *Orient* V (1844), p. 178, 207; and *Allgemeine Zeitung des Judenthums*, VIII (1844), p. 405.

21. R. Schwemer, *Geschichte der Freien Stadt Frankfurt, 1814–1866*, vol. III, part 2 (Frankfurt: 1918), pp. 75–78, 209.

22. Jost *op. cit.*; I, pp. 95–103, III, pp. 205–218.

23. On the Reformverein, see M. Meyer, "Alienated Intellectuals in the Camp of Religious Reform: The Frankfurt Reformfreunde, 1842–1845," in *AJS Review*, VI (1981), pp. 61–86.

24. On Leopold Stein and his relations with the community, see R. Liberles, "Leopold Stein and the Paradox of Reform Clericalism" in *Leo Baeck Institute Yearbook*, XXVII (1982).

25. On the rabbis of Frankfurt in modern times, see P. Arnsberg, *Neunhundert Jahre "Muttergemeinde in Israel": Frankfurt am Main, 1074–1974, Chronik der Rabbiner* (Frankfurt: 1974). For the period through 1805, see M. Horovitz, *Frankfurter Rabbinen* (2nd ed.; Jerusalem: 1969).

26. On the founding of the I.R.G., see E. Schwarzschild, *Die Gründung der Israelitischen Religionsgesellschaft* (Frankfurt: 1896).

27. On life in the I.R.G. community, see the memoirs of Hermann Schwab, *Aus der Schützenstrasse* (Frankfurt: 1923), and *Memories of Frankfurt* (London: 1955).

28. On these controversies, see Schwab, *The History of Orthodox Jewry in Germany* (London: 1950), pp. 60–86. On the I.R.G. in the later nineteenth century, see J. Rosenheim, *Erinnerungen* (Frankfurt: 1970).

29. Arnsberg, *op. cit.*, passim.

30. W. Hanauer, *Zur Statistik der jüdischen Bevölkerung in Frankfurt a. M.* (Frankfurt: 1910), pp. 1, 4. See also J. Unna, *Statistik der Frankfurter Juden zum Jahre 1866* (Frankfurt: 1931).

31. K. Gerteis, *Leopold Sonnemann* (Frankfurt: 1970), pp. 57–58.

Istanbul Jewry 1750–1870

Joseph R. Hacker

WHEN CONSTANTINOPLE WAS conquered by the Ottoman Turks in May 1453, it became, under the name Istanbul, the capital of their empire, and so it remained until October 1923. Almost immediately, Meḥmed II the Conqueror adopted a policy of compulsory settlement in order to repopulate the city. Jews, as well as Christians and Muslims, were brought from the Asian provinces of the empire (Anatolia) and from the European provinces (Rumelia) to the ravaged megalopolis. Later on, improving economic and social conditions in the city and a lenient policy of the Sultan toward non-Muslim minorities stimulated voluntary migration to the city. Later still, Jews expelled from Spain (in 1492) and Portugal (in 1497) turned Istanbul into the dominant Jewish community of the Ottoman Empire; indeed, the city had the largest Jewish population in the world in the sixteenth century.

In 1535, 40,000 Jews were living in several quarters of Istanbul, and in 1690, 50,000 were counted in the city and its suburbs. During the eighteenth and nineteenth centuries, however, the Jewish population decreased considerably because of both emigration to expanding economic centers in the West and internal migration, which had begun in the seventeenth century, especially to Smyrna (Izmir). As the focus of world commerce shifted from the Mediterranean to the Atlantic coast of Europe, many Jews made their way to Holland, England, and even to the central and eastern parts of the continent, especially to Danubian Europe.

Nevertheless, the estimated Jewish population of Istanbul in the mid-nineteenth century was still about 40,000. Around the turn of the twentieth century the number of Istanbul Jews again began to increase rapidly. In 1904 the community was estimated to number 65,000, thanks mainly to immigration from the Balkans (especially Bulgaria) and Russia and to internal demographic growth.

The basic structure and character of the Jewish community of Istanbul were shaped in the fifteenth and sixteenth centuries, and some features and trends of that period still prevailed through the nineteenth century.

As a result of the policy of repopulation in the 1450's and 1460's, Jews were settled in various neighborhoods of the city according to their geographic origins. Every group was given its own quarter and was allowed to build its own synagogues and other institutions. Among the communities in Istanbul we find: Great and Little Istanbul (composed of the Jews of Byzantine Constantinople), Antalya (Adalia), Bursa, Sinop, Great and Little Selânik (Salonika), Tire (Tyre), Siroz (Serres), Izdin (Lamía), Agriboz (Negropont), Edrine (Edirne-Adrianople), Ohri (Ohrid), Kesriye (Kastoria), İştip (Stip), and several others. These Jews were given a special juridical status (sürgün), according to which they were prevented from leaving the city without express permission of the authorities. This and related regulations, which were still in force at the end of the seventeenth century, had a profound impact on the structure of the entire Jewish community, the system of taxation, and other major issues.

As a result of this pattern of settlement and communal organization, whenever new groups of Jews settled in the city, voluntarily or by force (as a result of conquest), they did so as autonomous communities. Ashkenazi Jews and Spanish and Portuguese refugees were also organized in quarters according to their origins. They comprised the communities of: Cordova, Calabria, Catalan (Catalonia), Aragon, Sicilia (Sicily), Gerush and Señora (both from Castile), Portugal, and so on. These Jews were called kendi gelen (those who come of their own accord) and, in contrast to earlier arrivals, were free to leave Istanbul without obtaining the consent of the authorities.

During the seventeenth century, more than forty congregations were recognized by the government, but in fact there were many more, largely owing to factions within some groups. In Istanbul (in contrast to Salonika, for example), any Jew, provided that he had paid his taxes, was free to leave his congregation and to join another. Because of this mobility and since over the years there had been many marriages between Jews of different origins, after the second half of the seventeenth century the membership of any given Jewish community no longer reflected necessarily the geographical origins and ethnic traditions of the old community. Muslim popular pressures and Muslim religious zeal, on one hand, and the deterioration of influence exercised by prominent Jews after the 1580's, on the other, also contributed to breaking up the original pattern of settlement in the city. Jews were frequently forced to move from neighborhoods recognized thenceforth as exclusively Muslim (or too close to mosques and other Muslim institutions) to other quarters (*mahalles*) of the city, usually less attractive and more heterogeneous in population. These intracity "migrations" were usually triggered by accidental or deliberate fires, which quickly destroyed the wooden houses of the period, or by popular disorders accompanied by looting and physical aggression. After each move, Jews were forced to rebuild their community life. Since, under Muslim law, obtaining permission to construct a synagogue (even to replace an old one) was a complex procedure, in the Ottoman Empire, it was accomplished usually only after substantial bribes had been paid to the appropriate officials. All these considerations led to even greater mixing and crossing of community lines within Istanbul Jewry. Therefore, from the eighteenth century on, the pattern of settlement was based mainly on quarters and the bonds of the community organization were loosened.

In the eighteenth century there were three major Jewish groups, divided into various congregations: the Sephardim, the Romaniotes, and the Karaites. Nevertheless, in official documents Jews were still listed according to the traditional divisions, and they still paid taxes according to that system. The Sephardim (Spanish, Portuguese, and Oriental Jews of Spanish origin) constituted the largest group, dominant in the Jewish social, economic, and cultural life of Istanbul. The Romaniote (Byzantine-Greek) Jews were nevertheless also an influential segment of the Jewish population of Istanbul. The Ashkenazim and the Italian Jews were few in number and had limited influence, whereas the Karaite community was far richer and more influential; some of its members held high positions in the local administration and maintained good relations with the authorities.

The Jews lived in various quarters of the city, mainly those close to the seashore. There were also twenty to thirty Jewish *mahalles* within the walls of the old city; some, like the Baghčekapi Emīnönü (the neighborhood at the southern end of the Galata bridge), were almost exclusively inhabited by Jews already in the fifteenth century. As already noted, there was a considerable change in the distribution of Jews within Istanbul during the second half of the seventeenth century. Many moved to new neighborhoods outside the city walls, mainly Galata, Kuzgunçuk, or Kādīköy, and suburbs even farther out; and abandoned their older quarters like Samatya, Küçük Pazar, and several neighborhoods in the center of the city. There was a general trend toward settling on the shores of the Golden Horn and the Bosporus, a trend that continued through the nineteenth century.

At the turn of the eighteenth century the biggest Jewish *mahalle*s were Balat (on the southern shore of the Golden Horn) and Galata. In the eighteenth and nineteenth centuries wealthy Jews—bankers, merchants, agents, and members of the skilled professions—lived mainly in Kuzguncuk, Pera, and Galata. In the latter two the majority of the population consisted of Greek and Armenian Christians, and Muslims were in the minority. The European embassies were located in those areas, which were also centers of commerce. Most Jews, however, lived in *mahalle*s like Balat and Hasköy (on the opposite shore of the Golden Horn); indeed, Balat remained the most populous Jewish quarter of Istanbul into the twentieth century. However there was a strong tendency to move to the Galata area, and in the late nineteenth century, half of the Istanbul Jewry was living in Galata and Pera.

The conditions of the Jews in Istanbul and their relations with the authorities were in general satisfactory, though from time to time segments of the population, especially the Janissaries (members of the elite corps of the Ottoman army), inflicted humiliations on them. Every Muslim, including children, could insult and mock Jews, who were forbidden to respond. The Janissaries, who significantly increased in numbers in the eighteenth century, however, had special relations with the minorities, including the Jews. On one hand, they protected them, especially during the violent revolts of the first half of the eighteenth century, which swept away the main accomplishments of the Tulip Period (1717–1730). On the other, they exploited their own growing power, they competed with the Jews as *eṣnāf* (artisan-merchants) and continually committed arson in Jewish quarters in order to be able to loot them.

From time to time, new laws restricting the dress of Christians and Jews were proclaimed as a result of increased popular tensions. Usually they forbade the wearing of certain colors, and the *ketkhudā*s (chiefs) of the guilds were warned that members were not to sell certain fabrics to these minorities. When urban violence erupted in 1730 and 1740, both Jewish houses and Greek churches were plundered. In 1740, however, the *eṣnāf*, including both Jews and Christians, were armed by the authorities and helped the Janissaries to suppress the popular uprising. But the special, rather uncertain relationship of the Istanbul Jews with this powerful group ended early in the nineteenth century, when Sultan Maḥmūd II (1806–1839) eliminated the Janissary corps (1826).

The eighteenth and the nineteenth centuries were a period of decline to the Empire and to the city of Istanbul. Stagnancy if not contraction was the prevailing condition of the economy. The superiority of the West was increasing and the Empire was forced into a series of wars and retreats, started in 1689 and culminating in 1774. These and later wars resulted in huge expenditures and led to repeated imperial concessions to Austria, Russia, France, and Great Britain. The effects were apparent in various aspects of Turkish life: decay of Ottoman power and integrity, weakness in the body politic, incompetence and waste in the army and bureaucracy, fiscal extortion, sale of public offices, inflation, agricultural stagnation, and speculation. The overall result was material and moral decline. Repeated efforts through the eighteenth century to reorganize, secularize, and Westernize the army and the administration were only partly successful. In opposition to reform-minded people and statesmen a faction led by the *'ulemā'* (Muslim religious authorities) was influential in mobilizing the masses against modernization.

All these trends affected conditions of daily life in Istanbul. Taxes were increased to cover war expenditures, and constant fighting brought an influx of refugees and immigrants. As desperate people flowed into the city, the unemployed competed with guild members for work. The prices of food also rose, partly as a result of severe shortages and debasement of the currency.

Throughout this difficult period those who were able to obtain immunity and protection through foreign embassies (thanks to the capitulations granted to diplomatic legations and other foreigners) managed to sustain and even to improve their positions. They were granted privileges of extraterritoriality, were free from local jurisdiction and thus from administrative abuses and taxes. At first the European embassies granted these privileges to non-Muslim embassy employees, to merchants, and others, but later to whoever could afford to buy them. The Armenians and Greeks were particularly successful in this respect, and by the mid-nineteenth century half of the population of Galata had obtained such protection. Nevertheless, most Istanbul Jews did not enjoy these safeguards, and the gap between Christians and Jews as well as between the few rich Jews and the many poor in Istanbul was thus widened still further.

Although, despite occasional abuses and popular upheavals, the Jews' relations with their Muslim neighbors were in general satisfactory, the attitude of the Christian population was in general hostile. As soon as Greek merchants rose to prominence as ship owners and merchants controlling external trade, in the seventeenth century, they pushed the Jews out of these fields. The Greek Orthodox population in various suburbs and villages along the Bosporus frequently assaulted Jews, and, whenever an incident occurred (for example, the disappearance of a Christian or a quarrel between a Jew and a Christian), the Armenians, the Greeks, and the Bulgarians would immediately unite to accuse the Jews. Violence and economic boycotts frequently ensued. Several incidents of this kind are recorded from the seventeenth century on, and they became increasingly common in the nineteenth century, when dawning nationalism reinforced religious zeal.

Substantial changes in the status of all minorities occurred in the nineteenth century, as a result of the penetration into Ottoman society of ideas propagated during the French Revolution. For example, the idea of granting equal citizenship to members of different religions was strongly urged by European states and came to be accepted by the Ottoman government and society. Certain guarantees were granted to minorities in 1839, with the promulgation of the *Ḥaṭṭ-i şherīf* (noble rescript) of Gülhane. In 1856 the *Ḥaṭṭ-i hümāyūn* (imperial rescript) went even further. It abolished restrictions imposed on non-Muslims, who were formally declared equal citizens, banned abusive references to non-Muslims and guaranteed their free worship. The constitution of 1876 embodied similar provisions, but nevertheless into the twentieth century Jews and other minority members were still not required or permitted to serve in the Ottoman army but instead were taxed in compensation.

Already in 1835 the first *Ḥakham Bashi* (Chief Rabbi) of Istanbul was appointed; this was the first step toward the creation of a Jewish millet as a special entity with recognized communal leaders. The first one was Rabbi Abraham Ha-Levi, and his task was to represent Ottoman Jews in dealings with the government; thus the *Ḥakham Bashi* was the highest-ranking Jewish figure in Istanbul. His authority was great, but private individuals like Abraham Camondo (a wealthy banker, financier, philanthropist, member of the Commission for Regulation of the City of Istanbul, French-protected citizen, and leader of the reform trend in Jewish society of Istanbul) were highly influential behind the scenes in Istanbul Jewish life and decisive in dealings with government circles. Furthermore, other Jews were close to the various levels of authority during the eighteenth and nineteenth centuries, though their numbers and influence were far smaller than in the sixteenth century.

The wealthy Jews of Istanbul were mainly bankers, moneylenders and agents. A few were merchants engaged in foreign trade. Most merchants functioned as intermediaries and brokers handling the trade of their European, mainly French, Venetian, and English counterparts; very few participated directly in international commerce, for Jews owned no ships, and their official protection was not comparabale to that afforded to the Greeks and Armenians. Even in the field of finance these groups outnumbered the Jews, but the latter Jews were quite numerous in proportion to the comparatively small size of their community. Indeed, as early as 1751, a British observer in Istanbul wrote that the Jews in the city had "truly fallen . . . in company with the Armenians." There were also physicians who, because of the special nature of their calling, had the ears of the *'ulemā'* and the higher functionaries of the administration.

At the end of the eighteenth and the beginning of the nineteenth centuries Istanbul Jews had still been little affected by European ideas. On the other hand, the Greek and Armenian élites of Istanbul were comparatively well versed in European culture and languages, which ensured them positions of strength in the city's administration and economy. As soon as Jews acquired the right to be Austrian subjects in 1769, Ottoman Jews became involved in European commerce, and several settled in Vienna.

On the whole, however, the well-to-do group of Istanbul Jews was quite small. The majority of the Jewish population consisted of craftsmen and peddlers; in Galata alone there were 1,500 Jewish artisans in the mid-nineteenth century. Many Jewish craftsmen were organized in guilds. In Ottoman society individual guilds were usually confined to people of specific communities, though a few were mixed. The tin smelters, the refiners, the pearl merchants, the tailors, and the parchment makers were mainly Jews. There were also Jewish boatmen and many Jewish textile manufacturers. The later ones declined, and the plans of the government to improve this industry in the eighteenth century failed. Jews also worked as water carriers, grocers, cloth merchants, wine-shop keepers, jewelers, dealers in second-hand clothes, and tinkers. Toward the end of the nineteenth century many Jewish girls in particular worked in tobacco factories, some of which were owned by Jews.

The deteriorating political and economic situation of the eighteenth and nineteenth centuries had marked effects on Jewish community life in Istanbul. Living conditions, especially in Balat and Hasköy were very poor, and many Jewish families owned practically nothing. According to visitors, most of the streets in those quarters were unpaved, the air unhealthy, and the entire environment unclean. These conditions brought about frequent deadly plagues and epidemics.

The Jewish communities in the city had a central organization that dealt with general common problems such as government taxation and representation in governmental affairs. Since the fifteenth century there had been a high court that ruled on appeals against lower level community court decisions. The *Maamad* (lay leadership) of the city consisted of delegates from the several communities, and its decisions were binding. There was also a

45

Va'ad Issur Ve'Heter, which controlled the ethical and religious conduct of the people. From 1835 on, the *Hakham Bashi* became the head Jewish official. He exercised great influence on the city's Jewry (as well as on the entire Jewish community in the Empire), and became the head of the Jewish court. But still the lay leadership was acting on behalf of the communities.

But the political and economic crises that caused rises in taxes and economic stagnation also deeply influenced Jewish community organization. After the end of the seventeenth century the centralized organization of the Istanbul community was forced into great debt, and its incentives were blocked by fiscal crisis. In 1742 the debt of the central organ was close to 250,000 kuruş. Interest was high; in fact it was the main item in the budget. The situation did not improve until 1772, when, however, interest on loans still accounted for 35 percent of the budget of the central body. This central body was composed of directors from the subdivisions of the larger community and paid taxes on behalf of the poor, salaries of the rabbis, and aid to the needy (especially at Passover); it also sent money to the Land of Israel (6 percent of the budget in 1772). Nevertheless, the deficit grew.

It is no wonder that, as time passed, the central governing body of the Istanbul Jews lost influence and the separate local communities took over most of its functions. Those included old responsibilities as well as new ones, especially those related to education, charity, caring for the sick, and burying the dead. These local Jewish communities had always enjoyed considerable autonomy, and they exercised it especially vigorously in times of fiscal crisis. In the nineteenth century, when, as a result of government initiatives and interventions, centralizing tendencies prevailed in Istanbul as well as elsewhere in the Ottoman Empire, the larger Istanbul Jewish community and its leadership exercised great influence on Ottoman Jewry both in religious and cultural affairs and in daily life.

The Jews of Istanbul were instrumental in helping Jewish communities throughout the Empire in times of tension or catastrophe. They frequently intervened with the authorities on behalf of Jews in cases of blood libel (like the renowned Damascus affair, initiated mainly by Christians) or misbehavior by local governors. They were also active in ransoming Jewish captives from slavery (as during the upheavals in Poland and Lithuania in 1648–49) and were extremely important in financing and organizing the Jewish communities of Palestine. In the eighteenth century, the Istanbul *Va'ad Pekidei Kushta* (body of governors) even chose the leaders of the Jerusalem community; they decided who was to receive financial aid, who would be welcome to travel to Palestine, and who would not.

The scholars of the capital were asked for opinions about communal matters by rabbis throughout the Empire, and their academies were frequented by students and scholars not only from the Empire but also from European countries. Still, the halachic literature of this period was not at the peak of Ottoman Jewish achievement in this field. Even though study was extensive and rabbinic life was vital and creative, no intellectual leaders emerged in the city from the eighteenth century on. The halachic literature was stagnant, and the homiletic literature became dominated by halachic *pilpul*. On the other hand, several literary works and anthologies written in the eighteenth and nineteenth centuries, like *Me'am Lo'ez*, are still popular today. Indeed, Ladino literature flourished in Istanbul, especially in the second half of the nineteenth century, and a number of books were written, translated, and printed in that language. Overall, however, compared with the great centers of Jewish and secular studies in eastern and western Europe, Istanbul was undoubtedly experiencing a period of cultural and economic decay in modern times, though it seems to have been barely touched by the Shabbatean movement at the end of the seventeenth century.

Istanbul was naturally the center of Romaniote (Byzantine) Jewry, and this community preserved its unique customs and rites in the city into the nineteenth century, after those of other communities had been partly submerged in the more homogeneous whole, shaped largely by the Sephardim, who dominated the Jewish cultural and economic life of the city.

After the middle of the nineteenth century there was a strong drive for reform, especially in education, encouraged mainly by the wealthy Jews of the city and the Alliance Israélite Universelle in Paris. In 1854 a Jewish high school was opened in Hasköy, and in 1868 another was opened by the government for all religious groups, with 10 percent of the student body being Jewish. The Alliance opened its schools in Istanbul only later: in Hasköy in 1874, in Balat and Galata in 1875, and so on.

These initiatives, as well as the beginning of instruction in Turkish, dismayed those who followed Jewish tradition strictly and caused bitter confrontations between reformers and supporters of the Alliance, on one hand, and the rabbis and traditional Jewish society, on the other. At the end of the nineteenth century children who attended "modern" schools constituted only a small part of the Jewish population, whereas those attending the Talmud Torah schools were much more numerous; in Balat the ratio was 120 to 700 in the 1870s.

Although the Jews of the capital had maintained their own way of life with dignity through a long period of Imperial crisis and had offered necessary aid to their brethren throughout the Empire, especially in Eretz Yisrael, as members of a decaying society they played only a minor role in modern Jewish history after the sixteenth century. Standing far from the crossroads of European history, they were isolated from the modern centers of knowledge, Enlightenment, and technology and were almost unaffected by these Western influences.

BIBLIOGRAPHY

I. *General*

1. G. Baer, "Monopolies and Restrictive Practices of Turkish Guilds," *JESHO* (*Journal of Economic and Social History of the Orient*), 13 (1970), pp. 145–165.
2. O. L. Barkan; T. Stoianovich; K. Karpat *et al.*, in: *Istanbul à la jonction des cultures balkaniques méditerranéennes, slaves et orientales au XVIe–XIXe siècles* (Istanbul: 1977).
3. B. Braude; J. Hacker; S. Rosenthal; A. Tietze *et al.*, in: *Christians and Jews in the Ottoman Empire* (ed. B. Lewis; B. Braude) (New York: 1982) (in print).
4. R. H. Davison, *Reform in the Ottoman Empire* (Princeton: 1973).
5. H. A. R. Gibb; H. Bowen, *Islamic Society and the West*, vol. 1, 2 parts: Islamic Society in the Eighteenth Century (London: 1950–57).
6. H. Inalcik, Istanbul, *Encyclopaedia of Islam*, vol. IV, fasc. pp. 63–64, 224–248.
7. C. Issawi, *The Economic History of Turkey 1800–1914* (Chicago: 1980).
8. B. Lewis, "The Impact of the French Revolution on Turkey," *Journal of World History*, 1, 1 (1953), pp. 105–125.
9. *Id.*, "Ottoman Observers of Ottoman Decline," *Islamic Studies*, 1 (1962), pp. 71–87.
10. *Id.*, *Istanbul and the Civilization of the Ottoman Empire* (Norman, Okla.: 1963).
11. *Id.*, *The Emergence of Modern Turkey* (Oxford: 1968.)
12. *Id.*, "L'Islam et les non-Musulmans," *Annales ESC*, 35, 3–4 (1980), pp. 784–800.
13. R. Mantran, *Istanbul dans la seconde moitié du XVIIe siècle* (Paris: 1962).
14. *Id.*, "Minoritaires, metiers et marchands étrangers à Istanbul aux XVI° et XVII° siècles," dans: *Minorités Techniques et Métiers* (ed. J. L. Miege) (Aix en Provence: 1979).
15. P. Masson, *Histoire du commerce français dans le Levant au XVIII siècle* (repr. New York: 1967).
16. R. W. Olson, "The Patrona Ḥalil Rebellion of 1730 in Istanbul . . . ," *JESHO*, 17 (1973), pp. 329–344.
17. *Id.*, "Jews, Janissaries, Esnaf and the Revolt of 1740 in Istanbul," *JESHO*, 20 (1977), pp. 185–207.
18. S. J. Shaw, *Between Old and New. The Ottoman Empire under Sultan Selim III, 1789–1807* (Cambridge: Mass., 1971).
19. T. Stoianovich, "The Conquering Balkan Orthodox Merchant," *Journal of Economic History*, 20 (1960), pp. 234–313.
20. N. Sousa, *The Capitulatory Regime of Turkey* (Baltimore: 1933).
21. M. A. Ubicini, *Letters on Turkey: An account of the Religious, Political, Social etc. . . . . ,* 2 vols. (London: 1856) (repr. New York: 1973).

II. *The Jews in Istanbul and the Empire*

1. A. Danon, "The Karaites of European Turkey," *JQR*, XV (1925), pp. 285–360; XVII (1926), pp. 165–198, 239–322.
2. P. Dumont, "Une source pour l'étude des communautés juives de Turquie: Les archives de l'Alliance Israélite Universelle," *Journal Asiatique*, CCLXVII (1979), pp. 101–135.
3. *Id.*, "La condition juive en Turquie à la fin du XIXe siècle," *Les Nouveaux Cahiers*, no.

57 (1979), pp. 25–38.

4. M. Franco, *Essai sur l'histoire des Israelites de l'Empire Ottoman* (Paris: 1897) (repr. Paris, 1980).

5. A. Galanté, *Histoire des Juifs d'Istanbul*, 1–2 (Istanbul: 1941–42).

6. *Id., Documents officiels turcs concernant les Juifs de Turquie* (Stamboul: 1931); *Appendice* (Istanbul: 1941).

7. *Id.*, "Recueil" and "Nouveau recueil" of "Documents officiels turcs," no. 1–7 (Istanbul: 1941–58).

8. *Id., Les synagogues d'Istanbul*, repr. from: *Hamenora* (Istanbul: 1937).

9. U. Heyd, The Jewish Communities of Istanbul in the Seventeenth Century, *Oriens*, 6 (1953), pp. 299–314.

10. H. Z. Hirschberg, "The Oriental Jewish Communities," in: *Religion in the Middle East* (ed. A. J. Arberry), vol. 1 (Cambridge: 1969), pp. 119–225.

11. A. Cohen, *An Anglo-Jewish Scrapbook, 1600–1840* (London: 1943).

12. N. A. Stillman, *The Jews of Arab Lands. A History and Source Book* (Philadelphia: 1979).

III. *The Jews in Istanbul and the Empire* (Hebrew)

1. J. Barnai, "On the History of the Jewish Community of Istanbul in the Eighteenth Century," *Miqqedem Umiyyam* (Studies in the Jewry of Islamic Countries) (Haifa: 1981) pp. 53–66.

2. *Id.*, "The Leadership of the Jewish Community in Jerusalem in the Mid-Eighteenth Century," *Shalem*, 1 (1974), pp. 271–315.

3. *Id.*, "The Status of the "General Rabbinate" in Jersualem in the Ottoman Period," *Cathedra*, 13 (1979), pp. 47–69.

4. *Id.*, "Blood Libels in the Ottoman Empire in the 15th–19th Centuries," *Antisemitism Through the Ages* (ed. Sh. Almog) (Jerusalem: 1980), pp. 211–216.

5. A. Danon, "Five Victims," *Mizrach Umaarav*, 1 (1920), pp. 271–284.

6. A.M. Lunz, "The Ḥacham Bashë in the Ottoman Empire," *Jerusalem*, 4 (1892), pp. 188–202.

7. S. Rozanes, *The History of the Jews in Turkey and the Eastern Countries*, 1–6 (1930–1938; 1945).

8. A. Yaari, *Hebrew Printing at Constantinople* (Jerusalem: 1967).

GLOSSARY * denotes word defined elsewhere in the Glossary.

amulet—an object believed to serve a protective function. The efficacy of Jewish amulets is considered to depend on their being inscribed with one or more names of God or of His angels.

Ashkenazi—in Hebrew lit. "German"; conventional term used to designate Jews of Western or Eastern European origin.

bimah—a raised platform at the front or center of the synagogue from which the Torah* is read.

chronogram—the writing of a date by means of words or biblical verses, based on the numerical value assigned to each letter in the Hebrew alphabet.

eternal light—a continuously burning lamp that hangs before the Torah ark* in a synagogue.

etrog—citron, a fruit resembling a lemon, that is one of the four species of plant used during the liturgy of the Sukkot* holiday.

gabbaim—plural of *gabbai*, an officer of a communal organization who was responsible for the collection and distribution of funds. The term is also used to designate a lay synagogue functionary.

Haggadah—the liturgical order of service for the *seder*. Also the term for the book containing the service.

ḥakham—(Turk. ḥāḥām) in Hebrew lit. "wise man"; title given to senior Sephardi* rabbis.

halakhah—generic term for Jewish law based on the Torah*, the Talmud*, and rabbinic exposition.

ḥallah—in Hebrew lit. the portion of dough removed from each baking and given to the priest in ancient Israel or burned after the destruction of the Temple; by synechdoche the name given to the bread used *par excellence* on Sabbaths and Festivals.

ḥamsa—in Arabic lit. "five"; a hand-shaped amulet.* It is commonly used by both Muslims and Jews as an apotropaic device against the evil eye.

Hanukkah—a Jewish holiday commemorating the victory of the Hasmoneans over their Greco-Syrian overlords in 165 B.C.E. and the establishment of religious freedom in ancient Israel.

havdalah—in Hebrew lit. "separation"; a ceremony held to mark the end of Sabbaths and holidays and the beginning of the workday week.

ḥuppah—a canopy under which the bride and groom stand during their wedding ceremony.

Judengasse—in German lit. "Jewish street"; the main street in the Jewish ghetto of Frankfurt.

kabbalah—in Hebrew lit. "that which has been received" or "tradition"; generic term for the Jewish mystical tradition and the esoteric teachings of Judaism.

Karaite—in Hebrew *Karai*, "one who studies the scriptural text"; the name given to a Jewish sect that followed only the scripture and rejected rabbinic interpretation.

ketubbah—in Hebrew lit. "that which is written"; a Jewish marriage contract.

kiddush—prayer of sanctification over wine recited on Sabbaths and Festivals.

kohen—a descendant of Aaron, the biblical high priest.

Ladino—Judeo-Spanish; the spoken and written language of Sephardi Jews.

matzah—unleavened bread eaten during Passover*.

megillah—a scroll, *e.g. Megillat Esther*, the Book of Esther, written on a scroll.

menorah—a seven-branched candelabrum as used in the biblical sanctuary and Jerusalem Temple; a similar candelabrum found in a synagogue; an eight-branched candelabrum used during the Hanukkah* festival.

mirror—central panel of an Ashkenazi Torah curtain*.

Mishnah—body of Jewish oral law or *halakhah* edited by Rabbi Judah ha-Nasi around the beginning of the third century C.E.

Passover—the spring pilgrimage festival commemorating the Exodus from Egypt.

pinqas—Hebrew from the Greek *pinaxes*, "register" or "list"; a book of minutes or records of a society within the Jewish community.

rimmon(im)—in Hebrew lit. "pomegranate(s)"; adornment for the staff of a Torah scroll.

Rosh Hashanah—the New Year, holy days occurring on the first and second days of the Hebrew month of Tishri.

Shabbetai Zevi (1626–1676)—a self-proclaimed messiah active in the Ottoman Empire, the central figure of Shabbateanism, the largest messianic movement in Jewish history since the destruction of the Temple in Jerusalem.

ṣah—a Turkish mark indicating that a silver object has been officially inspected.

seder—in Hebrew lit. "order"; term given to the fourteen-part order of liturgical home service for the first two nights of Passover*, which include recitation of the story of the Exodus from Egypt accompanied by ritual eating and drinking.

sêfer—Hebrew for "book".

Sephardi—in Hebrew lit. "Spanish" or "of Spain"; conventional term used to designate Jews of Spanish and Portuguese ancestry.

shammash—in Hebrew lit. "servant" or "one who ministers"; used to designate a synagogue functionary (sexton) and, specifically, the candle or light on the Hanukkah lamp that kindles (serves) the eight lamps.

Shavuot—Feast of Weeks, a two-day festival commemorating the giving of the Torah* at Sinai and the bringing of offerings to the Temple in Jerusalem, which occurs seven weeks after the second day of Passover*.

50

shiviti—a plaque hung in a synagogue inscribed with the verse *shiviti hashem lenegdi tamid*, "I have set the Lord always before me" (Ps. 16:8).

shofar—a rams' horn sounded during the services on Rosh Hashanah* and Yom Kippur as a call to repentance.

spice box—a container for the spices used during the *havdalah** service.

sukkah—in Hebrew lit. "booth"; a temporary shelter erected during the Festival of Sukkot* (Feast of Tabernacles) to recall the homes inhabited by the ancient Israelites during their wanderings in the desert.

Sukkot—Feast of Tabernacles; in Hebrew lit. "booths"; Festival which falls four days after Yom Kippur*, at the time of the autumnal harvest.

tallit—a prayer shawl (plural: *tallitot*).

Talmud—in Hebrew lit. "study" or "learning"; rabbinic commentary on the Mishnah*. The Babylonian Talmud was compiled *c.* 500 C.E., the Jerusalem Talmud *c.* 400 C.E.

tefillin—two leather boxes enclosing passages from the Torah* that are worn during morning prayer, except on Sabbaths and Festivals.

Torah—a parchment or leather scroll inscribed with the first five books of the Hebrew Bible.

Torah ark—a cabinet set in or against one wall of a synagogue. It holds the Torah scrolls and is the focus of prayer.

Torah binder—a band that holds the two staves of a Torah scroll together when the Torah is not being read.

Torah curtain—a curtain hung in front of the Torah ark* in synagogues. It generally consists of a curtain and a valence.

Torah mantle—a cover of silk or other precious fabric that encases the Torah scroll and is removed for reading.

Torah pointer—a small rod of wood or precious metal used by the reader of the Torah to follow the text.

Torah shield—an ornamental metal plaque hung from the staves of a Torah, sometimes having small interchangeable plates inscribed with the names of holy days, indicating the appropriate readings.

tughrā—(Arabic, in Turkish *ṭugrā*) the Ottoman sultan's official signature, written in ornamental fashion.

wimpel—the Ashkenazi* name for a Torah binder*.

yarmulke—Ashkenazi* term for a small cap worn by a Jewish man; in Hebrew "*kippah.*"

yeshivah—an academy or school for Jewish learning.

Yom Kippur—in Hebrew lit. "Day of Atonement"; a day of fasting and prayer that falls on the tenth day of the Hebrew month of Tishri.

z.l.—*z[iḥrono] l[ivraḥah]* (Fem. *ziḥronah levraḥah*), in Hebrew lit. "may his (her) remembrance be for a blessing"; a Hebrew honorific used after the name of a deceased person.

Notes to the Catalogue

IN THE ENTRIES maximum dimensions are given, in the following order: height or length, width, depth. For circular objects, height is followed by diameter, designated dm. A glossary of terms used in the entries begins on p. 48. In accordance with guild regulations, Frankfurt silver from the period covered by the exhibition generally bears two hallmarks, one for the city and one for the master. These marks help to establish dates and authorship. They are frequently designated here by numbers in standard reference works on the subject; the abbreviated titles of these and other works appear in the Bibliography of Frequently Cited Sources, which begins on p. 167. In contrast, the marks on Turkish silver give no indication of the master; they do, however, provide *termini ante quem* for manufacture. The entire subject of Turkish silver marks remains to be studied in depth.

The transcriptions of Hebrew inscriptions are complete, except for the omission of standard honorifics, indicated by ellipses. The only notable exception is the term *z.l.*, which contributes significantly to the meaning of the inscriptions. Another interesting feature of Hebrew inscriptions is the use of chronograms, based on the numerical value traditionally assigned to each letter. The chronograms that appear on objects included in this exhibition all omit the first digit of the Hebrew year. The remaining numbers are sometimes incorporated into quotations from Scriptures or the liturgy, with relevant letters marked by accents. Because of printing limitations, the range of diacritical marks used in the inscriptions could not be reproduced exactly here, but an attempt has been made to suggest their variety.

Translations of verses from the Five Books of Moses (the Torah) have been taken from the new translation by the Jewish Publication Society of America (2nd ed.; Philadelphia: 1974). Quotations from the Prophets and Writings have been taken from the J.P.S. edition of 1955. Other translations are by the authors of the entries unless otherwise indicated.

The transliteration of Hebrew terms is according to the system set forth in the *Encyclopaedia Judaica*, except for names and terms that have entered English usage, which have been given their most common spellings. Ottoman Turkish terms have been transliterated according to the system established by the *International Journal of Middle East Studies*.

Each entry is followed by the initials of its author.

A Tale of Two Cities: Catalogue

"The coexistence through many centuries of two Jewries like the Ashkenazim and the Sephardim is a remarkable phenomenon in Jewish history. There is almost no department in which they did not differ. These differences range from anthropological and sociological distinctions to differences of custom in the observance of religious laws which culminated in the crystallization of two separate legal systems. There is also another fact which makes the coexistence of Ashkenazi and Sephardic Jewries something unique in history. Although deviating from each other in their way of life they have always been united in their desire to serve Judaism; although divided in their customs they have always been in harmony with each other where religion itself was concerned; although adhering strictly to its own traditions each Jewry has respected highly the tradition of the other Jewry; and finally, although each of them has always defended its legal system, the representatives of one community have always enjoyed the confidence of the other." (Zimmels, *Ashkenazim and Sephardim*.)

1. View of the Galata Bridge, Istanbul

Istanbul, late nineteenth century
Photograph on paper
7-7/8 × 10-1/8 in., 20.0 × 25.7 cm.
The Jewish Museum, New York, JM 158-68

The Galata Bridge spans the Golden Horn, connecting two sections of the city, the original peninsula, Stamboul, and Galata, where Europeans lived during Ottoman times. This photograph was taken from the Galata side of the bridge, looking towards the old city. The Yeni Çami (New Mosque), just on the other side of the bridge, was built in the early seventeenth century on the site of the former Karaite Jewish quarter. The Karaites were evicted by Sultan Meḥmed III (1595–1603) when he began construction of the mosque. At the left is the Mosque (formerly the church) of Hagya Sofya.

E. D. B.

2. Postcard of Rothschild Family House and Synagogue, Frankfurt

Frankfurt, c. 1904
Printed on paper
5-1/16 × 3-5/8 in., 12.8 × 9.2 cm.
Leo Baeck Institute, New York

In this view down the Judengasse, the Rothschild house can be seen in the foreground on the right-hand side of the street. It is distinguished by six lozenge shapes beneath each window on the second and third stories, which serve to articulate each bay, and by the pointed gable roof. Two buildings separate it from the main synagogue (or Börnestrasse Synagogue), with its imposing onion domes (see no. 84). The caption reads, *Frankfurt a. M. Rothschilds' Stammhaus und Synagoge*, "Frankfurt o[n the] M[ain], Rothschilds' Family House and Synagogue." The card is postmarked from Frankfurt, March 19, 1904, and was sent to a woman in Vienna.

The Judengasse (Jewish Street) formed the heart of the Frankfurt ghetto, which was established in 1460 (see no. 44). Over the centuries the Judengasse came to symbolize not only the persecution and isolation of the Jews of that city, but also the rich spiritual and communal life that flourished behind the ghetto walls, as well as the many achievements of its inhabitants, among whom the Rothschilds figured prominently. Even after the abolition of the ghetto in 1811, some members of the Jewish community continued to live in the Judengasse. Gudule Rothschild (see no. 105) remained in the family house pictured here, even after her children had moved away and her husband had died.

E. D. B.

Common Origins, Beliefs and Observances

According to tradition, the patriarch Abraham was the first individual to recognize one God and to follow His directive to settle in the land of Canaan (later Israel). Abraham's descendents continued to inhabit the land except for a period of slavery in Egypt (c. 1600–1200 B.C.E.).

Later, Nebuchadnezzar's victories led to the destruction of the Solomonic Temple in Jerusalem and to exile to Babylon (586–539 B.C.E.). After the return, the Jews built the Second Temple which stood until the Roman conquest in 70 C.E.. Records of the Second Temple period indicate that Jews had already then begun to migrate to nearby lands. By the ninth century, a continuous Jewish presence had been established in northern France and the Rhineland and another in Spain. These two areas became the centers of the two major Jewish groups: the Ashkenazim and the Sephardim. During the formative period of the Early Middle Ages, the two centers were separated geographically and evolved under completely different cultures and political systems. Though the Ashkenazim and Sephardim developed different attitudes towards their common heritage, they remained linked by their common traditions and their common ideals, beliefs and customs.

In Spain an important portion of the Jewish community was intimately involved with Muslim and Christian life. Jewish culture there developed as a synthesis of Judaism and the two Spanish cultures which had reached levels of sophistication far surpassing those of any other European country. This is evident in Sephardi values which are influenced by Muslim and Christian philosophy, science, language and worldliness. For example, the Sephardim created a rich secular literary tradition and stressed language skills such as grammar and precise expression. In contrast, the Jews of Ashkenazi background were far more isolated from medieval Christian culture which was comparatively backward north of the Pyrenees until the High Middle Ages. Consequently, Ashkenazi Jewry was inner directed and stressed values like humility and piety which had been present in the Palestinian and Babylonian traditions.

On the level of popular belief and customs, both Ashkenazim and Sephardim were deeply influenced by the practices of the people among whom they lived. In matters of *halakhah* (Jewish law) and the study of Talmud, both Sephardim and Ashkenazim based their studies on the Babylonian Talmud and on Midrash and Gaonic literature. Both depended on the commentaries of Rabbi Solomon Itzhaki (Rashi), but while the Ashkenazim utilized literature written by scholars in Franco-German centers (*Tosafot*) the Sephardim relied on other sources (for example the *novellae* of R. Solomon b. Adret, R. Nissim and Nachmanides).

As a result of better communication and migrations in the late Middle Ages, the two groups interacted to a greater degree and scholars wrote works which synthesized the varied halakhic traditions, for example the famous *Tur* of Rabbi Jacob b. Asher, who left Germany and settled in Spain in the fourteenth century.

The Patriarchal Period

All Jews consider themselves descendants of the patriarchs Abraham, Isaac, and Jacob. Their strong and vital ties to the land of Israel are ultimately based on God's covenant with Abraham, the promise that Abraham's descendants will inhabit the land forever (Gen. 12:7). At the close of the patriarchal period c. 1700 B.C.E., the Jewish nation was enslaved in Egypt for more than 400 years until its liberation under the leadership of Moses. After a period of forty years spent wandering in the desert, the Jews entered the Promised Land, where they established an independent state that lasted until conquest by the Babylonians in 586 B.C.E.

54

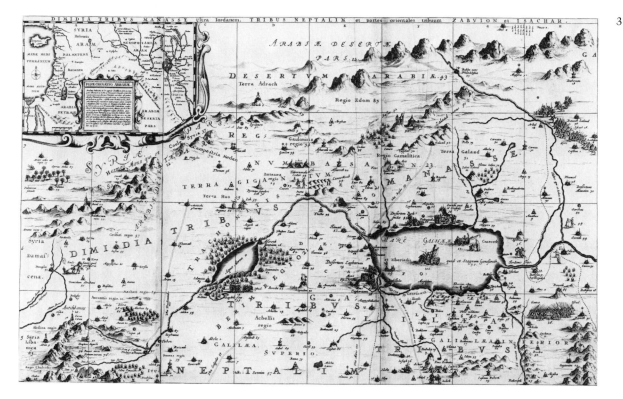

3. Map of Tribal Territories in the Holy Land

Amsterdam, 1658
Jan Jansson (1588–1664)
Engraving on paper
16-3/4 × 27-3/4 in., 42.5 × 70.5 cm.
The Jewish Museum, New York, gift of Mr. Charles R. Gordon, '79-154

This map, entitled *Dimidia Tribus Manasse Ultra Iordanem Tribus Neptalim et Partes Orientales Tribum Zabvion et Isachar*, is one in a sequence of seven maps of the Holy Land published in Jansson's *Novus Atlas*. Oriented toward the east, it shows the territories of half the tribe of Manasseh, the tribe of Naphtali, and the eastern portions of the tribes of Zebulun and Issachar, territories established under Joshua, successor to Moses. The cartouche at upper left, labeled *Peregrinato Abrahae*, encloses a map of the Near East showing the wanderings of Abraham.

E. D. B.

4. Mizrach

Kassel, 1838
Adam Rosenzweig (b. 1826)
Water color and ink on paper
6-7/8 × 7 in., 16.3 × 17.8 cm.
The Jewish Museum, New York, gift of Dr. Guido Schoenberger, JM 75-64

This small painting was designed to indicate to the worshiper the proper attitude and direction of prayer. At the top, partially framed by a wreath held by two angels, is a quotation from Psalms 16:8:

שויתי ה' ל[נגדין] תמיד

I have set the Lord always b[efore me].

The emphasis on the Lord's name through enlargement of the letters and placement of the crown above it necessitated abbreviation of the next word in order to maintain the symmetry of the composition. At the center, in large letters, is the word מזרח ("east"), which also serves as a mnemonic device for the saying written below:

מצד זה רוח החיים

From this direction comes the breath of life.

The initial letters of this epigram are emphasized by diacritical marks, and all the letters are decorated with *taggim*, the ornaments placed by scribes above letters of the Torah. The lively polychrome treatment of the letters is similar to that employed in the decoration of Torah binders (see no. 62).

For centuries, the Temple in Jerusalem was the central focus of Jewish religious observance. After its destruction, Jews continued to turn toward Jerusalem during worship, and it became common practice to place signs in synagogues and homes to indicate the correct direction. For Jews in the West, this direction was east, and the sign thus came to be known as a *mizrach*, the Hebrew word for "east."

Adam Rosenzweig was born in Kassel on February 1, 1826. This *mizrach* was executed when he was only twelve years old. Later Rosenzweig became known as an engraver of woodcuts. He was the uncle of Franz Rosenzweig, the famed Jewish theologian, who was also born in Kassel but who spent the later portion of his life in Frankfurt.

V. B. M.

The Babylonian Exile

After the conquest by Nebuchadnezzar II in 586 B. C. E., most of the leaders of Judah were exiled to Babylonia, leaving the rest of the population behind in Palestine. Eventually strong communities and great *yeshivot*, or schools of learning, were established by the exiles. The Babylonian Talmud, a compendium of legal discussions that became the basis of later Jewish law for both Ashkenazim and Sephardim, was compiled in the academies of Sura and Pumbedita.

In this period, differences in observance and custom already existed between Palestinian and Babylonian Jewry.

6

5. Babylonian Talmud

Istanbul, 1782
Published by Hayyim Elia Faro
Ink on paper
13-5/8 × 9-7/16 × 7/8 in., 34.6 × 24.0 × 2.2 cm.
The Library of the Jewish Theological Seminary of
America, New York

This edition of the first Talmudic tractate, *Berakhot*, dealing mostly with matters of ritual and liturgy, was printed for the use of students at Jewish schools in Istanbul. This particular copy contains numerous examples of doodling throughout. On f. 16a, a student signed his name: Menahem b. Israel.

M. S. C.

Monotheism

Though other nations of the Near East briefly experimented with monotheism, it was the Israelites who established belief in one God as the central tenet of their faith. The quintessential expression of monotheism in Jewish liturgy is the prayer, Shma Yisrael, "Hear O Israel, the Lord our God the Lord is One." (Deut. 6:4). Belief in one God is incorporated into the Ten Commandments and is expressed by the wording of all blessings, which begin "Blessed art Thou O Lord our God, King of the Universe..."

6. Shiviti

Germany, 1834–1835
Abraham ben Leibschutz
Paint and ink on paper
14-5/8 × 11-7/16 in., 37.2 × 29.0 cm.
The Jewish Museum, New York, gift of Dr. Harry G.
Friedman, F 3949

This painting combines visual imagery and texts. At the sides are two flat ornamental pilasters decorated with fanciful motifs painted in blue, red, yellow, green, and gold. They are joined below by a thin red strip serving as a ground line and above by an inscription in large letters also filled with flat decorative forms in similar colors. In the center a red arch bears a crown supported by lions perched in trees growing in a verdant garden. Beneath the arch is a depiction of the sun with a human face and an inscription in cursive characters:

ממזרח שמש עד מבואו מהולל שם ה'

From the rising of the sun to the going down thereof the Lord's name is to be praised.
(Ps. 113:3).

Between this composition and the pilasters are two roundels framed in red, green, and yellow. Two additional roundels bordered in red are set within the pilaster bases; they contain the painter's name and the date on which he completed the *shiviti*:

אברהם / בן כהרב ליבשיץ / עשה הציור / הזה.

נעשה ונגמר / ראש חודש/חשבון (כך!)

תקצה/לפ"ק.

Abraham son of Leibschutz made this drawing. [It was] made and finished on the New Moon of Ḥeshvan 5[595] (1835).

According to the inscriptions, this composition was designed to serve three purposes. The largest inscription reads:

שויתי ה' לנגדי תמיד

I have set the Lord always before me.
(Ps. 16:8).

This sentence is commonly found on plaques used in synagogues as invocations to worshipers. On the pilaster bases are the letters מז/רח , "east," indicating the direction of prayer (see no. 4). Finally, the two largest roundels contain the beginnings of the blessing recited after wine is drunk and after food (other than bread) is eaten. The main body of the text, common to both prayers, appears in the lower portion of the painting. The concluding section of the blessing with alternative readings for Sabbaths, new moons, and holidays are arranged in the small roundels at the bottom. From this combination of texts it may be supposed that this *shiviti* was created for a synagogue and was hung in a room where services were held and food eaten. That the synagogue was in Germany is indicated by the style of the lettering and its ornamentation, which have close parallels in German Torah binders (see no. 62), and by comparison with a similar *shiviti* in the Feuchtwanger Collection painted in Leuterhausen, Germany, in 1833.[1]

1. Shachar, *Jewish Tradition in Art*, no. 111.

V. B. M.

Giving of the Torah

The paramount event in the early history of the Jewish nation was the receipt of the Torah, the Five Books of Moses, at Sinai, an event which took place after the Exodus from Egypt. The belief that the Torah was given by God and freely accepted by the entire Jewish nation laid the foundation for a continuing Jewish commitment to the laws and precepts contained within it. These written laws of the Torah were elaborated in the "oral law," the Talmud.

8

7. Moses Presenting the Tablets of the Law to the Israelites

France, late seventeenth century
Jean Lepautre (1617–1682)
Etching on paper
8-7/8 × 12 in., 22.5 × 30.5 cm.
The Jewish Museum, New York, U 7143-38

8. Torah Scroll

Nuremberg, 1700–1751
Johann Conrad Weiss (staves and fittings)
Marks: R³3767, 4279
Ink on vellum; staves, wood with silver, cast and engraved
Scroll: 6-9/16 in., 16.7 cm.; staves: 15-3/8 in., 39.0 cm.
The Jewish Museum, New York, gift of Samuel and Lucille Lemberg, JM 54-52

This small, finely written Torah scroll is rolled on wooden staves fitted with silver handles and finials of baluster form. The latter are joined to circular caps with incised scalloped borders, which are fitted over the wooden cores of the rollers.

Similar scalloped borders with incised lines occur on other eighteenth-century German Judaica, particularly circumcision implements (see no. 36). There are two other works by Weiss in the collection of The Jewish Museum: a pair of *rimmonim* (F 70) and a spicebox (F 383). The small size and the absence of any dedicatory inscription on the handle plates suggest that this Torah scroll was commissioned by a private individual for his own use.

V. B. M.

9. Babylonian Talmud

Frankfurt, 1720
Published by Johann Kellner
Ink on paper
13-3/8 × 9-1/4 × 2-1/16 in., 34.0 × 23.5 × 5.2 cm.
The Library of the Jewish Theological Seminary of America, New York

This volume contains the tractates *Bava Kamma* and *Bava Mezia*, which deal with different aspects of torts and civil legislation. A Latin summary of the contents and the imperial seal are included on the title page.

M. S. C.

10. Mishneh Torah, Volume 4

Istanbul, 1509
Published by Abraham Yaish
Ink printed on vellum
13-5/16 × 8-15/16 × 2-1/8 in., 33.9 × 22.8 × 5.4 cm.
The Library of the Jewish Theological Seminary of America, New York

This magnificent volume contains the section of Maimonides' great code of law (*Mishneh Torah*) that deals with sexual and dietary prohibitions. Although the text of this work had been printed before, this edition is the first to include some of the commentaries that were to become standard. As was customary in early printed Hebrew books, the title page faces the opening page of the text. This volume belongs to the only complete set printed on vellum known to have survived to our day; this entire set is in the collection of The Jewish Theological Seminary. The colophon in the eighth and final volume reads:

> . . . [a]nd I, the young Abraham, son of my lord, teacher and rabbi, Joseph, son of Yaish, may his pious memory be for a blessing . . . and [the work on] this worthy book was completed in the First Adar, in the year 5269 A.M. [1509] in Constantinople, the great city that is under the rule of our lord and king, Sultan Bāyezid, may his glory be magnified and his majesty exalted in his days, and in our days, may Judah be redeemed and may Israel dwell securely. Amen, may such be the will of God.

Maimonides (1135–1204), a great scholar and physician, was born in Cordoba to a Sephardi family who left Spain in 1148. He was active as a physician and scholar in Fustat (old Cairo), and wrote works on science, philosophy, and Judaism that became classics. The *Mishneh Torah* is a synthesis and systematization of laws contained in the Talmud and became one of the bases of all later codifications, both Ashkenazi and Sephardi.

M. S. C.

Daily Worship

Until the destruction of the Second Temple in 70 C.E., the Jewish worship of God was based on offerings and sacrifices made in His Holy Temple in Jerusalem. Still, prayer was not unknown in the Temple period, and the antiquity of this institution is suggested by the Jewish tradition that ascribes the establishment of the daily order of prayers—for the morning, the afternoon, and the evening—to the three patriarchs Abraham, Isaac, and Jacob, respectively. After the destruction and exile of the Jewish people, prayer assumed greater importance.

11. Tefillin

Turkey, nineteenth century
Leather, dyed, and ink on parchment
1-1/2 × 1 × 3/4 in., 3.4 × 2.4 × 2.0 cm.
United States Museum of Natural History, Smithsonian Institution, Washington, D.C., 130276

The *tefillin* are a pair of leather boxes containing passages from the Torah written on parchment; one is worn on the head, the other on the arm, and both are held in place by means of straps. Each box contains four biblical passages;[1] those in the box for the head are inscribed on one parchment, those for the arm are on separate pieces each placed in its own compartment.

The commandment to wear *tefillin* is recorded in the following passage: "Bind them as a sign on your hand and as a symbol on your foreheads" (Deut. 6:8, 11:12). It is generally taken to apply to a male worshiper during the morning service, though on fast days *tefillin* are not worn until the afternoon and on Sabbaths and festivals they are not worn at all. There is evidence that in some periods of Jewish history *tefillin* were worn the entire day, but it is uncertain how widespread the practice was. The word *tefillin* has no English translation. "Phylacteries," a term derived from Greek and often used for amulets, is inappropriate.

1. The passages are from Ex. 13:1–10, 11–16, and Deut. 6:4–9, 11:13–21. The composition of *tefillin* is uniform among all Jews; the only difference is in the order of the passages. Recent archaeological discoveries show that the

59

customs followed today were also practiced in the first centuries of this era. See *Encyclopaedia Judaica*, XV: 904.

REFERENCE: Casanowicz, 1929, no. 12, pl. 2.

V. B. M.

12. Tefillin and Cases

Germany, nineteenth century
Marks: MW and 13
Case: silver, engraved; *tefillin*: leather, dyed, and ink on parchment
2-1/8 × 3-1/8 in., 5.4 × 7.9 cm.
The Jewish Museum, New York, gift of Dr. Harry G. Friedman, F 2329a, b

12

In order to be fit for ritual use (kosher) *tefillin* boxes cannot be damaged. There thus arose the necessity for covering and protecting the leather while the *tefillin* are not being worn. These cases are fashioned of silver, each side engraved with a flower set within a rectilinear border. On top of each is a crowned cartouche, one engraved של/יד ("for the hand"), the other של ראש "for the head").

Such cases were mainly made in nineteenth-century Germany and Poland.[1]

1. *Cf.* Barnett, nos. 581–583.

V. B. M.

The Sabbath

The Fourth Commandment of the Decalogue enjoins the people of Israel to remember and observe the Sabbath, the only holy day explicitly mentioned in that text (Ex. 20:8–11; Deut. 5:12–15). Various reasons for this observance are suggested in the Torah: that in resting Israel imitates God, Who rested on the seventh day of Creation; that observance of the Sabbath sanctifies life; and that it is humane to allow one's servants and animals to rest. Over the centuries the Sabbath became not only a period of cessation from work but also a time of prayer, study, and spiritual renewal. It is celebrated with ceremonies both in the home and in the synagogue.

13. Die Sabbaths Ceremonien

Sabbath Ceremonies from Paul Christian Kirchner, *Jüdisches Ceremoniel*
Nuremberg, 1724
Johann Georg Puschner (active c. 1705–1750)
Etching and engraving on paper
Page: 7-3/16 × 8-3/4 in., 19.8 × 22.2 cm.; plate: 5-3/4 × 7 in., 14.5 × 17.8 cm.
The Library of the Jewish Theological Seminary of America, New York

The third plate in Kirchner's book on Jewish ceremonies depicts the celebration of the Sabbath. Inset at the top is a picture of the celebration in the home. On Friday evening the wife lights the Sabbath candles, which can be seen on the table; the hanging Sabbath lamp (*Judenstern, cf.* no. 116) has already been lowered and lit. At the back the father blesses his two children. In the foreground Puschner has shown part of the *havdalah* ceremony at the close of the Sabbath: The father holds a wine cup and spice container. The figure of a man seated at the laid table is most likely intended to refer to the festive meals that are part of the celebration of the Sabbath.

In the main portion of the plate the interior of the Fürth synagogue during a Sabbath morning service is depicted. At the right is the Torah ark with a decorated curtain before it (*cf.* no. 57); a *menorah* (*cf.* no. 59) stands beside it. In the center of the room

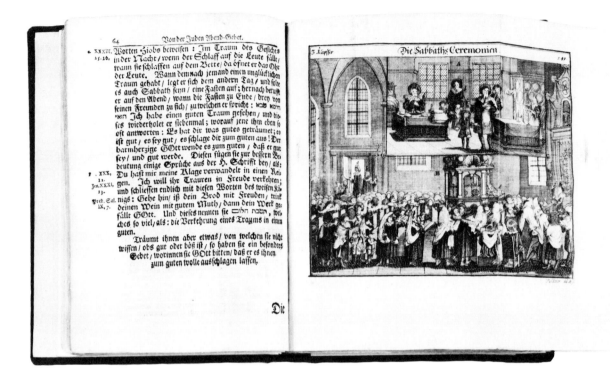

is the *bimah* and a man reading from an open Torah scroll (*cf.* no. 8). The man standing in the doorway performs the ritual washing of the hands before entering the sanctuary; his neighbor kisses the *mezuzah*[1] on the door post.

1. A *mezuzah* is a parchment scroll inscribed with biblical passages (Deut. 6:4–9, 11:13–21) that is affixed to the doorposts of Jewish homes and communal buildings, usually encased in a protective cover.

REFERENCE: Rubens, *Iconography*, 1981, no. 542.

E. D. B.

14. Kiddush Cup

Turkey, late nineteenth century
Silver, cast and engraved
2-3/16 × 2 in. dm., 5.6 × 5.1 cm.
The Jewish Museum, New York, U7607

The cup is shaped like a squat urn to which a cast

handle in scroll form was later soldered, obscuring a portion of the inscription. Both the base and rim are decorated with beadwork. Below the rim an inscription is engraved:

קדוש ליום השבת עובדי/בן יעקב הכהן

Kiddush for the Sabbath day, Ovadia[h] son of Jacob ha-Cohen

The remainder of the exterior surface of the cup is decorated with an engraved flowering vine on a stippled ground.

The decorative features of this cup—the engraved design on a stippled ground, the beadwork around the rim, and the scrolled handle—are similar to those of a charity box also in the collection of The Jewish Museum that bears the *ṭughrā* of 'Abd al-Hamīd II (see no. 210) and to those of a related box in the Jewish Museum, London, described as of the early nineteenth century.[1] The decoration of the exhibited box is more regular and mechanical than that of the cup, suggesting that the latter is somewhat earlier.

1. Barnett, no. 578.

V. B. M.

The High Holidays

The high holidays of the Jewish Year are Rosh Hashonah (Head of the Year), which falls on the first two days of the Hebrew month of Tishrei, and Yom Kippur, the Day of Atonement, which falls on the tenth day of the same month. These holy days and the period between them are known collectively as the Days of Awe, a time of prayer, penitence, and self-examination in which each Jew reviews his conduct over the preceding twelve months and prays that the coming year will bring life and blessing.

type: "Emil Grünebaum, *Litohgr.* [*sic*] *Atelier* Frankfurt a. M." The field is enclosed in a rectangle defined by a thin wavy line with decorative bells and flowers at the corners. Along the outside of the rectangle are phrases taken from the prayer *Avinu Malkenu* ("Our Father, Our King"), which is recited on the High Holidays:

כתבנו בספר חיים טובים / חדש עלינו שנה
טובה / זכרנו בזכרון טוב לפניך / כתבנו
בספר זכיות

Inscribe us in the book of good life; renew unto us a good New Year; remember us with good favor; inscribe us in the book of merit.

The entire card is framed by strips of undulating ribbon.

E. D. B.

16

15. New Year's Postcard

> Frankfurt, 1877
> Emil Grünebaum
> Lithograph on paper
> 3-5/8 × 5-1/16 in., 9.2 × 12.9 cm.
> Leo Baeck Institute, New York

Greetings for the New Year, printed in German Gothic and set within a decorative oval comprised of leaf and scroll forms, occupy the central portion of this card:

> *Herzliche Gratulation zum Neuen Jahre*
> *5638.* התרל"ח
> Best wishes for the New Year 5638 (1877–1878). [5638, the date repeated in Hebrew]

They are surmounted by the traditional Hebrew message:

"לשנה טובה"

For a good year.

Along the lower edge the name of the lithographer and the city are printed in Latin boldface and italic

16. Shofar

> Germany, eighteenth century
> Horn, engraved
> 16 × 3/4 in., 40.7 × 1.4 cm.
> The Jewish Museum, New York, gift of Dr. Harry G. Friedman, F 502

The edge of the *shofar* is decorated with dots arranged in a series of triangles, with three short lines projecting from the apex of every other triangle. At the opening and just above the curve of the *shofar* are bands of crosshatching bordered by similar triangles and lines. A broken loop projects from the outer edge near the wide opening. The following quotation is engraved along the length of the *shofar*, beginning at the large opening on one side and ending at the mouthpiece on the other:

תקעו*בחדש*שופר*בכסא*ליום*חגינו*
כי*חוק*לישר[אל]/הוא משפט*לאלקי*
יעקב*בחצוצרות*קול**שופר*

62

Blow the horn at the new moon, at the full moon for our feast day. For it is a statute for Israel, an ordinance of the God of Jacob. (Ps. 81:4–5). With trumpets and the sound of the horn. (Ps. 98:6).

These sentences are part of the Rosh Hashanah service, during which the *shofar* is sounded one hundred times as a call to penitence.

Identical decoration appears on two other *shofarot* in the collection of The Jewish Museum (D 117 and F 1746), on one in the Israel Museum[1] the entire group may be dated by the inscriptions on two other examples, which include the year in addition to the same verses found on all the others.[2]

1. Shachar, *Jewish Tradition in Art*, no. 312.
2. Barnett, no. 195; Sotheby Parke Bernet, New York, *Good Judaica and Related Works of Art*, Sales catalogue, May 13, 1981, no. 111.

V. B. M.

17. La Pénitence des Juifs Allemans dans Leur Synagogue

The Penitence of German Jews in Their Synagogue, from *Cérémonies et coutumes religieuses de tous les peuples du monde*, Vol I.
Paris, 1741
Pieter Tanjé (1706–1761), after a design by Louis-Fabricius du Bourg (1693–1775)
Engraving on paper
Page: 14-3/4 × 10 in., 36.5 × 25.3 cm.; plate: 12-1/2 × 8-3/8 in., 31.8 × 21.2 cm.
The Jewish Museum, New York, gift of Dr. Harry G. Friedman, F 5863

The ten days between Rosh Hashanah and Yom Kippur, the Days of Awe, are traditionally a time of reflection, self-scrutiny, and repentance for Jews. Prayer and fasting are part of the observance of these days, and in some communities it is customary to receive symbolic lashes (*malkot*) on the eve of Yom Kippur. The lashes are administered as the repentant Jew recites the *Ashamnu*, a short confessional prayer. The man who strikes the blows invokes God's mercy, saying, "For He is merciful and forgives iniquity."

Cérémonies et coutumes religieuses de tous les peuples du monde (*Religious Ceremonies and Customs of All the Peoples of the World*) was a collab-

17

oration between the Amsterdam publisher J.F. Bernard and the French-born artist Bernard Picart (1673–1733), who settled in Amsterdam in 1711. The first volume, which included the section on Jews, was published in 1723, though the final volume did not appear until 1743. Picart designed and engraved most of the plates, taking great care to depict religious observances accurately. His prints are thus a valuable source of knowledge of eighteenth-century Jewish customs.

La Pénitence is one of two plates that appeared only in the Paris edition, which was published in 1741. Although produced under Picart's supervision, they were designed by du Bourg and engraved by Tanjé, both Amsterdam artists.

REFERENCE: Rubens, *Iconography*, 1981, no. 458.

E. D. B.

63

18. Prayer Shawl for the High Holidays

Ottoman Empire, eighteenth or nineteenth century
Silk brocade embroidered with metallic threads and metal foil; cotton
17-1/4 × 70 in., 43.7 × 177.7 cm.
The Jewish Museum, New York, H. Ephraim and Mordecai Benguiat Family Collection, S55

This prayer shawl, or *tallit,* is fashioned mainly of white silk woven in a diamond pattern. Metallic threads interwoven with the silk form a narrow border at each end. To each of these borders is attached a relatively short band of cotton embroidered in metallic threads and foil forming two patterns: a row of segmented scrolls, and a continuous flowering vine. The lower edge of the cotton is fringed, and ritual fringes of wool (*ẓiẓiyot*) are attached to the corners. Because metallic threads and foil of copper, silver, and gold were used, the embroidery exhibits subtle polychrome effects.

Among Sephardim the custom of wearing a white *tallit* on the high holidays as a sign of purity was not widespread, as it was among the Ashkenazim, but the cantor (*hazzan*) often did so.

V. B. M.

18

Pilgrim Festivals

When the Jewish nation lived in ancient Israel, each of these festivals was a time of pilgrimage to the Temple in Jerusalem and the bringing of offerings, rites that are today commemorated through prayer. Today each holiday is also linked with the historical experience of ancient Israel: Passover recalls the Exodus from Egypt, Shavuot the giving of the Torah at Sinai, and Sukkot (Tabernacles) the wandering in the desert. The annual celebration of these holidays among both Ashkenazim and Sephardim is a continual reminder of the common origins and religious principles that unite the two groups.

Sukkot

In celebration of the holiday of Sukkot, which falls four days after Yom Kippur, Jews build booths (*sukkot*) representing the homes inhabited by the ancient Israelites in the years between the Exodus from Egypt and their entry into the land of Canaan. During the holiday it is customary to eat all meals in the *sukkah.*

The Torah also commands that on Sukkot each Jew hold together four species of plants that grew in the land of Israel and recite blessings over them. They are the palm, the willow, and the myrtle (which are bound together with strips of palm to form a *lulav*), and the citron.

19. Members of the Benguiat Family Outside Their Sukkah

Izmir, last quarter of the nineteenth century
Photograph on paper
7-3/16 × 9-3/16 in., 18.2 × 23.3 cm.
The Jewish Museum, New York, Benguiat Document File

Hadji Ephraim Benguiat is shown standing in front of his *sukkah,* holding the traditional *arba'ah minim* (four species): the *lulav* (palm, willow, and myrtle branches) and *etrog* (citron). The two women are probably his wife and daughter (for further information on Benguiat, see pp. 20-23).

This photograph shows the Turkish Jewish custom of creating the "walls" of the *sukkah* by hanging decorative fabrics from a wooden frame. A curtain tie (see no. 20) is used to hold back the textile hanging over the entrance. In the foreground are a laver and basin used in the ritual washing of the hands (see no. 161).

E. D. B.

20. Curtain Tie

Turkey, early eighteenth century
Cotton and silk, embroidered with polychrome silk and metallic threads
71 × 8-5/8 in., 180.4 × 21.9 cm.
The Jewish Museum, New York, the H. Ephraim and Mordecai Benguiat Family Collection, S 106

The embroidered portions of the towel ends are bordered by thin rows of metallic and silk drawn stitches. A diamond-shaped field is centered on each; it frames a stylized vase of flowers in which are perched two birds. These shapes are woven of white silk and embroidered with gilt threads. They are set on a ground of openwork. Floral designs fill the corners; each consists of two green tulips with blue stamens, a single carnation, and metallic leaves, in an axial arrangement. Only the colors of the carnations differ: Two are white and gold, and two are white and pink with red outlines. All the embroidery is very finely worked.

According to H. Ephraim Benguiat, this tie was made by a Jew of Izmir in the seventeenth century and was used to hold back the curtain that hung over the entrance to the *sukkah*. Comparisons with dated textiles in Swedish collections suggest an early eighteenth-century date, however, and the extremely fine quality of the workmanship may even belong to a court atelier.[1]

1. Geijer, *Oriental Textiles*, nos. 145, 148, 149, 151, 153, pls. 76–78, 85.

REFERENCES: Adler and Casanowicz, 1901, no. 42, pl. 27; Adler and Casanowicz, 1908, no. 106; *Fabric of Jewish Life*, no. 195.

V. B. M.

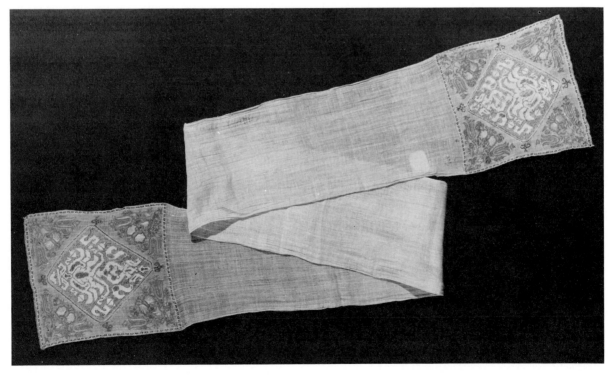

21 22

21. Etrog Container

Germany, nineteenth century
Silver, cast and hammered
4-3/4 × 5-3/8 in., 12.1 × 13.7 cm.
The Jewish Museum, New York, gift of Dr. Harry
G. Friedman, F 87

This container was intended to hold the *etrog* (citron) for the Sukkot holiday. Its shape is modeled on that of the fruit itself: a hollow citron supported by a thick stem rising from a leafy base. The undulating surface, achieved by means of hammering, simulates the texture of the fruit.

The earliest extant example of a fruit-shaped *etrog* container was made in Augsburg in 1670–1680 (The Jewish Museum, F 4390). Judging by the number of such containers known from the nineteenth century, the form was especially popular at that time. There are three similar pieces in the collection of The Jewish Museum (F 6a, F 6172, and D 74) the marks on which date them to the nineteenth century.[1]

1. *Cf. Danzig 1939*, no. 40.

V. B. M.

22. Etrog Container

Turkey, nineteenth century
Silver, cast, repoussé, engraved, and punched
5-7/16 × 3 in., 13.7 × 7.6 cm.
The Jewish Museum, New York, the H. Ephraim
and Mordecai Benguiat Family Collection, S 108

This container is in the form of a covered urn on a stepped circular base. Rows of leaves are the main decorative motifs. They occur on the base, the cover, and as a border motif on the urn itself. Festoons of flowers executed in repoussé with engraved details encircle the body of the urn. The style of the flowers

and leaves is similar to that of other works stamped with the *tughrās* of the Ottoman sultans, for example, no. 203. Above and below the festoons, the following inscriptions are set off against a stippled ground:

ולקחתם / לכם ביום / הראשון / פרי עץ הדר

/ פרי הדר

On the first day you shall take the product of *hadar* trees (Lev. 23:40). The product of *hadar* [trees].

The cover is hinged to the body of the container; its handle is a knob finial rising from a circle of leaves. From the position of the inscriptions and their execution, they seem to have been added at a later date.

V. B. M.

Passover

The profound spiritual significance of Passover lies in its commemoration of the Israelites' attainment of physical and spiritual freedom after more than 400 years of bondage in Egypt. Their experience as slaves, the process of emancipation, and the Exodus are recalled by the recitation of the *Haggadah*, a compilation of prayers, historical narratives, and hymns, and by the eating of special foods at the Passover meal, the *seder*. Bitter herbs and a mortar-like mixture known as *haroset* evoke the years of slavery; they are placed on a special *seder* plate together with meat recalling the paschal sacrifice formerly offered at the Temple in Jerusalem. During Passover, only *matzah* (unleavened bread) is eaten, enabling Jews to relive the experience of their ancestors, who left Egypt in such haste that they did not have time to wait for bread to rise.

The laws regarding food on Passover are stringent, requiring that all Jewish households possess special utensils and dishes for this festival, but groups of Jews like Ashkenazim and Sephardim differ in the foods eaten during the holiday.

23. Seder Plate

Frankfurt, 1791
Johann Georg Klingling

Pewter, engraved
Marks: Figure of Justice holding scales, deer at its right
12-9/16 in. dm., 31.9 cm.
The Jewish Museum, New York, gift of The Lamport Estate, JM 48-51

The center of this plate contains an imperial symbol, a large double-headed eagle. Around the eagle are the three main symbols of the *seder* with accompanying labels: מרור, מצה, פסח *matzah, pesach* (the paschal sacrifice), and *maror* (the bitter herbs). Flowers, rosettes, and a border of palmettes and acorns fill the remainder of the field. A sentence from the *Hagaddah* is engraved on the rim:

וזכת [כך:] את יום צאתך מארץ מצרים כל
ימי חייך ועשית פסח לה' אלקיך תקנ"א

And remember "the day of your departure from the land of Egypt as long as you live." (Deut. 16:3) "And offer a Passover sacrifice to the Lord your God" (Deut. 16:1) [5] 551 (1791).

It is followed by ee (?), the owner's monogram, and כ"ה טבת (25 Tevet), perhaps the date of completion. A running vine with acorns and flowers emanates from the ascenders of some of the letters, a stylistic characteristic also found on eighteenth-century Ashkenazi Torah binders. (For other plates by Klingling, see no. 127.)

V. B. M.

23

24. Two Leaves of a Haggadah

Probably Istanbul, 1515
Ink on paper
7-3/8 × 4-3/4 in., 18.8 × 12.1 cm.
The Library of the Jewish Theological Seminary of America, New York, Very Rare Collection 5637
Yaari 5 (Haggadah Catalogue); Yaari 28 (Istanbul Catalogue)

These two leaves, plus a third in the same collection, are from what is probably the oldest illustrated printed *Haggadah.* Although precise dating is difficult, it seems likely that they come from an original set of twenty-four leaves printed in Istanbul in about 1515. Two of the three were reproduced by the Soncino Gesellschaft in Berlin in 1927.[1] Another leaf was subsequently identified by A. M. Habermann[2] and four more have been published by Alexander Scheiber,[3] thus bringing to eight the total of known leaves from this early work. Some authorities date the book even earlier, to about 1504; if they are correct, then it is likely that the type and illustrative plates were brought to Turkey by Jewish exiles, probably from Portugal. It is not entirely out of the question that the leaves themselves were printed in the Iberian peninsula before the expulsions of 1492 and 1497.

1. *Haggadah: Das Fragment der ältesten mit Illustrationen gedruckten Haggadah . . .* (Berlin: 1927)
2: A. M. Habermann, "An unknown leaf of the Hagadah, Constantinople? 1515?" *Kirjath Sefer* 38 (1963), p. 273.
3. A. Scheiber, "New Pages from the First Printed Illustrated Hagaddah," *Studies in Bibliography and Booklore* 7 (1965), pp. 26–36.

M. S. C.

25. Passover Banner

Frankfurt, c. 1900
E. Mannheimer, designer; Verlag von J. Kauftmann, printer
Undyed cotton: block printed
47-1/2 × 16-3/8 in., 120.5 × 41.5 cm.
The Jewish Museum, New York, given in memory of Siegmund Halli by his children, JM 28–53

This banner provides a synopsis of the *Haggadah*, the service book read at the Passover *seder*. Its texts include biblical passages commanding the observance of Passover such as

את חג המצות תשמור

"You shall observe the Feast of Unleavened Bread" (Ex. 23:14)

which is printed on the crowned shield held by the two confronted lions at top. Other passages from the *Haggadah* follow, accompanied by notation of their textual sources where relevant. Eight of these serve as tituli for scenes from the Passover story which are based on illustrations of the popular Amsterdam *Haggadah* of 1695. In the space between these scenes is the order of the *seder* and representations of the four cups of wine, drunk during the service to symbolize the redemption of the Israelites from bondage in Egypt. Below is a listing of the ten plagues accompanied by illustrations of each and, finally, a depiction of the Temple in Jerusalem whose rebuilding symbolizes the messianic age in Jewish thought and prayer. It is accompanied by passages which link the promise of salvation to the observance of divine teaching

זכרו תורת משה / עבדי

"Remember the law of Moses My servant." (Malachi 3:22)

הנה אנכי שלח לכם את אליה הנביא

"Behold I will send you Elijah the prophet." (Malachi 3:23)

Thus pictorially and textually, the decoration of the banner expresses the belief that as the Lord redeemed Israel from slavery in Egypt, so He will again save His people by sending the Messiah, whose herald is Elijah the prophet. The final words of the banner articulate the hope that this future redemption be imminent.

לשנה הבאה בירושלים

"Next Year in Jerusalem."

V. B. M.

Shavuot

The third of the pilgrim festivals falls seven weeks after the first day of Passover and is therefore called Shavuot (Weeks). The interval between the two holidays is marked by the ceremonial counting of the days between them, known as the "counting of the *Omer*." In Jewish tradition the two holidays are linked by more than their calendrical relationship; Shavuot is regarded as the fulfillment of Passover. Only by accepting the moral and religious law of the Torah at Sinai did the Jewish people become spiritually free, completing the process of liberation begun at Passover with the Exodus from physical bondage in Egypt.

26. Ketubbah for Shavuot

Istanbul, 1570–1573
Ink on paper
3-5/8 × 3-3/8 × 1/4 in., 9.2 × 8.6 × 0.6 cm.
The Library of the Jewish Theological Seminary of America, New York, Very Rare Collection, 5670 Yaari 178.

This volume is the only copy known to have survived to the present. The beginning pages are missing, but on the title page to the second section there is an inscription:

כתובה ליום שני של חג השבועות לאומרה
בעת הוצאת ספר תורה. . . . . לרב סעדיה נ'
יוסף . . . .

A *ketubbah* [marriage contract] for the second day of Shavuot, to be recited when the Torah scroll is removed from the ark . . . by Rav Saadia ibn Joseph (Gaon). . . .

This "marriage contract" is actually a poetic reaffirmation of the bond of love and almost conjugal trust that exists ideally between Israel and God. The author (probably not Saadia) has chosen to express that idea by means of a "contract" between God the bridegroom and Israel the bride.

M. S. C.

Hanukkah and Purim

Two minor holidays of the Jewish year are not biblical in origin, but were instituted by the rabbis of the Talmudic period to commemorate historic events.

In the year 165 B.C.E., Jewish patriots under the leadership of the Hasmonean family rebelled against their Greco-Syrian rulers and established religious and political freedom. Soon after attaining independence, they cleansed the Temple in Jerusalem, removing idols set up by the Syrians, and restored the ancient order of worship. One of the objects replaced was the *menorah*, the seven-branched lampstand. According to one account of these events, the Hasmoneans found only enough consecrated oil for one day, yet the small cruse burned for eight days until new oil could be manufactured. restored the ancient order of worship. One of the objects restored was the *menorah*, the

By the first centuries of this era, the holiday of Hanukkah (whose name means dedication and refers to the restoration of the Temple) was celebrated by the kindling of lights. The lamps used over the centuries took many forms, some recalling the shape of the Temple *menorah* and others, deriving

from local types. They all have in common the number of lights, eight, one for each day of the Hanukkah festival.

Purim, the second minor holiday, commemorates events that occurred during the Babylonian exile under the rule of the Persian King Ahasuerus (probably Artaxerxes II). The King's vizier, Haman, plotted to kill the Jews of Persia and cast lots (*purim*) to determine the date of the attack. They fell on the fifteenth day of the Hebrew month of Adar. Haman's plans were foiled by Ahasuerus' beautiful Jewish queen, Esther, and her wise uncle, Mordecai. Haman and his allies were hanged on the gallows, and the Jews of Persia rejoiced and sent gifts to one another. The entire story is recorded in the Book of Esther, which is read annually on Purim from a scroll, the ancient book form. It is also customary for Jews to send gifts of food to friends, to give charity, and to eat a festive meal celebrating the salvation from destruction of the Persian Jews.

27. Hanukkah Lamp

Frankfurt, 1748–1776
Rotger Herfurth (1722–1776)
Marks: Scheffler 153b, 287
Silver, cast, ajouré, repoussé, and engraved
5-3/8 × 5-1/2 × 2-1/4 in., 13.7 × 14.0 × 5.4 cm.
The Jewish Museum, New York, gift of Mrs. Adele Ginzberg to the Harry G. Friedman Collection, F 5237

This lamp consists of a chest-shaped container for oil supported by four cast lions and joined to an ornamental backplate formed of two rampant lions holding a crowned cartouche bearing the representation of an eight-armed *menorah*. The rampant lions stand on an irregularly shaped base. All interstices between the lions and the cartouche and base are open. A removable servitor with pennant flag is attached at right. The tail of the lion at left and the upper part of the crown have been restored.

The elements described above constitute what has been called the typical Frankfurt Hanukkah lamp. Gundersheimer and Schoenberger have suggested that Herfurth developed the type from the basic

chest form without backplate; they viewed the rococo base supporting the lions as the vestige of a more elaborate architectural arcade. Only one example of Herfurth's composition with complete arcade is known, that in the Franklin collection, now in the Jewish Museum, London.[1] The type that became popular was the reduced composition represented here. A somewhat larger example of the same design, also by Herfurth, is in the collection of The Jewish Museum (F 2812). Others are in the Israel Museum (nos. 118/214 and 118/65) and the Jewish Museum, London. Two additional pieces were in the Feinberg collection[2] and the collection of Jacob Michael.[3]

The popularity of silver lamps among Frankfurt Jews is clear from the large numbers still extant and is also attested to in *Yosef 'Ometz*, a book on Jewish customs published by R. Joseph Juspa Hahn in 1723 (see no. 48). There the author recommends having a silver Hanukkah lamp or at least a lamp in which one of the lights is of silver.[4]

1. Barnett, no. 240.
2. "The Charles E. Feinberg Collection," Parke-Bernet Galleries, New York, sales catalogue, November 29–30, 1967, no. 452.
3. In *Notizblatt* XXXIV (1937), no. 4, there is a listing of Hanukkah lamps known in 1937. M. Narkiss believed that the addition of a backplate was owing to eastern European influence; see Narkiss, pp. 61–62.
4. J. J. Hahn, *Yosef 'Ometz* (Frankfurt: 1723), f. 1322.

V. B. M.

28. Hanukkah Lamp

Ottoman Empire, eighteenth century
century
Brass, cast, ajouré, punched, and engraved
15-3/8 × 11-7/8 × 2-3/8 in., 39.0 × 30.2 × 6.0 cm.
The Jewish Museum, New York, gift of The Eva Morris Feld Judaica Acquisitions Fund

This lamp consists of a backplate with suspension piece and a tray holding eight small pans for oil. Each pan is an oval distended at one point to form a pouring spout. A ninth pan is soldered to a hook that can be inserted in the backplate; it serves as *shammash* (servitor). The backplate has three parts: the suspension piece, the central plaque, and the perforated brass sheet to which the plaque is attached. The plaque appears to have been originally intended for a different purpose: It has a rim around the back, as would be found on the top piece of a brazier. A border of beads in repoussé surrounds the central openwork design: a vase from which emerges a symmetrical arrangement of leaves and tulips. Details are rendered through engraved lines and a series of overlapping ring punchmarks, the latter used principally to outline the forms.

The closest published parallel for this lamp is an example in the Magnes Museum, Berkeley, described as a gift from the Jewish community of

28

Cairo.[1] It exhibits similar forms and identical articulation by means of circular punchmarks. A lamp with related but cruder decoration in a Jerusalem collection has been compared to the pierced cover of a seventeenth-century Dutch pan in the Victoria and Albert Museum;[2] the latter is very similar to the backplate of the exhibited lamp but is executed in a more illusionistic style. Still another work belonging to this group is in the Jewish Museum, London, and was also acquired in Jerusalem.[3] All these works, including the pan cover, have been dated to the seventeenth century and, except for the Berkeley example, all have been described as Dutch. All the lamps first came to light in the Ottoman empire, except for the exhibited lamp, which was acquired in Italy, a country in close contact with Turkey. It seems reasonable to suggest that this group may be Ottoman in origin and is perhaps based on Dutch models.

1. R. Eis, *Hanukkah Lamps of the Judah L. Magnes Museum*, Berkeley, 1977, no. MC 12.
2. Narkiss, figs. 122 and 126.
3. Barnett, no. 228.

V. B. M.

29. Scroll of Esther (See color plate, p. 12)

Frankfurt, 1806–1807
Illustrated by Jacob b. Bezalel
Paint and ink on parchment; wooden roller
Roller: 12-1/8 in., 30.8 cm.; parchment: 5-7/8 in., 14.9 cm.
The Jewish Museum, New York, gift of Mrs. Karl R. Finestere, F 3597

Preceding the main text of the story of Esther is a symmetrical composition consisting of an escutcheon containing a rampant lion on a red-and-gold striped field surmounted by a knight's visored helmet, which bears a lion seated in a crown; the whole is flanked by two flags and two hearts. The two flags and the heart on the right are inscribed with the three blessings recited before the reading from the scroll on the holiday of Purim. In the heart on the left is the blessing said at the completion of the reading. The date of the writing is repeated three times, flanking the helmet: בשנת תקס"ז , "in the year [5]567 (1806-1807)"; flanking the escutcheon in a chronogram: נהפך להם מיגון לשמחה לפ"ק ,

"[and the month] which was turned unto them from sorrow to gladness" (Est. 9:22), and below the escutcheon: בפראנקפורט / 'דמיי' תקס"ז / לפ"ק , "in Frankfurt am Mai[n] [5]467 (1806–1807)." The name of the artist occupies the lower left corner:

המצייר יעקב ב"ר בצלאל

the illustrator Jacob son of Rabbi Bezalel.

Jacob has arranged the text of the Book of Esther in a series of octagonal fields with decorative frames separated by fanciful columns, each consisting of a base and two segments of a baluster supporting the Tablets of the Law surmounted by a crown.

It is unusual to find a hand-painted *megillah* (scroll of Esther) that is signed.

V. B. M.

30. Scroll of Esther

Turkey, 1869–1870
Ink on parchment; ivory roller
Roller: 13-1/2 in., 34.2 cm.; parchment: 5-1/2 in., 14.0 cm.
The Jewish Museum, New York, gift of Dr. Harry G. Friedman, F 4420

30

The text of this scroll is of the *hamelekh* type; that is, the sentences are arranged so that as many columns as possible begin with the word *hamelekh* ("the king"), referring to Ahasuerus, the monarch of the Esther story. The parchment is attached to an ivory holder, the handle of which is plain except for a series of parallel incised lines near the cup supporting the scroll. Above is a tiered finial, with the following inscription on the lowest tier:

נסים ביניציה הי"ו   5630

Nissim Benezia . . . 5630 [1869–1870]

The three upper tiers are in openwork, each representing a stylized skyline including domed buildings and minarets; surmounting the whole is a crescent, the most common finial for Ottoman domes.

A similar scroll and holder are to be found in the collection of the Wolfson Museum, Hechal Shlomo, Jerusalem.[1]

1. Bialer, *Jewish Life*, p. 169.

V. B. M.

31. Quflas di Purim

Istanbul, 1786
Published by Judah Yerushalmi b. Samuel
Ink on paper
6-5/8 × 4-7/16 × 3/8 in., 16.8 × 11.3 × 0.9 cm.
The Library of the Jewish Theological Seminary of America, New York, Yaari 502

This book contains an interesting sampling of Ladino poems and texts for Purim. Of special interest is the text of a *ketubbah* (marriage contract) for Haman and his wife Zeresh, which is a parody of the standard wedding document. This copy is lacking several leaves and has a damaged title page.

M. S. C.

Kashrut, the Dietary Laws

One of the basic principles of Judaism is that all aspects of life should be sanctified, raised to a spiritual level: "And ye should be holy unto Me" (Lev. 20:26). Sanctity is not achieved through denial of physical pleasure, but rather through pursuit of such pleasure within the parameters established by religious law.

Eating is governed by a system of dietary laws, some of which are specifically mentioned in the Bible. Among them is the commandment to eat only the flesh of animals that both chew their cud and have split hooves, and only the meat of fish that have both fins and scales (Lev. 11:3, 9). Another is the requirement that milk and meat be separated: "Thou shalt not seethe a kid in its mother's milk" (Ex. 23:19, 34:26; Deut. 14:21). The third major component of the dietary laws consists of regulations pertaining to the proper slaughter of animals; they are part of the oral tradition recorded in the Mishnah and the Talmud. Food that meets the requirements of Jewish religious law is called *kosher*.

32. Hilkhot Terêfot

Istanbul, 1515–1518
Ink on paper
8-3/16 × 5-15/16 in., 20.8 × 15.1 cm.
The Library of the Jewish Theological Seminary of America, New York, Very Rare Collection, 8669
Yaari 71

These five leaves (of an original nine) constitute one of the few surviving fragments of *Hilkhot Terêfot* by David ibn Yaḥya; it deals with the laws of *kashrut* pertaining to the slaughter of animals and to meat in general. The colophon, which is missing in this copy, usually reads:

72

תמו הלכות טרפות הסירכא למה״ר דוד אבן
יחייא מתושבי אשבונה המהוללה ברוך
רופא כל בשר ומשליט האדם ביצורי
האדמה אמן. תם.

Furnished here are the dietary laws regarding
meat, as they pertain to questions of internal
injury and adhesions by our teacher David
ibn Yaḥya from the inhabitants of *Ashvona*
the great, blessed is the healer of all flesh
who causes man to rule creations of the
earth. Amen. The end.

M. S. C.

34

33. Set of Knives in Cases

Germany, nineteenth century
Handle: bone; mount: copper; blade: steel
a) case: 1-1/16 × 21-1/2 × 2-3/8 in., 2.7 × 54.6
× 6.0 cm.; knife: 17-3/4 in., 45.1 cm.
b) case: 7/8 × 14 × 2-1/2 in., 2.2 × 35.5 × 6.3 cm.;
knife: 12-3/8 in., 31.3 cm.
c) case: 5/8 × 8-5/8 × 1-1/2 in., 1.6 × 21.9 × 3.8
cm.; knife: 7-1/8 in., 18.2 cm.
The Jewish Museum, New York, gift of Maurice
Herrmann, S 428 a, b, c

Animals must be slaughtered by an individual thor-
oughly trained in the laws of *sheḥitah* (slaughter).
He kills an animal by slitting its throat with a sharp
blade that is repeatedly checked for imperfections
in order to avoid causing the animal unnecessary
pain. Vital organs such as the lungs are then examined for defects and other evidence of disease. If they
are present, the meat is not *kosher*.

A *shoḥet*, slaughterer, generally owns a set of
knives, from which he chooses, depending on the
size of the animal. The mount of the smallest knife
in this set is stamped "Grunewald" and the blade of
the largest "Claemmerheit" presumably the name
of the makers. Other portions of the knives are un-
marked, indicating that some of them are replacements.

REFERENCE: *The Jewish Encyclopedia*, XI (1905), p. 256
(ill.).

V. B. M.

34. Dish

Germany, eighteenth–nineteeenth century
Mark: angel with scales and sword and deer
running left in a quatrefoil frame, letters illegible
Pewter, cast and engraved
7/8 × 8-1/4 in., 20.3 × 21.0 cm.
The Jewish Museum, New York, gift of Dr. Harry
G. Friedman, F 973

This shallow dish is decorated with a single incised
line around the rim and with an engraved heart-
shaped shield containing the inscription:

וויש / חלב

Wiss/milk.

Wiss is presumably the name of the owner, though
it could be a transliteration of *Fisch* (German for
"fish"). The word "milk" is also incised on the back.

As Jewish dietary laws require the separation of
foods cooked with milk from those cooked with
meat, some means of identifying the different dishes
used is necessary. In an age when pewter was the
most common tableware, engraved inscriptions
served that purpose.

V. B. M.

73

Judaism, like other religions, marks the important events in the lives of individuals by appropriate ceremonies. Some of these ceremonies are universally observed; others are specific to ethnic groups or even to individual communities. Circumcision of a male child on the eighth day of life is an example of a rite practiced by all Jews, as is the marriage ceremony centered on the writing and transferral of a *ketubbah* (contract) specifying mutual obligations of bride and groom.

In other cases, local customs influenced the observance of a life cycle event. The hazardous nature of childbirth before the modern era led to the making of amulets for the protection of mothers and their newborn children. In Germany these amulets were generally written on paper and parchment; in Turkey, on the other hand, mothers wore bonnets embroidered with the names of protecting angels. The varying forms of tombstones in Frankfurt and Istanbul also reflect local usage.

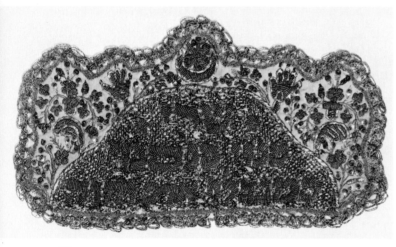

35

of a newborn child. The central mound-shaped area bears an embroidered inscription executed in metallic thread against a tinsel ground:

שדי / סנוי סנסנוי /סמנגלוף אדם וחוה

Almighty, Sanvai, Sansanvai, Semanglof, Adam and Eve.[2]

The remainder of the panel surrounding the inscribed section is composed of ivory silk embroidered with flowering branches, two *ḥamsas* (open hands, an ancient apotropaic symbol), and, at the top, the star and crescent found on much late Turkish Judaica. An edging of metallic lace surrounds the whole. The textural effects produced by means of different types of metallic thread is similar to that on an embroidered bridal dress (no. 186) whose original owner came from Gallipoli. Yet the spiky *ḥamsas* on this amulet and the profusion of sequins suggest comparison with embroideries from Izmir.[3] Because of such varied similarities, it is difficult to localize much of the gold embroidery produced in the late Ottoman Empire.

Frankfurt books of *minhagim* (customs) also record that mothers of newborn infants received visits and gifts, but the elaborate dressing of the bed and the wearing of special objects like bonnets are Turkish Jewish customs.

1. There is an entire bonnet in the collection of the Ethnography Department of the Israel Museum.
2. Sanvai, Sansanvai, and Semanglof are angels thought able to neutralize the power of Lilith; see T. Schrire, *Hebrew Amulets* (London: 1966), pp. 18, 51.
3. For example, see Juhasz, nos. 68 and 98.

REFERENCE: *Fabric of Jewish Life*, no. 142.

V. B. M.

35. **Amulet for the Mother of a Newborn**

Turkey, mid-nineteenth century
Silk, embroidered with metallic threads, tinsel, and sequins; metallic lace
6-1/2 × 11-1/2 in., 16.5 × 28.5 cm.
The Jewish Museum, New York, gift of Dr. Harry G. Friedman, F 646

This oblong panel with scalloped upper edge was once the front part of a bonnet[1] worn by the mother

36. **Carved Box with Circumcision Implements**

Germany, 15th or 16th century, with later additions
Box: fruitwood, carved and painted
Flask: glass and silver, cast and engraved
Knife: handle, silver filigree, gilt; blade, steel
Box: 9-1/2 × 2-1/16 × 1-9/16 in., 24.0 × 5.5 × 4.5 cm.
Flask: ht: 4-5/16 in., 11.0 cm.
Knife: l: 8-1/4 in., 21.0 cm.
The Jewish Museum, New York,
gift of Mr. and Mrs. Norman Zeiler in memory of Mrs. Nana Zeiler, JM 35-66

36

Carved decoration covers the entire surface of the box: zodiac signs in roundels separated by flower-filled vases and other motifs on the front and back, single birds on the end panels, inhabited vine scrolls on four of the five panels of the cover and discontinuous vines flanking a mnemonic inscription on the fifth panel of the lid. The inscriptions reads:

ב א י ו א מ ה א ק ב ע ה ת צ ח ל[פק]

B[lessed art] T[hou] O L[ord] o[ur God] K[ing of] t[he Universe] w[ho] h[as sanctified us] a[nd commanded us] c[oncerning] c[ircumcision]. [5]498 (1737–1738).

Inside the box were a knife with filigree handle, a glass flask with silver mounts, a sharpening stone, and a small rhomboid piece of glass of indeterminate use painted with gilt flowers.

This box belongs to a group of late medieval caskets known as *Minnekästchen* or *Briefladen*, which were given as gifts by men to women, as bridal gifts, or as New Year's gifts. Guilds and societies also used them to hold important documents. In size and form the box exhibited here is closest to two *Minnekästchen* of about 1300,[1] but its carved decoration suggests a later date. The end panels may be compared to the back of a casket once in the Kunstgewerbemuseum, Berlin, which was carved in the fifteenth century with similar birds in low relief and decorated with dots.[2] The sides of the Berlin casket were not carved until 1540; the same is true of the sides of the box in The Jewish Museum. The closest stylistic parallels for the zodiac signs with human figures are three wooden playing pieces in the Bayerisches Nationalmuseum in Munich, which are datable to about 1530–1540. These pieces are carved with similar stocky forms with enlarged arms, broad,

flat cheeks, and small facial features; they entirely fill their frames.[3] At the time when the front and back of the exhibited box were decorated, the interior of the lid was also hollowed out, so that it is semicircular in cross section; it was then covered with fabric. Some of the glue by which the fabric was attached still remains.

In 1738 the box was converted for use by a *mohel*, or circumcisor. A wooden inset, rhomboid in cross section, was fitted into the lid in order to hold the knife; this alteration necessitated an oak patch at one end, and the inscription was carved on the remaining plain panel of the cover. The flask dates to about the same time. Its scalloped border appears on German circumcision knives of the late seventeenth and eighteenth centuries.[4] The filigree handle of the knife is similar to one dated about 1800 in the Feuchtwanger collection, which has been tentatively attributed to Germany,[5] and to the handle of a Torah pointer in The Jewish Museum, which bears an eastern European hallmark dated to 1851 (F 2568). The knife thus appears to be a later replacement of German or eastern European origin.

1. H. Kohlhausen, *Minnekästchen in Mittelalter* (Berlin: 1928), nos. 18, 21.

2. J. Lessing, *Holzschnitzereien des Fünfzehnten und Sechszehnten Jahrhunderts in Kunstgewerbe Museum zu Berlin* (Berlin: 1882), pl. 28.

3. G. Himmelheber, *Spiele: Gesellschaftsspiele aus einem Jahrtausend* (Munich: 1972), nos. 60–62, pl. 75.

4. *Danzig 1939*, no. 1, now attributed to Germany; Shachar, *Jewish Tradition in Art*, no. 13.

5. Shachar, *Jewish Tradition in Art*, no. 20.
ish Art, IX (in press).

REFERENCE: V. Mann, "A Sixteenth-Century Box in The Jewish Museum and its Transformation," *Journal of Jewish Art*, IX (in press).

V. B. M.

37. Marriage Contract

Istanbul, 1866
Ink, pencil, and crayon on paper
38-3/16 × 21-15/16 in., 97.0 × 55.7 cm.
The Jewish Museum, New York, gift of Edouard
Roditi, JM 200-68

The space of this large oblong marriage contract (*ketubbah*) is divided by means of colored lines into a wide border and three central compartments. Pairs of divided heart-shaped leaves joined by rosettes decorate the border and form a rectangular arch in the top central section. Above the arch is the abbreviation בס״ט , standing for בסימן טוב , "with a good sign," and at the very top is a *ḥamsa,*[1] an open hand, inscribed שדי , "Almighty." Beneath the arch is an Aramaic saying often found on Sephardi and Oriental *ketubbot:*

בסמנא טבא ובמזלא מעליא

With a good sign and with exalted luck.

Two other aphorisms are enclosed in medallions at the bases of the arch:

אשת חיל עטרת בעלה

A virtuous woman is a crown to her husband. (Prov. 12:4)

מצא אשה מצא טוב

Who finds a wife finds a great good. (Prov. 18:22)

The main text reveals that the contract was written between the groom

דוד רודיטי בן נסים ישראל רודיטי
לונה בת נפתלי גיאפיליטי

David Roditi son of Nissim Israel Roditi [and the bride] Luna daughter of Naphtali Galipoliti

in an area of Istanbul near Kuzguncuk on 24 Elul 5626 (September, 1866). The signatures of the witnesses and the stamp of the rabbinate of Istanbul can be seen below the main text. The other texts, stamps, and signatures provide information on the later history of the Roditis. The lower compartment contains an Italian translation of the contract. Officials of Belgium, and the United States, as well as the Grand Rabbi of Paris, M. Dreyfus, signed in the available empty spaces.

Until the modern period, illuminated marriage contracts were found only among Sephardi and Oriental Jews, with the exception of a single fourteenth-century example from Kremsmunster in Austria. Most of the extant decorated contracts date from the seventeenth through the nineteenth centuries.

1. The *ḥamsa* can be traced back to the Phoenicians.

V. B. M.

38. Frankfurt Jewish Cemetery

Frankfurt, 1917
Photograph
6-7/8 × 9-3/8 in., 17.5 × 23.8 cm.
Leo Baeck Institute, New York, Arnsberg collection

This photograph shows the so-called "Rabbis' corner" in the old Jewish cemetery on Battonstrasse. The vertical headstones are markers for underground burials and are decorated with Hebrew inscriptions.

E. D. B.

39. Jewish Cemetery in Istanbul

From Preziosi, *Stamboul, Souvenir d'Orient*
Paris, 1865
Colored lithograph on paper
16-3/16 × 12-5/16 in., 41.2 × 31.2 cm.
The Jewish Museum, New York, gift of Dr. Harry
G. Friedman, F 5885

Preziosi remains an enigmatic artist of obscure origin. He was probably Italian and is known to have worked as a genre and landscape painter in Istanbul, where he died in 1882. He recorded this view of a Jewish couple in the Istanbul cemetery in a watercolor dated 1857, which was then published along with other scenes of that Ottoman city by Lemercier in *Stamboul: Souvenir d'Orient* in Paris, in 1865.

Instead of the vertical headstones found in European Jewish cemeteries, including the ones in Frankfurt (see no. 38), the tombs depicted here are cenotaphs, which resemble ancient examples in form. The cupolas and minarets of one of Istanbul's many mosques and the Bosphorus, with its sailing vessels, are visible in the background.

REFERENCE: Rubens, *Iconography*, 1981, no. 2425.

E. D. B.

39

Relations Between Man and Man

Judaism incorporates a comprehensive legal system governing all aspects of human relations. Because most Jews have lived outside the land of Israel for the last two millennia, and their lives have been ruled by local laws, the civil and economic laws of Judaism have sometimes fallen into disuse.

Frankfurt and Istanbul were both centers of Hebrew publishing. The first Hebrew book printed in Istanbul was Jacob b. Asher's *Tur* (Row) of 1493, a code of law, which was also the first book ever printed in Turkey.

40. Shulḥan Arukh

Istanbul, 1736
Published by Jonah ben Jacob
Ink on paper
6-9/16 × 4-7/16 × 2 in., 16.7 × 11.3 × 5.1 cm.
The Library of the Jewish Theological Seminary of America, New York

The *Shulḥan Arukh* (*Prepared Table*) was written by Rabbi Joseph Caro in the sixteenth century; it represents an attempt to synthesize Ashkenazi and Sephardi practices in one code. His work became and remained the single most authoritative code of Jewish law in the world. This volume, which contains the first section, entitled *'Oraḥ Ḥayyim*, was printed in Istanbul.

41. Sefer Kenesset Haggedolah

Istanbul and Izmir, seventeenth century
Hayyim Benveniste
Published by Jonah b. Jacob and Naphtali b. Azriel
Ink on paper
15 × 20-1/2 in., 38.1 × 52.1 cm.
The Library of the Jewish Theological Seminary of America, New York

This work is the most important compendium of Jewish law written in Turkey between the seventeenth and nineteenth centuries. The author organized his text according to the *Shulḥan Arukh* and its model, the *Tur* (*Gate*) of Rabbi Jacob b. Asher. The volume exhibited includes dietary laws and laws concerning interest.

J. H.

Frankfurt: An Ashkenazi Community

The Establishment of an Ashkenazi Community: Frankfurt Until 1750

The early history of the Jews of Frankfurt was marked by repeated attempts to establish a community in the face of periodic persecutions. The first mention of Jews in Frankfurt dates to the eleventh century. Two hundred years later, in 1241, nearly the entire community of 200 people was massacred, an event commemorated in the liturgy of Frankfurt Jews for the ninth of Av, the annual fast observed by all Jews in remembrance of the destruction of the Temple in Jerusalem.

In 1270, city officials interested in the financial exploitation of Jews invited a few Jewish families to settle in the city, and within two decades they had established communal institutions: a synagogue, a cemetery, a bath house, a hospital, and a marriage hall. Jewish life in Frankfurt, as in so many European cities, was again disrupted by persecutions resulting from the Black Death of 1348, an outbreak of bubonic plague that decimated the population of Europe and was blamed on the Jews by superstitious Christians. After 1360 the community again gradually increased in size. During this period Jews lived in the finest area of Frankfurt, near the cathedral. In 1424 the city council of Frankfurt first issued the *Stättigkeit*, a series of regulations governing relations with the Jewish community, and in 1460, under pressure from the Emperor Frederick III and the Church, the council established a specific quarter for the Jews in an area near the Main river. Although originally large enough, the Frankfurt ghetto, called the Judengasse, soon became overcrowded. By the end of the sixteenth century living conditions were extremely poor, yet the ghetto sustained an intensive Jewish communal and religious life.

The most serious disturbance of Frankfurt Jewish life after the institution of the Judengasse was the anti-Semitic outbreak led by Vincent Fettmilch in 1614. Fettmilch's insurrection against the city council was motivated by economic and political interests combined with strong anti-Semitism. On August 22, 1614, the rebels sacked the Judengasse. Eventually, in 1616, Fettmilch and his associates were executed, but in the same year the city council formulated a new and more restrictive *Stättigkeit*, which limited the number of households on the Judengasse, the number of Jewish marriages in each year, and the economic opportunities open to Jews.

Yet, despite severe difficulties, the Jews of the Frankfurt ghetto were successful as traders, wholesalers, pawnbrokers, and money-lenders, and created a rich intellectual and communal life. Residents of the city included learned rabbis like Isaiah Horowitz (1565–1630) and Joseph Juspa Hahn (d. 1637), the author of *Sêfer Yosef 'Ometz*, a compendium of laws and customs. In 1711 Naphtali Kohen, a kabbalist, was chief rabbi. A fire that began in his house spread and engulfed the Judengasse, necessitating the rebuilding of the synagogue and other structures. An inventory of 1700 records that even a poor Jew, Seligmann zur goldenen Krone, who lived with his family in only two rooms and had few household possessions, owned ninety-eight Hebrew books. The community also supported a *yeshivah*, a traditional school of Jewish learning. Frankfurt rabbis and their courts were so highly respected that Jews outside the city often consulted them on matters of Jewish law and custom.

42. Oldest Jewish Headstones from Frankfurt

Frankfurt, *c.* 1952
Photograph
5-1/2 × 9-1/4 in., 14.0 × 23.5 cm.
Leo Baeck Institute, New York, Arnsberg collection

These headstones, dated 1284, reflect the vicissitudes of Jewish life in Frankfurt. They attest to the reestablishment of a Jewish community in Frankfurt in 1270, after the massacre of 1241. When the new community was wiped out in 1349 during a violent anti-Jewish outbreak at the time of the Black Death, the cemetery was desecrated. The headstones were used for the new altar of the Cathedral as a symbol of the triumph of Christianity over the Jews,[1] and were rediscovered only in 1952, because of severe damage the building sustained during bombardment in World War II.

1. Historical Museum Frankfurt, *Documentation Guide*, p. 275.

E. D. B.

43. Der Juden zu Frankfurt Stättigkeit und Ordnung

Frankfurt, 1613
Published by Johann Saurn
Ink on paper
7-5/8 × 6-1/16 × 3/8 in., 19.3 × 15.4 × 0.9 cm.
The Library of the Jewish Theological Seminary of America, New York

This edition of the *Stättigkeit* (which was periodically updated and republished) is based on the original, handwritten parchment text of 1452; in it the privileges extended to the Jews of Frankfurt by the city council are specified. This edition was printed in 1613, precisely in the middle of the Fettmilch disturbances, which resulted in an attack on the Judengasse on August 22, 1614 (see no. 46). Jewish community life was not reorganized in Frankfurt until 1616, when the Judengasse was placed under the protection of the Emperor.

M. S. C.

44

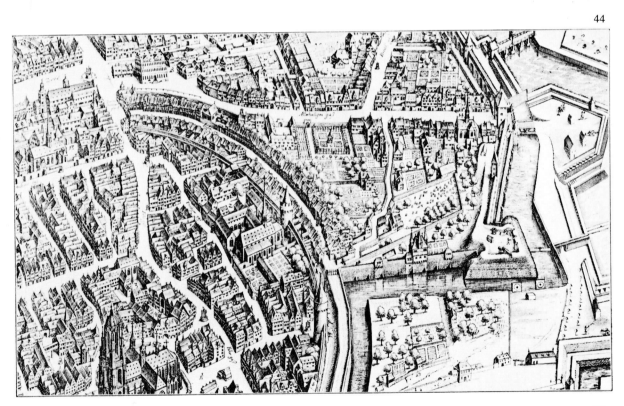

44. The Frankfurt Judengasse

Frankfurt, 1628
Matthäus Merian the Elder (1593–1650)
Photograph: detail after Merian

This detail of Merian's city map of Frankfurt shows the row of cramped houses arranged in an arc that constituted the Judengasse, or Jewish street, in the first half of the seventeenth century.

Until the fifteenth century the Jews had lived among the Christians in the best section of the city, between the River Main and the cathedral (lower left). In 1460, after repeated demands by both Emperor Frederick III and representatives of the Church, the Frankfurt city council decided to create a special Jewish quarter. They selected an area that was only sparsely inhabited, near the Main and beyond the oldest city wall. On Merian's map, the towers of this old wall bordering the ghetto are visible, as is the river, at the end of the Judengasse.

Merian was born in Basel, Switzerland, and in 1624 moved to Frankfurt, where eventually he inherited the printing firm of his father-in-law, Johann Dietrich de Bry. He is known for his maps of European cities and for the illustrations of several works by J. L. Gottfried, including the *Historische Chronica* of 1642 (see no. 46).

E. D. B.

45

45. Die Judensau (The Jewish Swine)

Germany, 1460–1480
Woodcut on paper
17-5/16 × 11-1/4 in., 44.0 × 28.5 cm.
The Library of the Jewish Theological Seminary of America, New York

Die Judensau, the most popular image of anti-Semitic propaganda, was already in use in the medieval period and remained highly visible until the beginning of the nineteenth century. Although pigs were used for other defamatory images in the fifteenth century,[1] the association with Jews was particularly frequent,[2] partly because of Jewish dietary laws forbidding the eating of pork. In order to mock these strictures, the slanderous pictures included scenes of Jews eating pigs' excrement and of Jewish children drinking milk from a pig's udder. The inscription on this particular print addresses these same points:

> Because we do not eat pork, we are considered obscene. Our breath stinks. Look dear people, what kind of a mother Jewish children have. We Jews shall always remember how close we are to the pig. Suck hard, dear brother, on its tail, while I blow into the ass. We must not forget that we can't eat pork.

Two bearded and cloaked men, representing rabbis, stand beside and behind the pig. The other figures wear short jerkins and pointed Jewish hats. The *Judenhut*, or Jewish hat, was a distinctive feature of Jewish medieval dress and in Europe became a symbol of Jewry.[3] Ill-formed Hebrew letters written backward decorate the hem of the figure who straddles the pig and lifts its tail to his lips. On the reverse of this woodcut is an image of the crucifixion and the collector's mark of Fritz Hasselmann.[4]

Another image of the *Judensau* with similar iconography was painted on the gateway of the *Bruckentürm* (the tower at the beginning of the Old Bridge) at Frankfurt.[5] Visible to every passerby, it combined the *Judensau* with a picture of a tortured boy, referring to alleged ritual murder of Christian children. The painting, known as the *Spott- und Schandgemälde* (picture of derision and infamy), remained until the destruction of the bridge tower in 1801. The power of this image, exhorting all who entered Frankfurt to beware of Jews, was attested to in Johann Wolfgang von Goethe's recollections of his childhood experiences in the Jewish ghetto of Frankfurt, written in 1811:

> It took a long time till I ventured into it alone . . . the ancient tales of cruelties of the Jews committed against the Christian children . . . loomed gloomily before my young mind. And although the people in modern times entertained a better opinion of them, yet the huge picture of derision and infamy which could still be seen quite plainly on a wall of an arch under the bridge tower, bore extraordinary witness to their dishonor: for it had not been made by private wanton sport, but at the public expense of the authorities.[6]

1. W. Brückner, *Populäre Druckgraphik Europas Deutschland: Vom 15 bis zum 20 Jahrhundert* (Munich: 1969), p. 24, fig. 23.

2. See Wilhelm Molsdorf, *Christliche Symbolik der Mittelalterichen Kunst*, (Leipzig: 1926), p. 183, no. 1017.

3. Rubens, *Jewish Costume*, pp. 92 ff. The *Judenhut* was used as a symbol by Jews as well. It appears in Hebrew manuscripts, for example, in the Birds' Head Haggadah, southern Germany, and in the Regensburg Pentateuch, Bavaria, both *c.* 1300. See B. Narkiss, *Hebrew Illuminated Manuscripts* (Jerusalem: 1969), pp. 28–29.

4. F. Lugt, *Les marques de collections de dessins et d'estampes* (Amsterdam: 1921), no. 1012.

5. Illustrated in Schudt, II, following p. 256.

6. J.W. von Goethe *Aus meinem Leben: Dichtung und Wahrheit* (*Goethes Werke*), VIII (Berlin and Weimar: 1966), p. 160.

REFERENCES: Brückner, p. 24, fig. 22; Historical Museum Frankfurt, *Documentation Guide*, p. 265.

E. D. B.

46. Plunder of the Frankfurt Ghetto, 1614

From J.L. Gottfried, *Historische Chronica*
Frankfurt, 1642
Matthäus Merian the Elder (1593–1650)
Engraving on paper
11-3/4 × 7-3/8 in., 29.7 × 18.7 cm.
Leo Baeck Institute, New York, 82.5

In 1612 a revolt of the guilds against the patrician rulers broke out in Frankfurt; it lasted several years. The Fettmilch Insurrection, named for one of its instigators and leaders, Vincent Fettmilch, was provoked by unjust political and economic conditions.

As was often so, the anger and dissatisfaction of the city's population found expression in intensified hatred for the Jews, and the participants in the uprising demanded their expulsion. After much vacillation by the city council, the mob took matters into its own hands and stormed the ghetto on August 22, 1614. The Jewish population resisted but was ultimately overcome and had to flee to the cemetery. Mobs eager for booty streamed into the Judengasse. What could not be carried off was vandalized, desecrated, or burned, including holy books and synagogue furnishings. Most of the Jews were not harmed, but they were forced to leave the city until the Emperor Matthias intervened on their behalf and they were allowed to return, in August 1615. With the execution of Fettmilch in 1616 the uprising ended. The rabbinate proclaimed 19 Adar a fast day in Frankfurt, where it was known as Purim Vincz.

Merian's engraving depicts the mayhem that ensued when the mob broke through the barricaded gates of the ghetto. The Jews can be distinguished by their dress: The male inhabitants wear the *barette*, the *Jüdenkragen* (Jewish ruff), and the badge. Originally a hat worn by European scholars in the fifteenth and sixteenth centuries, the *barette*, a beret made of felt and wool, became the daily headgear for Jewish males, though later it was reserved for synagogue wear.[1] The women also wear the ruff and Jewish badge, as well as the Jewish bonnet with cone-shaped earpieces (see no. 47).[2]

For further information on the career of Merian, see no. 44.

1. Rubens, *Jewish Costume*, p. 115. A nineteenth-century example is in the Bayerisches Nationalmuseum, *Monumenta Judaica* E 490 (ill.).

2. Ibid.

REFERENCES: Rubens, *Jewish Costume*, fig. 160.; Rubens, *Iconography*, 1981, no. 1302.

E. D. B.

47. Franckfurther Jud und Jüdin

(Jew and Jewess from Frankfurt), from Abraham A. S. Clara, *Neu-Eröffnete Welt-Galleria*
Nuremberg, 1703
Published by C. Weigel
Etching and engraving on paper
9-3/8 × 7 in., 23.8 × 17.8 cm.
The Moldovan Family collection, New York

This print illustrates the characteristic attire of Frankfurt Jews at the beginning of the eighteenth century. The man wears a broad-brimmed hat, replacing the earlier Jewish beret (*barette*; see no. 46), which was now reserved for the Sabbath. A knee-length coat, a gown, and a lace collar complete his outfit. The woman wears the Jewish ruff (*Jüdenkragen*), which originated in the sixteenth century and remained a distinctive feature of Jewish dress until the nineteenth century.[1] Her bonnet, with cone-shaped earpieces, is also characteristic. These elements were commented upon by Skippon, who visited the ghetto toward the end of the seventeenth century:

> Most of the men wear ruffs and the women are habited with a black mantle; their head dress is of linen, which sticks out much on either side; several of the women also wear ruffs. All the Jews wear a little yellow mark upon the clothes for distinction.[2]

1. Rubens, *Jewish Costume*, p. 117.
2. P. Skippon, *An Account of a Journey* (London: 1746), p. 442, in ibid.

REFERENCES: Rubens, *Jewish Costume*, fig. 162; Rubens, *Iconography*, 1981, no. 1309.

E. D. B.

48. Sêfer Yosef 'Ometz

Frankfurt, 1723
Joseph Juspa Hahn Nördlingen (c. 1570–1637)
Published by Johann Kellner
Ink on paper
6-5/8 × 3-15/16 × 1-5/8 in., 16.8 × 10.0 × 4.1 cm.
The Library of the Jewish Theological Seminary of America, New York

". . . this book is a volume that contains all things: laws that apply to the entire year, laws for the new moon, Sabbath and festivals . . . and especially all of the customs of this place, the holy congregation of Frankfurt am Main . . . May this book be studied among all Jewish study circles, and may the merit of such study suffice for God to send us the Redeemer."—from the title page.

M. S. C.

49

49. The Synagogue in Frankfurt am Main

Frankfurt, c. 1845
William Lang, after Jakob Fürchtegott Dielmann (1809–1885); published by Carl Jügel
Hand-colored etching on paper
Page: 8-3/16 × 11-3/8 in., 20.8 × 28.9 cm.; plate: 6-3/16 × 8-3/4 in., 15.8 × 22.2 cm.
The Jewish Museum, New York, JM 158-67

On January 14, 1711, a fire broke out in the home of Chief Rabbi Naphtali Kohen (see no. 50); it ended in the destruction of the entire ghetto, including the synagogue that had been built in 1603. The construction of a new synagogue of identical proportions on the same site was begun shortly after the disaster; the cornerstone was laid on March 25. Johann Jakob Schudt (see no. 53) commented on the enthusiasm with which the building was accomplished: "It was a joy and pastime to see how every man, young and old, wanted to work at it with great earnestness and zeal, and paid the mason journeymen generously just to be allowed to help."[1]

The master mason, Daniel Kayser, was promised a bonus for every week that he was able to pare from the construction schedule; at the end of September 1711 it was possible to hold the services for the High Holydays in the new building.[2] The new synagogue, a rectangular, two-story structure with a flat roof, differed dramatically from the other architecture in the ghetto, as can be seen in this print.

Dielmann concentrated on the west side of the building, which faced the Judengasse. The facade was characterized by four small square windows on the ground floor and two pairs of arched windows on the second story. Linking the two stories were tall, slender columns, one at each end; they may have been allusions to the two free-standing pillars *Jachin* and *Boaz* that stood before the Temple of Solomon in Jerusalem (I Kings 7:15–22, 41–42; II Chron. 3:15–17).

The men's entrance to the synagogue was on the south side and was reached by a large courtyard.

The most striking feature of the interior was the vaulted ceiling in Gothic style. Small arched windows on the north side and larger windows of the same shape spanning both stories on the south side echo the predominant motif of the west facade.

This building was torn down in 1854 so that a larger synagogue could be built to accommodate a growing and increasingly affluent community (see no. 84). For Dielmann and Jügel see no. 55.

1. Schudt, II, p. 29, in Freimann and Kracauer, p. 137.
2. Ibid., pp. 137–138.

REFERENCES: Hammer-Schenk, pp. 30–31, figs. 22–23; Rubens, *Iconography*, 1981, no. 1313. *Bilder zur Frankfurter Geschichte*, 1950, no. 159; Weizsäcker and Dessoff, II, p. 31.

E. D. B.

50. Rabbi Naphtali Kohen (1649–1719)

Germany, twentieth century
Photograph of a lithograph, mounted on a card
4 × 2-1/2 in., 10.1 × 6.3 cm.
The Library of the Jewish Theological Seminary of America, New York

Beneath this picture of Rabbi Naphtali Kohen is the following inscription:

צורת הגאון מ"ו/ה"ה"נפתלי כהן ז"ל
א[ב] ב[ית] ד[ין] דק"ק פאזנן ופ[ראנק] פ[ורט]
דמ[יין] וכו"

Image of . . . Naphtali Kohen of blessed memory. Chief Rabbi of [the] h[oly] c[ongregations of] Posen and Frankfurt on the Main, etc.

An abbreviated German translation appears below the Hebrew.

Rabbi Naphtali Kohen was a tragic figure, unfortunately best remembered because the fire in the Frankfurt ghetto in 1711 began in his house. Born into a rabbinical family in the Ukraine, he had spent part of his childhood as a prisoner of the Tatars. He escaped and returned to his native town of Ostroj, where he succeeded his father as rabbi. In 1690 he went to Posen, where he served as chief rabbi until he was called to Frankfurt in 1704. A learned scholar and author, Kohen owned a valuable library of rare kabbalistic manuscripts. His interest in the Kabbala gave rise to many rumors and accusations, which brought about his downfall after the fire broke out on January 14, 1711 (see no. 49). Dazed by the flames, Kohen lost all presence of mind: he neither tried to quench the flames, nor did he call for help. He was therefore held responsible for the spread of the fire, which raged through the night and eventually destroyed the entire ghetto. Both Jews and gentiles saw the catastrophe as an act of divine punishment. For a period of fourteen years after the fire Jews refrained from the usual Hanukkah and Purim celebrations and masquerades and from playing all games except chess.

Rabbi Kohen was arrested for his alleged role in the fire and remained in prison for several months until bail was raised. After his release he left Frankfurt, never to return. He died in Istanbul in 1719, en route to the Holy Land.

This representation is based on a larger picture of the Rabbi studying with two young pupils, which bears a French inscription identifying it as "the unfortunate rabbi kabbalist, after a painting by Nothnagel 1772."[1] This widely distributed image of Rabbi Naphtali Kohen is thus a fanciful posthumous rendering and not a true portrait.

1. *Bilder zur Frankfurter Geschichte*, 1950, no. 156.

E. D. B.

51. Sêfer 'Êtz Ḥayyim

Frankfurt, 1720
R. Isaiah Horowitz
Published by David Jacob Kronie

Ink on paper
7-3/4 × 6-5/8 × 13/16 in., 19.7 × 16.8 × 2.1 cm.
The Library of the Jewish Theological Seminary of America, New York, The Joffe Collection

This Yiddish abridgement of one of the classic encyclopedic compendia of kabbalistic ethics and ritual is from the collection of rare Yiddish books of Judah A. Joffe, now part of The Library of the Jewish Theological Seminary.

M. S. C.

52. The Marriage Hall in the Judengasse

Frankfurt, 1864
After a watercolor by Karl Theodor Reiffenstein (1820–1893)
Color lithograph on paper
8-15/16 × 14-1/8 in., 22.7 × 35.8 cm.
Leo Baeck Institute, New York, 78.597

This reproduction of a watercolor painted by Reiffenstein in 1864 depicts part of the exterior of the Jewish marriage hall in Frankfurt. The ambiance of the Judengasse is suggested by a clothing stall set up on the cobblestone street and the woman who stands in the doorway observing the life of the neighborhood.

The marriage hall, also called the *Tanzhaus* (Dance Hall), was maintained by the community,[1] as private homes were generally too small and cramped to accommodate guests. Festive meals and entertainment associated with betrothal, as well as the celebration after the ceremony itself, were held in the marriage hall.[2]

Reiffenstein, a native of Frankfurt, was principally a painter of architectural views and landscapes; he executed numerous drawings and watercolors of local sites and scenes. From 1836 to 1846 he studied at the Frankfurt Städel'schen Institute, where Philipp Veit (see no. 100) was one of his teachers.

1. Dietz, *Stammbuch*, p. 440, no. 7.
2. See Pollack, *Folkways*, pp. 29 ff.

REFERENCE: Weizsäcker and Dessoff, II, pp. 116–117.

E. D. B.

53. Jewish Ceremonies: Wedding Procession

From Johann Jakob Schudt (1664–1722), *Jüdische Merkwürdigkeiten*
Frankfurt and Leipzig, 1714–1718
Peter Fehr (1681–1740)
Etching and engraving on paper

8-1/4 × 7-1/4 × 3 in., 21.0 × 18.4 × 7.6 cm.
The Library of the Jewish Theological Seminary of America, New York

Johann Jakob Schudt was a Frankfurt-born Orientalist who developed a special interest in the history and customs of the Jews. He first studied theology at Wittenberg before pursuing Oriental studies in Hamburg. Upon his return to Frankfurt, he began a teaching career.

The fire that destroyed the Frankfurt ghetto in 1711 prompted him to write his multivolume work *Jüdische Merkwürdigkeiten* (*Jewish Peculiarities*), which incudes a general history of the Jews in different parts of the world and a more specific account of the Jews of Frankfurt. Although much of this book is tainted with prejudice and is unreliable, it is also

53

a valuable source for the customs, clothing, and way of life of Frankfurt Jews in Schudt's time.

This illustrated page appears at the end (p. 74) of the third book of Part IV. It is divided into three registers, the central one of which depicts a wedding procession beneath the inscription:

Die Braut geht hier mit grossem Pracht.
The bride passes here in great splendor.

Led by four musicians, the heavily veiled bride walks beneath a *huppah* (marriage canopy) carried by four small boys, as female friends and relatives follow behind. Both men and women wear the distinctive Jewish ruff (see nos. 46 and 47). The women's headgear, the *viereckiger Schleier* (square veil), a cap with stiff, wing-like protrusions of starched linen, was a survival from the medieval period and was worn only on the Sabbath, on holidays, and for other religious ceremonies.[1] (For the cap worn every day at that time, see no. 47.) The men wear traditional Jewish *barettes* (see no. 46).

Musicians were an important part of wedding festivities (see no. 130), which brightened the drab and difficult life of the ghetto's inhabitants.

The plate was designed and executed by Peter Fehr, a Frankfurt engraver who specialized in book illustration.

1. Rubens, *Jewish Costume*, p. 117.

REFERENCES: Rubens, *Jewish Costume*, pl. 169; Rubens, *Iconography*, 1981, no. 1367b.

E. D. B.

54. Decree Specifying That Jews Are Permitted to Conduct Business Only in the Ghetto

Frankfurt, October 16, 1738
Printed on paper
13-3/4 × 8-1/4 in., 35.0 × 21.0 cm.
Leo Baeck Institute, New York

55. Die Judengasse in Frankfurt am Main

Frankfurt, c. 1845
William Lang, after Jakob Fürchtegott Dielmann (1809–1885); published by Carl Jügel
Hand-colored etching on paper

55

8-7/8 × 6-3/16 in., 22.5 × 15.7 cm.
The Jewish Museum, New York, JM 159-67

Jügel published numerous prints of city scenes and *vedute* after designs by Dielmann, including a view of the Frankfurt synagogue built in 1711 (see no. 49). Dielmann, a Frankfurt artist, was also known for his depictions of country life and landscapes in the Rhineland and in Hesse. The name Judengasse, Jewish Street, dates from 1552. At the time when the ghetto was established, this street provided adequate housing for the Jewish population. As this population increased, however, conditions grew steadily worse, because the Frankfurt city council refused to allow Jews to acquire more property for houses. Consequently, Jews were forced to fill every available bit of land with dwellings and to build vertically on top of already existing houses. Sanitary conditions were poor, people were crowded into cramped quarters, and the Judengasse acquired its gloomy, prison-like appearance.

With the abolition of the ghetto in 1811, the Jews

85

were no longer forced to live on the Judengasse. The street remained, however, the symbolic center of Jewish Frankfurt, with many landmarks, like the 1711 synagogue and the ancestral home of the Rothschilds (see nos. 2 and 104). The new synagogue, built in 1855–1860 (see no. 84) was built on the same site as its predecessors, though by that time the Judengasse had been renamed Börnestrasse in honor of the ghetto's famous son, Ludwig Börne, politician, journalist, and activist.

Johann Wolfgang von Goethe grew up in Frankfurt, and in his autobiographical work *Aus meinem Leben: Dichtung und Wahrheit* (1811) he described his youthful impressions of the Judengasse:

> To the forebodings which plagued the boy and somehow also the youth, belonged especially the condition of the Jewish city, actually called the Jewish street, because it hardly consisted of more than a single street which, in earlier times, might have been jammed in between city wall and moat, as if in a cage. The narrowness, the filth, the swarming multitude, the pronunciation of an unpleasant language, together made the most disagreeable impression, even if one only looked in while passing by the gate. It took a long time before I ventured into it alone, and I did not return again so quickly when I had escaped the importunities of so many people who demanded indefatigably that something be traded, or offered their wares for sale . . . . Meanwhile, they remained after all the chosen people of God, and went about, as it might have happened, as a memorial to the most ancient times. Moreover, they, too were humans, active, helpful, and one could not withhold respect for the obstinacy with which they clung to their customs. Besides, the girls were pretty, and did not dislike it when a Christian lad who met them on the Sabbath on the *Fischerfeld*, was friendly and attentive.[1]

1. *Dichtung und Wahrheit*, pp. 159–160.

REFERENCES: Weizsäcker and Dessoff, II, p. 31; Rubens, *Iconography*, 1981, no. 1314.

E. D. B.

The Frankfurt Synagogue

The reconstruction of the synagogue in this exhibition is based on photographs and sketches of Frankfurt synagogues that were in existence between 1750 and 1870, though it is not an exact replica of any of them. Instead, an attempt has been made to recreate the essential features of such a house of worship, incorporating, as much as possible, furnishings made in Frankfurt or surrounding Hesse; these furnishings are arranged as they would have appeared in the Schützenstrasse or Börnestrasse synagogues of Frankfurt.

56. Tablets of the Law

Danzig, 1818
Wood, painted and gilded
40 × 27 in., 101.5 × 68.5 cm.
The Jewish Museum, New York, gift of
the Danzig Jewish Community, D 283

The tablets bear the initial words of the Ten Commandments in raised and gilt lettering against a deep-blue ground. Gold paint also outlines the edges of the tablets and portions of the crown atop them. The remainder of the crown is painted red.

Extant engravings and sketches show that in Frankfurt synagogues, as in others throughout Germany, carved Tablets of the Law were set above the Torah ark. This practice can be traced back only to the seventeenth century.[1] According to Dr. Erwin Lichtenstein, last syndic of the Danzig community, these tablets came from the Schottland synagogue, which had been erected in 1818.

1. J. Gutmann, "How Traditional Are Our Traditions?" in *Beauty in Holiness*, p. 418.

REFERENCE: *Danzig 1939*, no. 53

V. B. M.

57. Torah Curtain (See color plate, p. 10)

Probably Frankfurt, 1752–1753
Silk brocade and velvet embroidered with polychrome silk and metallic thread; metallic fringe and ribbons
63 × 50-3/8 in., 160.0 × 128.0 cm., exclusive of fringe
The Jewish Museum, New York, gift of Dr. Harry G. Friedman, F 3524

Metallic ribbons frame the field of this curtain and serve to organize its decoration. At center is a mirror composed of two pieces of French brocade, of about 1750. The vertical framing ribbons continue to the top of the curtain, thus forming a smaller rectangular field containing two confronted lions flanking a crown labeled כתר תורה (Crown of Torah) above two blessing hands labeled כתר כהנה (Crown of Priesthood). The pictorial elements are executed in stumpwork. In the narrow vertical fields to right and left is an inscription, which begins at right:

ז"נ / ה"ה מ' אברהם / ב' הרב מ' ליב / כ"ץ
בן הגאון / המפורסם מ' / יעקב כ"ץ / ז"צל
א[ב] ב[ית] ד[ין] / ור[יש] מ[תיבתא] דק"ק
פ[ראנק]פ[ורט] / דמיין ומצד / שני נכד /
הגאון / המפורסם / מ' זלמן / מירלש / א[ב]
ב[ית] ד[ין] ור[יש] מ[תיבתא] / דק"ק
א[ל]טונא [ו]אניזבעק] ה[אמבורג] / ע[ם]
א[שתו] ה' והג[בירה] / מרת ריינה / תי' ב'
הקצין / מ' יאקב / בר"א נר"ו / לפרט /
שבתון זכרון / תרועה לפ"ק

T[his is the] d[onation of] Abraham son of . . . Leib Katz, son of Jacob Katz, chief rabbi of the h[oly] c[ongregation] Frankfurt am Main, and on the other side, the grandson of Meshullam Zalman Mirels, chief rabbi of the h[oly] c[ongregation] of Altona-Wandsbeck-Hamburg, and of his wife Reyna, daughter of Jakob son of A . . . by the era "Complete rest, a sacred occasion commemorated with loud blasts" (Lev. 23:24) [chronogram for 5(508) (1752–1753)].

Pictorial and literary references to the Crown of Torah are commonly found on Torah curtains. What is noteworthy is the inscription referring to the second crown, that of priesthood, which was included because the donor came from a family of *kohanim* (priests).[1] The inscription also demonstrates the great emphasis placed on family lineage (*yiḥus*) by Jews of the period. Abraham, son of Leib, mentions not only his father's famous father but also his mother's. Both grandfathers were chief rabbis of major Jewish communities.

1. *Ethics of the Fathers*, 4:17.

REFERENCE: *Fabric of Jewish Life*, no. 25.

V. B. M.

58. Valance for the Torah Ark

Probably Frankfurt, *c.* 1752, with later additions
Silk brocade, velvet embroidered with metallic threads, and metallic braid
18-3/4 × 61 in., 47.5 × 155.0 cm.
The Jewish Museum, New York, gift of Dr. Harry G. Friedman, F 2046

Although this valance has been heavily restored, the original portions suggest that it was made to match the Torah curtain no. 57. The four decorative panels are of the same mid–eighteenth-century brocade as the mirror on the curtain, and the embroidered letters of both pieces are identical in form and workmanship. In addition, the ribbon surrounding the inscription matches that of the Torah curtain, and the width of the remaining sections is comparable to that of the curtain. According to the inscription, the donor of the valance was the brother of Dinah, wife of Abraham son of Leib Katz, the donor of the curtain:

כ"ת / ז"נ כ"ה / מיכאל ז"ל בן / מוהר"ר /
יאקב / בר"א / ז"ל

C[rown of Torah]. T[his was] d[onated by] . . . Michael of blessed memory the son of . . . Jakob son of A. of blessed memory.

The form of the inscription reveals that Michael was already dead at the time when the valance was made.

REFERENCE: *Fabric of Jewish Life*, no. 25.

V. B. M.

59. Menorah for the Synagogue

Germany, eighteenth century
Brass, cast and engraved
21-1/2 × 26 × 6-1/2 in., 54.6 × 66.0 × 16.5 cm.
The Jewish Museum, New York, gift of Dr. Harry G. Friedman, F 195

The shaft of this *menorah* rises from a stepped base. Four rings encircling the shaft are fitted with sockets for the eight arms, cast as stylized branches. Each arm terminates in a pricket, and a ninth pricket is held by the cast figure of a Jew who stands atop the central shaft. He is dressed, as in many eighteenth-century depictions, in a long frock coat and Jew's hat (*barette*; see nos. 46 and 53).

Similar figures were incorporated in Judaica produced by Frankfurt silversmiths active in the eighteenth century, but a Frankfurt origin cannot be definitively ascribed to this *menorah*, for it is known to have come to New York from the synagogue of Creglingen, a town more than 200 kilometers southeast of Frankfurt.

REFERENCE: Kayser-Schoenberger, no. 146a.

V. B. M.

60. Eternal Light

Germany, mid-eighteenth century
Master AG
Marks: AG and 13
Silver, cast, ajouré, and repoussé
29 × 5-1/2 in., 73.6 × 14.0 cm.
The Jewish Museum, New York, gift of Dr. Harry G. Friedman, F 1494

The suspension ring of this hanging lamp is affixed to a small canopy from which hang three chains holding the lamp proper. At their lower ends, the chains are attached to scalloped handles decorated with rococo scroll and shell forms executed in repoussé. The center of the lamp is of baluster form with two knops. Below the second, smaller knop are

a cap of leaves and a ring (probably to hold a drip pan, now missing). The two knops are composed of three fields each; each field is a rocaille cartouche on a pierced ground. The inscription seems to be of a date later than the lamp:

הג' / יהודה / ליוואי / מהרל / מפראג / יח
אלול השס"ט

Rabbi Judah Loewy, Maharal of Prague, 18 Elul 5369 [1609]

A similar lamp hung in the Börnestrasse synagogue.[1] In the Cologne Historical Museum is another example, dated to the middle of the eighteenth century.[2]

1. H. Eschwege, *Die Synagogue in der deutschen Geschichte*, (Dresden: 1980), fig. 112.
2. *Monumenta Judaica*, no. 407.

61. Pair of Sconces with Candleholders

Danzig (?), nineteenth century
Brass, cast and engraved
13-3/4 × 21 × 16-1/4 in., 35.0 × 53.0 × 41.0 cm.
The Jewish Museum, New York, gift of the Danzig Jewish Community, D 334 a, b

A clenched fist serves as the socket for the main arm of each sconce, linking it to the oblong backplate. The arm forms an S curve terminating in a candleholder and drip pan, both engraved with circles. Two smaller sockets attached to the apex of the S curve hold smaller arms and candleholders. The numbers 9 and 10 engraved on the backplate indicate that this pair was once part of a series housed in a Danzig synagogue.

Sockets in the form of clenched fists are found on German Judaica as early as the seventeenth century.[1] These sconces, however, probably belong to the nineteenth century, as they appear to have come from one of the Danzig synagogues founded then. They are listed in the 1933 catalogue of that city's Jewish Museum and may also be those referred to in the 1904 edition.

1. See a synagogue *menorah* from Clèves dated to the seventeenth century in *Geschichte der Juden im Rheinland*, p. 1.

REFERENCES: Danzig, 1904, no. 124; Danzig, 1933, no. 148; *Danzig 1939*, no. 269.

V. B. M.

62. Torah Binder

Kronberg, 1839
Linen, painted
128-1/8 × 7-15/16 in., 324.0 × 19.0 cm.
The Jewish Museum, New York, gift of Dr. Harry
G. Friedman, F 687

According to its inscription, this binder was made
for

שלמה צבי בר אשר הלוי (קראנבערג)
לאורך ימים טובים נולד במזל טוב ביום
ו' ט"ז תמוז תקצ"ט לפק ה' יתן לגדלו
לתורה ולחופה ולמעשים טובים אמן סלה.

> Solomon Zvi son of Asher the Levite
> (Kronberg), may his days be long and good,
> born under a good sign on Friday, 16
> Tammuz [5]599 [June 28, 1839] . . . May God
> allow him to be raised to Torah and to the
> marriage canopy and to good deeds. Amen
> Selah.

All the large letters are outlined in red and their interiors filled with variegated designs. The ascenders
and descenders of some of the letters have been elaborated into animals, leaves, and scrolls. Instead of
diacritical marks, the artist used flowers, an animal,
and a crown to mark abbreviations. Two pictorial
elements are included. The first is an open Torah
enclosing the saying

תורה צוה לנו משה

> When Moses charged us with the Teaching
> (Deut. 33:4).

The second is an elaborate marriage canopy consisting of two columns with bases and capitals and a
cloth enclosing the word

ולחופה

and to the marriage canopy.

The binder is edged along its length with simple
stitches of varying colors. In the late medieval period, it became the practice among Ashkenazi Jews
to fashion Torah binders like this one out of cloth
used at circumcision ceremonies. The earliest examples were embroidered, but by the eighteenth
century many were being painted as well; the decoration consisted of the child's name, the date of his
birth and the final passages of the circumcision ceremony. On the boy's first or third birthday or on
some similar occasion of importance, the binder was
presented to the synagogue. The German name of
the father (Kronberg) painted below his Hebrew
name indicates that this binder comes from a city
near Frankfurt. Such indications of origin are rarely
found on Ashkenazi binders.

V. B. M.

63. Torah Mantle

Germany, eighteenth century
Silk brocade with silk appliqué
35 × 14-9/16 in., 89.0 × 37.0 cm.
The Jewish Museum, New York, gift of Dr. Harry
G. Friedman, F 702

The base fabric of this mantle is a cream-colored silk
brocade woven in a pattern of floral bouquets in ver-

62

63

The square form of the letters is typical of eighteenth century German Torah curtains and mantles, and the fabric is a French silk brocade of the same period. From the patching of the fabric at the bottom front and the use of the selvage (visible to the right of the center insert) it may be concluded that the mantle was made from a valued piece of cloth that was, however, not large enough.

V. B. M.

64

in vertical rows of alternating direction. Two strips of tan brocade with a pattern of yellow flowers superimposed on a dark brown stripe form the central portion of the front. Over these strips are applied two Hebrew letters and a diacritical mark cut from pink silk:

כ[ותר]ת̇[ורה]

the C[rown of] T[orah].

90

64. Torah Mantle

Frankfurt (?), c. 1700
Velvet with stumpwork and embroidery in polychrome silk and metallic threads
Oval top: 8-11/16 × 12-3/8 in., 22.0 × 31.0 cm.; body: 34-11/16 × 22-1/16 in., 88.0 × 56.0 cm.
The Jewish Museum, New York, gift of Dr. Harry G. Friedman, F 2634

The major decorative motif of this mantle is a fanciful crowned *baldacchino*, executed in stumpwork and laid and couched embroidery, which appears on both the front and back. At the base of the *baldacchino* a series of balustrades alternates with undulating bushes or trees. The lower portion of the *baldacchino* consists of a diamond-patterned cloth filled with rosettes and shells. It is topped by a crowned melon-shaped dome resting on an entablature from which hangs a valance with tassels. A single shell fills each lower corner of the front and back. Above each shell rises a row of inverted tulips and buds. Two confronted lions flank the crown on the front of the mantle, but there are no such lions on the back; instead, two additional shells top the rows of flowers flanking the *baldacchino*, and two more shells are embroidered on the top piece.

This mantle formerly belonged to a family from Altona and was said to have been given to an ancestor by a Portuguese Marrano in the late seventeenth century. If so, the mantle must have been fabricated in the area of Frankfurt or Mainz. The stumpwork diamond pattern is close in form and execution to that on the mirror of a curtain dedicated in Frankfurt in 1713 and to those on similar published curtains of the same period.[1]

1. See I. Posen, "Die Mainzer Torahschrein Vorhänge," *Notizblatt*, XXIX (1932), no. 10; and F. Landsberger, "Old-time Torah Curtains," *Beauty in Holiness*, figs. 7, 9.

V. B. M.

65. Torah Shield

Frankfurt, 1684–1718
Johann Michael Schuler (1658–1718)
Marks: Scheffler 120 (R³2004), 247
Silver, cast, ajouré, engraved, and gilt
6-1/4 × 9-1/2 in., 15.9 × 23.5 cm.
The Jewish Museum, New York, gift of Dr. Harry G. Friedman, F 740

65

The main portion of this shield consists of three cast sections, which have been joined together. A symmetrical composition of rosettes and vine scrolls organized along a vertical axis appears in full form on the two end sections; the central section is abbreviated. A symmetrical mask-and-scroll design repeated three times creates scalloped upper and lower borders. The side borders consist of animated vine scrolls, portions of which are now lost. (Other losses include a central bell once affixed to the lower border, a central chain attached to the hole at the top, and the suspension hook.) Two openwork columns, a crown with fleur-de-lis decoration, and a box holding plaques inscribed with the names of the readings have been soldered to the surface. The crown and columns are symbolic elements commonly found on Torah shields and probably represent the crown of Torah and the two free-standing pillars that once stood on the porch of the Temple in Jerusalem.[1]

This shield is closely related technically and stylistically to four others that are presumed to be the work of the same silversmith, though none bears his mastermark. One example is in the Wolfson Museum, Hechal Shlomo, Jerusalem: another is in the Cluny Museum, Paris. A third is in a private collection in Paris. The fourth was exhibited in London in 1887, and its present location is unknown.[2] A fragment of a fifth shield bearing the same master's mark—IMS in an oval field—is now in The Jewish Museum, New York (F 4391).

In 1966 Schoenberger identified the maker as Johann Matthias Sandrart, to whom he attributed a series of fifteen works, some bearing the oval IMS mark and two others stamped IMS in a trefoil field.[3] More recent research has revealed that the first mark belongs instead to Johann Michael Schuler, brother of Johann Valentin Schuler,[4] which probably explains the extremely close stylistic correspondences between some of their works, for example, the *menorah* by Johann Michael in the Cluny Museum and the *menorah* by Johann Valentin in the Frankfurt Historical Museum. This attribution also obviates Schoenberger's rather awkward explanation of why Sandrart used two different hallmarks.[5]

1. For the crown, see *Ethics of the Fathers*, 4:17; for the pillars, see I Kings 6:15 *ff*.
2. See respectively Bialer, *Jewish Life*, p. 115; *Synagoga*, no. 222; and *Anglo-Jewish Historical Exhibition*, no. 1459.
3. G. Schoenberger, "Der Frankfurter Goldschmied Johann Matthias Sandrart," *Schriften des Historisches Museums Frankfurt a. M.*, XII (1966), pp. 143–170.
4. Scheffler, nos. 312 and 360.
5. Schoenberger, op. cit., 164–165.

REFERENCES: Kayser-Schoenberger, no. 44; Scheffler, no. 312; and Schoenberger, "Der Frankfurter Goldschmied Johann Matthias Sandrart," *Schriften des Historisches Museums Frankfurt a. M.*, XII (1966), pp. 164–165.

V. B. M.

66. Torah Shield

Frankfurt, 1722–1762
Georg Wilhelm Schedel (1698–1762)
Marks: Scheffler 133(R³2010), 272(R³2059)
Silver, repoussé, cast, and parcel-gilt
15-9/16 × 8-1/2 in., 39.5 × 21.6 cm. (with chain)
The Jewish Museum, New York, Jewish Cultural Reconstruction, JM 21-52

A wide border of beadwork, parallel lines, and rosettes, all worked in repoussé, frames this rectangular shield with arcuated top. Two gilt columns with elaborate stepped bases and capitals "float" in the field. A pair of rampant lions, also gilt, have been placed above the capitals; they reach toward a gilt crown centered at the top. The rest of the field is filled with foliate scrolls, flowers, and strapwork, placed symmetrically about a vertical axis. At the center is a recessed holder for holiday name plates. Only one of the five bells originally suspended from the lower border survives; three of the existing bells

66

are later replacements. The cast suspension piece is an elaborate composition of masks, scrolls, and a cherub. Only two of the three original chains remain.

The composition of this shield lacks cohesiveness; the elements appear to float without clear relation to one another. Even the floral ornamentation consists of discrete forms without organic unity. Schedel also created a ceremonial goblet for the Burial Society of a Hessen community (F3297), a Hanukkah lamp in The Jewish Museum (F2820) and an *etrog* container in the Frankfurt Historical Museum (Inv. Nr. X61; 17).

V. B. M.

67. Torah Shield

Frankfurt, *c.* 1710
Johann Adam Boller (1679–1732)
Mark: 120
Silver, cast, ajouré, engraved, and stippled
9-9/16 × 9-1/16 in., 24.3 × 23.0 cm.
The Jewish Museum, New York, The Jewish Cultural Reconstruction, JM 28-52

67

portions of the foliage to suggest the three-dimensionality of curling leaves. Particularly noteworthy are the notched outlines and trilobed endings of the leaves. The workmanship of the lions reflects a similar concern for sculptural effects. Delicate stippling models the bodies, and fine engraving indicates texture. The lean, energetic bodies are executed in graceful curves.

The same stylistic characteristics are found on works bearing Johann Adam Boller's hallmarks. For example, identical acanthus vines with notched outlines and trilobed endings are executed in repoussé on the catch basin of a Sabbath lamp now in The Jewish Museum (F 4400), and the same foliage is engraved on the base of a Hanukkah lamp in a New York private collection, now on loan to The Jewish Museum. On the upper zone of the catch basin the acanthus vines are inhabited by dogs chasing prey, all portrayed in the same naturalistic style as are the lions on the shield. The tool marks on this Torah shield are also similar to those on the other works. Finally, it should be noted that, on a second Sabbath lamp in Temple Emanuel, New York, Boller used an openwork acanthus design for the main shaft. The attribution of this Torah shield significantly increases the acknowledged body of Judaica created by Boller beyond the hanging lamps, *menorot*, and burial beakers known earlier.

REFERENCES: Kayser-Schoenberger, no. 46; *Notizblatt* XXIII (1929), 7, fig. 6; Moses, 150, ill. 152a; Hallo, no. 19; *Mitteilunger* III/IV, ill. 24.

V. B. M.

In its present form this shield shows evidence of reworking, possibly on more than one occasion. The original shield was cast in openwork with a symmetrical design of acanthus vines inhabited by confronted lions supporting a crown surmounted by a palmette. Just below the center is a box for plaques edged by a fleur-de-lis design. The original plain border is broken at a number of points on the sides, bottom, and arcuated top. Apparently as a result of this damage, the shield was strengthened by means of attachment to a silver backplate with beaded border and scalloped edge. A fragmentary Frankfurt city mark appears along the lower edge of this outer border. The urn at the center bottom of the field may have been added at this time: It differs in style and workmanship from the main portion of the shield. The applied crown, of rude and heavy workmanship, may belong to this same reworking or to a later one.

Two aspects of the original shield are remarkable: the naturalistic style and the use of openwork. Despite the symmetrical composition, the acanthus leaves are executed as organic forms, their swelling outlines and exuberant curves transmitting a sense of growth. In several areas the silversmith stippled

68. Torah Shield

Frankfurt, before 1781
Rötger Herfurth (1722–1776)
Marks: Scheffler 147, 287
Silver, repoussé, hammered, and gilt
14-3/8 × 7-1/2 in., 36.5 × 19.1 cm. (with chain)
The Jewish Museum, New York, Jewish Cultural Reconstruction, JM 33-52

In its irregular outline, broken contours, and emphasis on shell and scroll ornament, this shield exemplifies the Rococo period. The center of the shield is filled with a diaper pattern framed by scrolls, shells, and flowers. The recessed box with plaques for readings is at the top held between the outstretched paws of two rampant lions. At the bottom

is a cartouche inscribed:

נתחדש ע״י הגבאים / מקלפי של צדקה /
כהרר ליב בעכהובין / וכמר עזריאל לוי /
בק״ק רעדלהיים / יו[ם] ה׳ כ׳ח תמוז / ת׳קפא׳ל

This was restored b[y] the *gabbaim* Leib
Beckhoven and Azriel Levy from the charity
boxes of the h[oly] c[ongregation] of
Roedelheim, Thursday, 28 Tammuz [5]521
[1781]. . . .

The original chain and suspension piece in the
form of a cartouche are still preserved.

In style and form this shield is closely related to
another in the collection of The Jewish Museum (F
4380), which has no marks but bears a date of 1757;
another in the Israel Museum (148/35); and a shield
that was exhibited in London in 1887.[1] Herfurth is
known to have produced many works of Judaica (see
nos. 27, 122).[2]

1. *Anglo-Jewish Historical Exhibition*, no. 1458
2. See also Scheffler, no. 444; *Synagoga*, nos. 230, 305,
373; *Notizblatt*, XXXIV (1937), 16–19.

V. B. M.

69. Rimmonim

Frankfurt, 1701–1741
Jeremias Zobel (1670–1741)
Marks: Scheffler 128 (R³ 2005), 256 (R³ 2050)
Silver, cast, repoussé, stippled, engraved, and gilt
18 × 7 in. dm., 45.7 × 17.8 cm.
The Jewish Museum, New York, gift of Dr. Harry
G. Friedman, F 3685

These *rimmonim* combine architectural and foliate
forms and are enriched by ornamental grotesques.
The supporting shafts are decorated with diagonal
bands of engraved foliage. They terminate in cushion shapes intermediate in size and form between
the slim shafts themselves and the bulbous lower
portions of the terminals. The latter are decorated
with acanthus leaves in repoussé on a stippled
ground. Above them rise three-storied hexagonal
towers, each surmounted by an openwork crown and
an orb with acorn finial. Each story of the tower
consists of a series of arches from the center of which
a bell is suspended. The surrounding "masonry" is
articulated by engraved lines, and the corners of each
story rest on columns with ornamental bases.

At the intersection of each story and corner a grotesque scroll obscures the basic outline of the *rimmon*. A series of grotesques attached to the bulbous

zone atop the shafts produces a similar effect. These *rimmonim* thus show a play between solid and void characteristic of much Frankfurt Judaica.

A nearly identical pair of *rimmonim*, also the work of Zobel, are now in the collection of the Frankfurt Historical Museum.[1] A pair of somewhat different design are in the Skirball Museum.[2] The same master was responsible for the *havdalah* candle and spice holder, no. 122.

1. Inv. no. X51 v-w; see *Synagoga*, no. 201.
2. F. Landsberger, "A German Torah Ornamentation," *Beauty in Holiness*, fig. 4.

REFERENCE: Kayser-Schoenberger, no. 29.

V. B. M.

70. Torah Crown

Berlin, 1821–1839
Johann Friedrich Wilhelm Borcke
Marks: Scheffler, *Berlin*, 14, 18, 331
Silver, cast, stippled, and gilt
12-1/4 × 9-1/8 in., 31.1 × 23.2 cm.
The Jewish Museum, New York, gift of Dr. Harry G. Friedman, F 1649

Eight bands rise from a circular base to meet at the center. Both bands and base are decorated with alternating lozenges and circles on a stippled ground. A cluster of three oak leaves marks each juncture with the base, and small gilt bells are suspended between the projecting side points of the bands. At the center of the crown is a gilt orb, below which is suspended a large gilt bell. The base is outfitted with a flat plate to which are attached two tubes meant to be fitted over the wooden staves of a Torah scroll.

In shape and decoration this crown is very similar to one dated 1821 that belonged to the Jewish community of Kassel.[1] Both works incorporate curved bands, decoration imitating inset gems, triple clusters of oak leaves, and the crowning orb. The Kassel crown was fashioned by Heinrich Wilhelm Kompff, who also made a death crown for Kurfürst Wilhelm I in 1821, evidently the model for the Kassel Torah crown. The crown belonging to The Jewish Museum is a variant of the Kassel design, made by a Berlin silversmith, Johann Friedrich Wilhelm Borcke, between 1821 and 1839. Thus if the Berlin crown was made as early as 1821, the origin of the design cannot be determined. In Scheffler's listing of Borcke's known works there is no other piece of Judaica.[2] In

the Danzig collection, however, there are two works made by Borcke during the same years indicated by the hallmarks on the crown (1821–1839), a pair of *rimmonim* and an alms dish.[3]

1. *Notizblatt*, XXIII (1929), p. 6, fig. 3.
2. Scheffler, *Berlin*, no. 1702.
3. *Danzig 1939*, nos. 218 and 274.

V. B. M.

71. Cloth Used to Cover the Torah

Munich (?), 1867–1868
Velvet, embroidered with white silk and metallic threads; metallic fringe and braid; sequins
18-1/8 × 21-1/4 in., 46.0 × 54.0 cm.
The Jewish Museum, New York, gift of Edward J. Sovatkin, through Dr. Harry G. Friedman, F 4289

The major decorative element of this cover is the dedicatory inscription:

זכור את יום השבת לקדשו.
אבי! אמצא חן בעיניך.
קבל מנחתי ותן לי ברכתך.
כ' יואל יעקב בארן פן הירש

Remember the Sabbath day to keep it holy.
(Ex. 20:8) My Father! May I find grace in Your
eyes.   Accept my offering and give me
Your blessing. Joel Jacob Baron von Hirsch.

A jeweled crown is embroidered above the inscription; the name of the donor and his coat of arms are below.

Diacritical marks above some of the letters in the first line indicate that the sentence forms a chronogram for the year [5]628 (1867–1868). Joel Jacob von Hirsch (1789–1876) was the brother of Joseph and the father of the philanthropist Maurice Baron von Hirsch.

As the biblical quotation refers to the Sabbath, this cloth may not have been used on other occasions. Some German synagogues were so well endowed with liturgical textiles that they could be changed frequently. Posen cites Torah curtains once in the Mainz synagogue whose inscriptions referred to specific readings from the Torah, indicating they were to be hung only on those Sabbaths when the particular lections were read.[1] Its small size suggests that this piece was probably used to cover the Torah between *alliyot* (lections). The absence of any abrasion marks on the embroidery indicates that it was not used to cover the cantor's lectern.

1. I. Posen, "Die Mainzer Torahschrein Vorhänge," *Notizblatt*, XXIX (1932), p. 5.

V. B. M.

72. Torah Pointer

Frankfurt, 1699–1743
Johannes Willems III (1666–1743)
Marks: Scheffler 255, 128(R³2005)
Silver, cast and engraved
12 in., 30.5 cm.
The Jewish Museum, New York, Jewish Cultural Reconstruction, JM 47–52.

The shaft of this Torah pointer consists of two spiral sections, each terminating in a knop engraved with inscriptions. The first reads:

חיים בינימין מאסלר

Hayyim Benjamin from Eslar [?]

The second reads:

ס[כום] ערכי מנחם מאסלר

A sum of the property of Menahem from Eslar [?]

Above the upper knop a rampant lion holds a blank scroll. Attached to its head is a suspension ring, which holds a second, larger ring. The opposite end terminates in a hand with extended forefinger. The lower knop is badly dented.

A similar Torah pointer, without marks but with an inscription dated 1735, is in the collection of the Frankfurt Historical Museum.[1] The rampant lion holding a scroll is commonly found on Frankfurt Judaica of the late seventeenth and early eighteenth centuries (see no. 121). According to Jewish Museum records, this pointer was probably used in the old synagogue of Frankfurt, whence it entered the collection of the Jewish Museum there.

1. Inv. no. X13779. See *Synagoga*, no. 240.

REFERENCE: Scheffler, no. 340; Kayser-Schoenberger, no. 66.

V. B. M.

73. Pair of Candlesticks for the Synagogue

Hamburg, 1841–1854
Adolf Ferdinand Fischer
Marks: R³2370, Scheffler, *Niedersachsen*, 1237 and 37
Silver, cast and engraved
21 × 8-3/16 in., 53.3 × 20.8 cm.
The Ernest and Erika Michael collection

The tall, tapering shafts of these candlesticks rise from hexagonal stepped and domed bases and relatively short baluster-shaped stems. The shafts are also hexagonal and decorated with various lightly engraved scroll and foliate motifs. Similar decoration is engraved on the upper bases, the central knops of the stems, and the lower portions of the candle holders.

These candlesticks were made for the Michael family synagogue in Hamburg and were brought to New York by Jakob Michael.

V. B. M.

72

96

74. Spice Box (See color plate, p. 9)

Frankfurt (?), c. 1550, repairs and additions, 1641
Silver, cast, engraved, and gilt
Marks: unidentified
9-5/16 × 2-15/16 × 2-7/8 in., 23.6 × 7.4 × 7.3 cm.
The Jewish Museum, New York, Jewish
Cultural Reconstruction, JM 23-52

This work, the second oldest extant spice box in tower form, was still in the synagogue of Friedberg (Hesse) until 1937–1938, when it, along with other precious items, was transferred to The Jewish Museum of Frankfurt (see nos. 72, 75, 76, 116).

The form is a four-storied masonry tower with varied openings; it is topped by a pinnacle with four surrounding turrets. The base is solid, except for a hinged "door" at the front. Above the door is a level with grilled "windows" on all four sides (the grills of two are missing). The third story is marked by rose windows at the front and back. A wide balcony with a balustrade of fleur-de-lis projects above, obscuring the base of the fourth story, which is articulated on each side by a set of "windows": two lancets and an oculus framed by an ogival arch. A band of rectangular fenestrations encircles the tower above, contributing to a feeling of lightness, despite the weightiness of the turreted roof. In the composition of the entire box there is a pleasing balance between the lightness provided by the openings and the heaviness of the articulated masonry, between the verticality of the tower form and the emphasis on horizontal moldings and balustrade separating the stories.

Many areas, including the balustrade, have been repaired: For example, a second, flat base has been riveted to the original, and there are silver patches on the turrets. An inscription on the back apparently dates the repairs:

Rahele daughter of Eliezer/Dayan [5]411
(1651)

The box itself was probably made about one hundred years earlier. It is similar to a somewhat more elaborate spice box, formerly in Kassel, that was engraved with the arms of two noble families united in marriage in 1543. Rudolf Hallo suggested that the Kassel box was a wedding gift from a Jew associated with the court of one of these families.[1]

1. Hallo, no. 74.

REFERENCES: *Mitteilungen* 1 (1900), fig. 1; Hallo, no. 74, pl. 20a; Moses, pp. 169–171; Kayser-Schonberger, no. 84, pl. XLII.; *Notizblatt*, XXIV (1929). p. 5, fig. 10; Shachar, *Jewish Year*, pp. 5–6, 24–25, pl. VIIIb (right); Hallo, *Jüdische Kult- und Kunstdenkmäler*, pl. III; *Towers of Spice*, p. 11, no. VI; M. Narkiss, "Origins of the Spice Box," *Journal of Jewish Art* 8 (1981), p. 28, fig. 3.

V. B. M.

75. Kiddush Goblet

Frankfurt, c. 1725
Mark: Scheffler 135(R³2001)
Silver, cast, engraved, and repoussé
3-1/16 × 3-1/16 in. dm., 7.7 × 7.7 cm.
The Jewish Museum, New York, Jewish
Cultural Reconstruction, JM 31-52

The short, flaring upper section of this goblet rests on a lobed lower portion. Thinner lobes decorate the domed base. A band of delicately engraved flowers and strapwork encircles the cup just beneath the rim. Below is a rudely executed inscription by another hand; it consists of two Hebrew letters in a rough frame: ע י (*ayyin, yud*), perhaps the owner's monogram.

V. B. M.

75

32   225

76. Ewer and Basin

Germany, 1875
Marks: E(?) A(?) and a pictorial mark
Silver, repoussé, hammered, engraved, and parcel-gilt
Ewer: 9 × 7-5/8 in. dm., 22.9 × 19.3 cm.; basin: 17-5/8 × 12-3/8 in., 44.8 × 31.4 cm.
The Jewish Museum, New York, Jewish Cultural Reconstruction, JM 38-52 a, b

A domed and stepped base supports the helmet-shaped ewer with scroll handle. Scroll, shell, and floral motifs worked in repoussé cover nearly the whole surface, leaving only a small plain area at the "front"; it is inscribed:

נדבת / כ' משה ב"כ אהרן / אפפנהיים /
ואשתו מרת קאפעליא / ר[אש] ה[שנה] שנת
תרל"ה לפ"ק

The donation of . . . Moses son of . . . Aaron Oppenheim and his wife . . . Copelia, R[osh] Ha[shanah] of the year [5]635 . . . [1875].

The identical inscription is repeated on the bottom of the basin, which has a scalloped border bearing the same decorative motifs as those on the ewer. A coat of arms has been applied to the side of the basin directly above the inscription.

Ewers and basins were used in synagogues for washing the hands of *kohanim* and Levites before the recital of the priestly blessing. According to Jewish Museum records, this set was used in the main synagogue of Frankfurt, probably the Börnestrasse synagogue (see no. 84). A Moses Aaron Oppenheim, son of Aaron Jantoff, is mentioned by Dietz;[1] he was born in 1833.

1. Dietz, *Stammbuch*, p. 221.

V. B. M.

76

77

77. Prayer Shawl

Germany, eighteenth century
White silk damask, polychrome silk brocade, metallic lace
66 × 79 in., 165.0 × 197.5 cm.
The Jewish Museum, New York, gift of Jakob Michael, JM 33-57

The major portion of this prayer shawl (*tallit*) is a white silk damask of floral design. A panel of polychrome silk brocade with floral motifs bordered in metallic lace and metallic ribbon is appliquéd to the upper edge of one side, and smaller squares of the polychrome brocade mark the corners; from them hang the ritual fringes (*ẓiẓiyot*). Two parallel bands of metallic lace run the width of the *tallit*, one just below the large brocade panel and another across the lower section.

The brocade panels are used for both aesthetic and

practical effects. The smaller squares reinforce the corners through which the ẓiẓiyot pass. The command to wear fringes is recorded in Numbers (15:38–41), where they are prescribed as reminders to observe the commandments.

Two similar *tallitot*, one from Altona, are in the collection of The Jewish Museum (JM 19-63 and JM 3-69).[1] A fourth example, a gift from a resident of Düsseldorf, once belonged to the Gesellschaft zur Erforschung jüdischen Kunstdenkmäler.[2] A fifth was published by Landsberger.[3] Jakob Michael, the donor of the *tallit* included in this exhibition, was born in Frankfurt but later lived in Hamburg. The known *tallitot* of this type thus all come from Germany, and a sixth is in the Prague Jewish Museum (No. B.C. 4) and Czechoslovakia, and all incorporate fabrics dated to the eighteenth century.

1. *Fabric of Jewish Life*, nos. 73 and 76.
2. *Mitteilungen*, 3–4 (1903), fig. 116.
3. F. Landsberger, *Einführung in die Jüdische Kunst* (Berlin: 1935), p. 14, pl. 6.

V. B. M.

Religious Life 1750–1870

Through the second half of the eighteenth century, Frankfurt remained a traditional Jewish community under the leadership of distinguished rabbis and scholars. Two major religious disputes raged in this period: the amulets controversy and the issue of the Clèves divorce (*get*).

The first dispute revolved around the writing of amulets with Kabbalistic content by Jonathan Eybeschütz (1690/95–1764), the renowned rabbi of Altona, Hamburg, and Wandsbeck. Jacob Joshua Falk (1680–1756), chief rabbi of Frankfurt from 1741 to 1751 and author of *P'nei Yehoshua* (see no. 79), a commentary on the Talmud, sided with the opponents of Rabbi Eybeschütz and excommunicated him. The second dispute involved a divorce granted in 1766 by Rabbi Israel Libschütz, head of the rabbinical court of Clèves; it was declared invalid by the rabbinical court of Frankfurt. To show their independence of the rabbinical authorities who opposed them, the rabbis of Frankfurt publicly burned the opinions written by their Polish colleagues.

As the century progressed, more and more Frankfurt Jews came to favor religious reform. The first changes took place in education. After several failed attempts, the Philanthropin School was established in 1804, it was the first Jewish school in the city to offer secular instruction. By 1807 Reform religious services were being held under its auspices. In the following decades the Reform members of the community demanded the erection of a new synagogue and innovations in the services. Their influence resulted in the appointment of Leopold Stein as deputy rabbi in 1843. He served Frankfurt for nearly twenty years and led efforts to develop a Reform liturgy for the new synagogue on the Börnestrasse. He was succeeded by Abraham Geiger, a native of Frankfurt and an outstanding scholar of the Science of Judaism (*Das Wissenschaft des Judentums*).

In response to Reform inroads on the traditional religious life of the community, a group of traditional Jews organized the Israelitische Religionsgesellschaft, a congregation of modern Orthodoxy. Samson Raphael Hirsch (1808–1888), then rabbi of Moravia, came to Frankfurt in 1851 to head the new Orthodox synagogue. Hirsch's ideal was expressed in the motto *Torah im derech eretz* ("the study of Torah and secular education"); he had himself studied at the University of Bonn, where he had become friendly with Abraham Geiger.

During the period 1750–1870, Frankfurt was thus a major force in Ashkenazi religious life and the center of two of the important religious movements of modern times, Reform Judaism and modern Orthodoxy.

78. Amulet

Prussia, *c.* 1810
Ink on parchment, ink on paper, silk, and linen
Pouch: 1-7/8 × 5/8 in., 4.8 × 1.6 cm.
Amulet: 1-1/8 × 1 in., 2.9 × 2.6 cm.
Paper: 4 × 3-1/4 in., 10.2 × 8.3 cm.
The Jewish Museum, New York, gift of Mr. and Mrs. Ulrich P. Wolff, 1981-315

This amulet came stitched in a black-silk pouch with attached strings for tying around the neck. It consists of a text written on parchment in the square script used to write Torahs; the words are arranged vertically:

ויעמד פינחם ויפלל ותעצר המגפה

Then stood up Phineas, and wrought judgment, and so the plague was stayed (Ps. 106:30).

The amulet was wrapped in a paper inscribed:

בשם ה' אלקי ישראל / לשמירה ברײנדיל
בת גולדא / מן הדבר ומן המגפה.

In the name of the Lord God of Israel, for the protection of Brendel daughter of Golda from pestilence and plague.

On the exterior of the paper was written:

הרבנית תחי'

"[For] the Rabbi's wife..."

The donor's family was descended from Rabbi Akiba Eger of Eisenstadt (1761–1837) whose second wife, Brendel or Breindel, died in 1836. With this amulet came a second one (1981-316) which is identical to the first, except for the names. It was written for Golda, daughter of Israel, presumably Brendel's mother. Akiba Eger was a leading German rabbi who established educational and benevolent institutions and was the author of many scholarly works.

V. B. M.

79. P'nei Yehoshua

Frankfurt, 1752
Jacob Joshua b. Zvi Hirsch Falk, (1680–1756), published by David Jacob Kronie
Ink on paper
12-1/16 × 8-3/16 × 2 in., 30.6 × 20.8 × 5.1 cm.
The Library of the Jewish Theological Seminary of America, New York

The author of this work served as rabbi in Lvov, Berlin, Metz, and Frankfurt. This volume contains his *novellae* on the Talmudic tractates of Berakhot, Shabbat, Pesaḥim, Beṣah, Rosh Hashonah, Sukkah Megillah, and part of Yoma. It is unusual in that it has a double title page.

M. S. C.

100

80. Sêfer Maaśeh Ḥoresh Veḥoshêv

Frankfurt, 1711
Moses b. Joseph Heide, published by Johann Kellner
Ink on paper
6-5/8 × 4-1/4 × 1-1/4 in., 16.8 × 10.8 × 3.2 cm.
The Library of the Jewish Theological Seminary of America, New York, Judah A. Joffe Collection

This charming mathematics textbook is in Judeo-German and covers all important aspects of arithmetic, including fractions and the measurement of time. It carries approbations from Rabbi Naftali Kohen, chief of the rabbinic court of Frankfurt (see no. 50), Rabbi Samuel Kohen Shottin, chief of the rabbinic court of the *kloiz* (house of study) of Frankfurt and Darmstadt, and Rabbi Hirsch Spitz Segal, chief of the rabbinic court of Worms. Such inclusions may seem odd to modern eyes, but in the author's day they were regarded as quite natural. The book opens with the author's philosophically oriented introduction justifying and recommending the study of mathematics.

M. S. C.

81. Medal Commemorating the Centennial of the Philanthropin School

Frankfurt, 1904
Leo Horovitz (1876–c. 1960)
Bronze, cast
2-9/16 in. dm., 6.5 cm.
The Jewish Museum, New York, gift of the Samuel and Daniel M. Friedenberg Collection, FB 204

Leo Horovitz, son of Frankfurt Rabbi Marcus Horovitz, specialized in Jewish medals, including portrait medals. The analogy between sowing in order to reap a good crop and properly educating children to ensure the future health of the community is incorporated into this design. On the obverse harvested sheaves of wheat bound together encircle the inscription:

Jahrhundertfeier des Philanthropins zu Frankfurt A. M. 1804–1904. Für Aufklärung und Humanität.
Centenary of the Philanthropin in Frankfurt a[m] M[ain] 1804–1904. For enlightenment and humanitarianism.

A beehive surrounded by swarming bees, a symbol of industry (see no. 131), separates the designations of the years.

On the reverse a man sows seeds in a wheat field, with the towers of Frankfurt visible in the distance. The inscription reads:

Die Jugend ist die Zeit der Saat
Youth is the time for sowing

For the history of the Philanthropin School, see pp. 00.

REFERENCE: Daniel M. Friedenberg, *Jewish Minters and Medalists* (Philadelphia: 1976), p. 87.

E. D. B.

82. Portrait of Leopold Stein (1810–1882)

Frankfurt: 1846–1850
Valentin Schertle (1809–1885), after a photograph by J. Seib; published by Eduard Gustav May
Lithograph on paper
11 × 7-13/16 in., 27.8 × 19.7 cm.
Leo Baeck Institute, New York, 78.80

A German legend below the portrait identifies the subject: "Leopold Stein, Rabbi of the Jewish congregation in Frankfurt am Main." Below this legend the following inscription appears in Stein's own handwriting:

Der Glaube an den einigen und einzigen Gott schliesst jede Ausschliessung aus. In ihm liegt die Burgschaft der Befreiung und Einigung des Menschengeschlechts zu einem heiligen Brüderbund. Leop. Stein.
The belief in the one and only God rules out any exclusion. In this belief lies the guarantee of deliverance and the unification of mankind into one holy brotherhood. Leop[old] Stein.

Stein was the rabbi in Frankfurt from 1844 to 1862 and was the moving force behind the building of the new synagogue on the Börnestrasse (see no. 84). For his role in the German Reform movement, see pp. 00.

Schertle was born in Villingen, studied in Munich, and worked in Dresden, St. Petersburg, and Warsaw before settling in Frankfurt in 1846. He made lithographic reproductions after the paintings of such Old Masters as Raphael and Guido Reni and of nine-teenth-century artists (for example, Delaroche and Rethel), beside executing portraits of nineteenth-century German personalities, many after photographs.

REFERENCE: Weizäcker-Dessoff, II, p. 130.

E. D. B.

83. Issue of Der Freitagabend

Frankfurt, December 16, 1859
Edited by Leopold Stein, published by Frans Benjamin Auffarth
Printed newspaper
9 × 5-3/4 in., 22.8 × 14.6 cm.
Leo Baeck Institute, New York

The weekly periodical *Der Freitagabend* (*Friday Evening*), subtitled *Eine Familienschrift* (*A Family Publication*), carried articles of interest to Frankfurt's Jewish community, as well as poems and stories with Jewish themes. It provides yet another example of Leopold Stein's prodigious activity in both the religious and literary realms (see p.   ).

The exhibited issue contains fifteen pages; the official newspaper seal of Frankfurt appears on the front page beside the title.

E. D. B.

84. The Börnestrasse Synagogue in Frankfurt

Frankfurt, c. 1866–1880
Eduard Sonntag (1813–1887)
Watercolor on paper
12-3/4 × 9-1/2 in., 32.4 × 24.1 cm.
The Jewish Museum, New York, gift of Dr. Harry G. Friedman, F 4423

Sonntag, an architect as well as a watercolorist, often chose buildings as subjects for his paintings. He had studied architecture in his hometown of Dresden and had practiced there until 1866, when he moved to Frankfurt, where he painted many city landmarks and designed several buildings.

The Börnestrasse synagogue was built between 1855 and 1860 on the site where the synagogues of 1603 and 1711 had stood (see no. 49). It derived its name from its location on the Börnestrasse (formerly the Judengasse), but was also called the Haupt-synagoge, or main synagogue.

Designed by Johann Georg Kayser (1817–1875), the new synagogue was built in the "Moorish-Byzantine" style then fashionable for German synagogues. Constructed of red sandstone, the main facade consisted of a central bay flanked by two projecting stair towers, each crowned by a large onion dome sur-

rounded by four small domes. The tripartite division of the facade reflected the interior organization of the building. The central hall contained seats for 514 men; the two side doors served as entrances to the two women's sections, which contained a total of 506 seats. The facade was unified by the main ogival

window, with its four slender colonettes supporting horseshoe arches. There were three open roundels in the tympanum.

The imposing size and ornateness of this building were in striking contrast to the unpretentious character of the synagogue built in 1711 (see no. 49). They reflected the new social and economic status of Frankfurt Jews in the nineteenth century. Furthermore, as Hammer-Schenk has suggested, the architectural sources of the building served two separate desires on the part of the congregation.[1] On one hand, "eastern" architectural motifs reflected the roots of Judaism: The ogival and horseshoe arches were inspired by Moorish buildings, the onion domes borrowed from Russian architecture. On the other hand, the members of the congregation wished to underscore their newly recognized identity as German citizens by affirming their ties with the Western architectural tradition. The tripartite organization of the building echoed the basic form of Western churches since the Middle Ages, and the stepped gable over the central bay was derived from German town houses. This eclecticism, typical of much nineteenth-century architecture, also reflected a general revival of interest in historical styles.

The Börnestrasse synagogue was commissioned by a Reform congregation (see pp.   ), which insisted upon its identity as both Jewish and German. This sentiment was expressed in the speeches delivered at the cornerstone-laying ceremony on June 28, 1855. Rabbi Leopold Stein declared:

> God has given us the German land, where we patiently bore so much, as a cherished Fatherland; and this German city, in which we suffered so greatly, has been given to us and to our children as a much beloved hometown [Vaterstadt].[2]

Stein associated the Hebrew tradition and language with the Jewish past and the German language and nation with the Jewish present. He looked ahead to a glorious future in the new synagogue, where both traditions would coexist harmoniously, together nurturing the development of the Jewish community:

> . . . here shall resound in days to come the holy language of the Scriptures, the inspired language of our past; with it, intimately

connected, our cherished and familiar mother tongue, the language of our present and of our future. Upon the base of both languages shall arise the sanctuary which we will build on the foundation of the past into the future.[3]

For a time, Stein's dreams were fulfilled, and the impressive new synagogue was both a reflection and a symbol of a thriving Jewish community in the nineteenth and early twentieth centuries. The synagogue was destroyed by Nazi hooligans on the night of November 10–11, 1938 (*Kristallnacht*), which marked the beginning of the end of this community.

1. Hammer-Schenk, pp. 296 ff.
2. Leopold Stein, *Jakob zu Bethel: Predigt nebst Gebeten, gehalten bei der feierlichen Grundsteinlegung der Hauptsynagoge zu Frankfurt a. M., Donnerstag den 28 Juni 1855, Frankfurt/M. 1855*, p. 8, in Hammer-Schenk, p. 299.
3. Stein, p. 12, in Hammer-Schenk, p. 300.

REFERENCES: Weizsäcker-Dessoff II, 146–147; Freimann and Kracauer, pp. 263 ff.; Hammer-Schenk, pp. 296 ff.

E. D. B.

85. Photograph of Dr. Abraham Geiger (1810–1874)

Germany, *c.* 1860
Modern copy of an unknown original
9-1/2 × 7-1/8 in., 24 × 18.1 cm.
Leo Baeck Institute, New York, Arnsberg collection

86. Issue of Wissenschaftliche Zeitschrift für Jüdische Theologie

Stuttgart, 1837
Ink on paper
8-5/16 × 5-1/16 × 1-1/8 in., 2.1 × 12.9 × 2.9 cm.
The Library of the Jewish Theological Seminary of America, New York

This journal was published by Abraham Geiger, the noted Reform Jewish scholar, in conjunction with the Verein Jüdischer Gelehrter. The Verein, an association of leading Jews and scholars of the day, had sixteen members in 1837 among them Zunz, Munk, Jost, Creizenach, Hess, Rappaport, and others.

M. S. C.

87. Portrait of Rabbi Samson Raphael Hirsch (1808–1888)

Germany, early twentieth century
Hermann Struck (1876–1944)
Lithograph on paper, 30/30
9-3/16 × 7 in., 23.4 × 17.8 cm.
Leo Baeck Institute, New York, 78.266

Struck made this posthumous portrait of Frankfurt Rabbi Samson Raphael Hirsch, the leader of modern Orthodox German Jewry (see pp.   ), from a popular photograph.

Himself an orthodox Jew, Struck was born in Berlin and had studied at the art academy there. Between 1898 and 1913 he traveled extensively in Europe and the United States; in 1903 he visited Palestine, where he was to settle permanently in 1923. He excelled in printmaking and taught graphic techniques to many of his colleagues, including Marc Chagall, Max Liebermann, and Lovis Corinth. In 1923 he published *Die Kunst des Radierens* (*The Art of Etching*).

Much of Struck's work is concerned with Jewish themes. He was particularly talented as a portraitist, and it is therefore not surprising that Hirsch should have interested him as a subject. Struck's initials HS and a Star of David appear as part of the lithograph; in addition there is a penciled signature. The monogram that appears on the sheet occurs frequently on the artist's earlier prints, some of which were even signed with his Hebrew name. This lithograph probably also belongs among his early works.

E. D. B.

88. 'Iggrot Tzafon: Neunzehn Briefe über Judentum

Frankfurt, 1920
Ben Usiël (Samson Raphael Hirsch)
Published by L. Sänger
8-3/4 × 5-11/16 × 1/2 in., 22.2 × 14.4 × 1.2 cm.
The Library of the Jewish Theological Seminary of America, New York.

S.R. Hirsch, founder of the modern Orthodox movement in nineteenth century Germany, was a prolific author as well as a political figure and rabbi. In 1936, Hirsch published his *Nineteen Letters*, at least in part to convince his publisher that an audience existed for works expounding his principles and theories. The author was chief rabbi of Oldenburg at the time he wrote this book, which was followed by his longer *Horeb: Essays on Israel's Duties in the Diaspora.*

89. Commemorative Medal of the Beit Tefilat Yeshurun Synagogue

Frankfurt, 1852
Silver, cast
1-1/2 in. dm., 3.9 cm.
The Jewish Museum, New York, gift of the Samuel and Daniel M. Friedenberg Collection, FB–194

On the obverse the main facade of the new synagogue is depicted with the inscription:

בית תפלת ישורון בק״ק פראנקפורט דמיין
הוסד יום ב׳ דר״ח אייר לשומרי ב׳ר׳ית׳ו
ועדותיו לפ״ק

Beit Tefilat Yeshurun Synagogue of the H[oly] C[ongregation of] Frankfurt am Main.
Founded on the second day of the n[ew] m[oon] of Iyaar. To the keeper of His covenant and His Congregation [chronogram for [5]612 (1852)].

On the reverse the inscription reads:

Denkmünze bei Erbauung einer Synagoge für die Israelitische Religionsgesellschaft zu Frankfurt am Main 5612/1852.
Medal commemorating the construction of a synagogue for the Israelitische Religionsgesellschaft in Frankfurt am Main 5612/1852.

The Israelitische Religionsgesellschaft (IRG) was founded by a group of Orthodox Frankfurt Jews dissatisfied with the increasingly liberal tendencies of the rest of the community (see pp.   and no. 91). In 1852–1853 the IRG, under the leadership of Rabbi Samson Raphael Hirsch and with the financial support of the Rothschilds, built its own synagogue on the Schützenstrasse.

J. W. Renk, a Frankfurt architect, designed the building. The western facade, shown on the medal, was to be flush with the sidewalk, prompting Renk to forgo a monumental entrance on that side. Instead, the synagogue was approached from the street

through arched gateways (visible at either side of the facade) fronted by low stoops (not represented on the medal).[1] These gateways led into narrow passageways, which served as vestibules to side entrances. Hammer-Schenk has pointed out that this unusual arrangement resulted not only from the building's location on the street but also from a desire for seclusion, which was in keeping with the very reserved philosophy of the IRG.[2]

1. See Hammer-Schenk, fig. 92.
2. *Ibid*, p. 117.

REFERENCE: *Coins Reveal*, no. 155.

E. D. B.

90. Interior of the Beit Tefilat Yeshurun Synagogue

Frankfurt, after 1853
Photograph
Courtesy of the Frankfurt Stadtarchiv

This photograph shows the Torah ark of the synagogue built by the Israelitische Religionsgesellschaft (IRG) in Frankfurt and dedicated in September 1853 (see pp.   and nos. 89 and 91). Two *menorot* (*cf.* no. 59) flank the ark, which is covered by a curtain and valence (*cf.* nos. 57 and 58). Above the ark is an inscription:

דע לפני מי אתה עומד

Know before Whom you stand [a variation on Babylonian Talmud, *Berakhot* 28b]

Above the inscription is the crown of Torah.[1] The ark is approached by two sets of steps terminating in a platform, upon which one would stand while removing and replacing the scrolls. A horseshoe arch on slender columns, in Moorish revival style, frames the entire complex.

The *bimah* from which the Torah scrolls were read during services was situated in the center of the sanctuary and is not visible in the photograph. This traditional central location of the *bimah* distinguishes the interior design of an Orthodox German synagogue in the post-Emancipation period. Reform congregations tended to place the *bimah* near the eastern wall, directly in front of the ark.

1. This image is derived from a verse in *Ethics of the Fathers* (4:17): "Rabbi Simeon said: there are three crowns: the crown of Torah, the crown of priesthood, and the crown of royalty; but the crown of a good name excels them all."

E. D. B.

91. Memorial Scroll from Cornerstone of Beit Tefilat Yeshurun Synagogue

Frankfurt, 1852
Handwritten on parchment
29-1/8 × 33-7/8 in., 74.0 × 86.0 cm.
Leo Baeck Institute, New York

This scroll, written for the cornerstone-laying ceremony for the synagogue of the Israelitische Religionsgesellschaft (IRG) on the Schützenstrasse (see pp. and nos. 89 and 90), reveals the hopes of the members for their new congregation, as well as the fears and conflicts that had prompted its founding. The Hebrew text is in a narrow column at the right, and the German version fills the rest of the sheet.

The founders spoke of the longevity and piety of the Jewish community in Frankfurt and recent threats to the principles of Torah and *avodah* (learning and practice):

> Leider haben wir eine traurige Umwandlung erlebt. Seit etwa dreissig bis vierzig Jahren zog ein Geist der Irre bei uns ein, der das jüngere Geschlecht dem Heiligtum entfremdete, für welches die Väter gelebt und gestorben. Als ob das ewige jüdische Gottesgesetz nur für die Zeiten des Drucks seine Geltung gehabt, lockerte man das hehre Band der jüdischen Religion, sobald das Joch des schweren Drucks durch Gottes Gnade sich zu lüften begann. . . .
> Unfortunately we have experienced a sad transformation. In the past thirty or forty years a spirit of wrong-headedness has set in, which has estranged the younger generation from the holiness for which our fathers lived and died. As if the eternal Jewish law of God were valid only for periods of stress, the lofty ties of the Jewish religion were loosened once the yoke of oppression began to be lifted through God's grace. . . .

The wrong-headedness perceived by the founders of the IRG was not confined to individuals but also permeated schools, synagogues, and other religious institutions:

> Und erst im Jahre 5610/1850 liess uns Gottes Gnade durch hohes Decret eines hohen Senates die Freiheit erlangen, unsere religiösen Bedurfnisse nach der Vorschrift unseres Gewissens ungehindert zu befriedigen. Und Gott sei Dank und Preis, der die Schwachen stärkt und die Machtlosen kräftigt. . . .
> And only in the year 5610/1850, God's grace gave us through the decree of a high senate the freedom to satisfy our religious needs without obstacles, in accordance with our conscience. Praised be the Lord who fortifies the weak and strengthens the powerless. . . .

The text goes on to tell of the growth of the Orthodox movement from a nucleus of only eleven men; enough brethren had joined by 1852 to permit resurrection of the patrimony. In conformity with the religious principles of the movement, Samson Raphael Hirsch (see no. 87) was brought from Hamburg as rabbi:

> . . . und stehen nun heute, den 30 September 1852 . . . um den Grundstein zu einem Gotteshaus su legen, welches uns und unseren Kinder die heilige Stätte werden solle, wo wir in gemeinsamer Andacht und Belehrung uns stets zur tätigen Erfüllung der herabgeerbten heiligen jüdischen Gotteslehre weihen und kräftigen wollen.
>
> . . . and today, September 30, 1852, [we] stand . . . in order to lay the foundation of a house of God that will be for us and for our children the holy place where we shall always consecrate and strengthen ourselves in communal devotion and teaching and fulfill the heritage of the holy Jewish law of God.

The scroll includes the information that 70 percent of the costs of the building, including a *mikveh* (ritual bath), had been defrayed by the house of Rothschild and that the remaining 30 percent had been paid by other members of the congregation.

The text concludes:

> Sein Wohlgefallen walte über all unser Tun und Sein heiligen Wille bleibe Grund und Stütze all unser es Schaffens und Wirkens für immer. Amen.
>
> May He be pleased by all our actions and may His holy will remain the basis and support for all our work and activities forever. Amen.

The scroll is signed by Samson Raphael Hirsch, Selig Moses Rothschild, and nine other members of the congregation.

E. D. B.

92. Sealing of Congregation Adas Jeshurun

Frankfurt, 1852
Plaster, painted
2-5/8 in. diam., 6.7 cm.
The Jewish Museum, New York, gift of the Samuel and Daniel M. Friedenberg Collection

The inscription on this sealing reads:

חותם תבני׳ קהל עדת ישרון י[בנה] ע[ירנו]
א[מן] פ[ר]אנקפפאר[ט דמיין

Seal of Congregation Adas Jeshurun, may our city [Jerusalem] be rebuilt, Amen, F[rankfur]t am Main.

V. B. M.

Political and Cultural Life

In 1750 the Jews of Frankfurt were still governed by the same ordinances that had ruled the lives of their ancestors in 1616. They were still "protected Jews," under the sponsorship of the ruler of Frankfurt, members of a self-governing community but not citizens. The first change in their status resulted directly from the Napoleonic wars. The French bombardment of the ghetto in 1792 and 1796 destroyed the walls that had confined the Jewish community, and the process of political emancipation thus began.

Despite the important role of the French in improving the status of Frankurt Jews, the community remained loyal to Germany. Its feelings were expressed by Ludwig Börne in an article written in 1814 ("Was wir wollen? . . . Wir wollen Deutsche sein . . ."; "What do we want? . . . We want to be Germans . . .") and in Moritz Oppenheim's masterpiece "The Return of the Jewish Volunteer" (see no. 99).

After much political activity by members of the community, the Jews of Frankfurt were finally granted citizenship in 1824, but full equality came only in 1864. The struggle for

106

Jewish emancipation in Germany as a whole was led by Gabriel Riesser, a brilliant polemicist who demanded emancipation for Jews on the grounds of honor and justice. In 1836 Riesser settled in Frankfurt for a few years. He was subsequently elected to the National Asembly, where he campaigned both for a unified Germany and for Jewish rights.

Jewish participation in the life of the larger Frankfurt community was also exemplified by the careers of Leopold Sonnemann, Moritz Oppenheim, and Leopold Stein. In 1866 Sonneman founded *Die Frankfurter Zeitung* as a liberal journal. He later served as a representative to the German Reichstag and as a member of the Frankfurt city council. Oppenheim was one of the first Jewish painters to emerge during the period of emancipation and the first to treat Jewish themes. Stein, who served as rabbi in Frankfurt for twenty years, was also a poet and dramatist whose plays were performed on the German stage.

93. The Last Jewish Postman in the Frankfurt Ghetto

Frankfurt, c. 1800–1811
Watercolor and pencil on paper
3-7/8 × 2-3/4 in., 8.7 × 7.0 cm.
Collection of Mr. and Mrs. Sidney G. Adler

This anonymous watercolor depicts Isaak Hayum Schuster (1781–1850), the last postman in the Frankfurt ghetto; the job of postman had been held by members of the Schuster family for three generations. The man who held this position was in the service of the Princes of Thurn and Taxis and was therefore their *Schutzjude* (protected Jew). Isaak's grandfather, Moses Marr Schuster, had gained favor with this royal house as a result of his talents as a chess player, according to descendants of the family. Prince Alexander von Thurn und Taxis had observed him playing, and had decided to employ him as a chess instructor; he also gave him the job of postman in Frankfurt's Judengasse.[1]

1. Dietz, *Stammbuch*, p. 274.

E. D. B.

94. Pinqas Frankfurt Demain

Frankfurt, c. 1801
Ink on paper
6-1/2 × 4 in., 16.5 × 10.2 cm.
The Library of the Jewish Theological Seminary of America, New York, 3672

This notebook (*pinqas*) contains a list of the Jewish deaths in Frankfurt between 1785 and 1801, as well as a list of marriages for about the same years. Both lists are arranged alphabetically, which suggests that they were compiled after 1801 from the official register. Toward the end of the volume, which consists of 142 leaves, there is a description of the appointment of Rabbi Hirsch Horowitz, son of the late Rabbi Pinḥas Horowitz.

M. S. C.

95. Extract from Protocoll der Judenschaft

Frankfurt, May 5, 1809
Ink on paper
13-3/4 × 8-5/16 in., 34.9 × 21.1 cm.
The Library of The Jewish Theological Seminary of America, New York

The embossed seal of the Frankfurt community marks the document as an official extract.

M. S. C.

96. Pass Permitting Jew to Leave the Ghetto

Frankfurt, 1790
Printed and hand-written on paper
6-1/4 × 7-11/16 in., 15.9 × 18.8 cm.
Leo Baeck Institute, New York

This pass, issued to Salmon Oppenheimer, granted him permission to leave the ghetto in order to witness the coronation of Emperor Leopold II in October 1790. Most of the text was printed, but the bearer's name was written by hand in black ink:

Vorzeiger dieses *Salmon Oppenheimer nebst seinen verwandten* kann auf bevorstehenden Krönungstag aus der Judengasse in die Stadt gelassen werden, um in einem Hause, oder auf einem Gerüste, nicht aber auf der Strasse, die Feierlich-keiten sehen zu können.
Frankfurt am Main . . . 8ten October 1790
Stadt Kanzlei
dahier

Bearer of this [pass] *Salmon Oppenheimer together with his relatives* is permitted on the forthcoming coronation day to leave the Judengasse and to enter the city in order to watch the festivities in a house or from a platform, but not on the street.

Frankfurt am Main . . . 8 October 1790
City Government

Throughout Frankfurt's history the Jews were often forbidden to walk in the city; they required special passes before venturing into streets beyond the ghetto. Despite increasing protests from the Jewish community, the Frankfurt city council decided once again to bar Jews from the streets during the coronation of 1790. Only a few rich and influential Jews were granted permission to leave the ghetto in order to watch the festivities, and even they were not always allowed to remain in the streets. Consequently, most Jews had to be content with a celebration in honor of Leopold II that was held in the ghetto on the same day as the festival of Simḥat Torah.[1]

1. Freimann and Kracauer, pp. 174–175.

REFERENCE: *The Jewish Encyclopedia,* V (N.Y.: 1906), p. 489 (ill).

E. D. B.

97. Appeal to Napoleon by the Jews of Frankfurt

Germany, nineteenth century
Ink on paper
14-11/16 × 18-5/16 in., 37.3 × 46.6 cm.
The Library of the Jewish Theological Seminary of America, New York

This long letter, written in mellifluous literary French, calls on Napoleon to grant citizenship to the Jews of Frankfurt:

Sire! Your Majesty has already exhausted all known glories and has left far behind all other conquerors and legislators. One single glory remains untouched and unnoticed by any before you: the glory of rescuing, with a single word, from civil and political nothingness, an immense number of people who will owe you more than life itself,

because they will owe you all that which makes life bearable and happy. The small number of heroes whose names have been mentioned before our century: Alexander, Caesar, Augustus, Charlemagne, have passed on without having done this glorious thing.

It has been reserved for you entirely, for the prince whom God has chosen to place above all of those heroes and centuries, for your majesty. . . .

M. S. C.

98. View of the Frankfurt Ghetto After the Fire of 1796

Frankfurt, *c.* 1796
Jeremias Paul Schweyer (1754–1813); published by Philipp Jacob Döring (1764–1841)
Etching on paper
6 × 7-15/16 in., 15.2 × 20.2 cm.
Leo Baeck Institute, New York, 82.3

The French bombardment of Frankfurt during the night of July 14, 1796 caused a huge fire, which destroyed most of the ghetto. As recounted in *History of the Bombardment of the City,* "The Jewish quarter . . . saw a particularly hard fate; on both sides of the street, 140 houses, from the entrance on the Fahrgasse, up until the synagogue, have been burned to the ground."[1]

This physical destruction of the Jewish quarter proved to be the first step in the emancipation of the Frankfurt Jews, though the ghetto was not officially abolished until 1811.

J.P. Schweyer, whose signature is visible at the lower right, recorded the scene of devastation and labeled the important buildings that remained standing after the flames had been extinguished. The inscription along the bottom reads:

Ansicht der Judengasse in Frankfurt am Main, nach dem Brandt. 1. Eingang der Judengas. 2. Synagoge. 3. die Judenmauer. 4. das neue Brauhaus. 5. die Windmühl. 6. Kramläden.

View of the Jewish street in Frankfurt on the Main after the fire. 1. entrance to the Jewish street. 2. Synagogue. 3. the Jewish wall. 4. the new brewery. 5. the windmill. 6. stalls

What is left of the ghetto wall on the entrance side stretches across the foreground. Before it lie piles of broken stones, and a number of small stalls in which shopkeepers display their wares have been set up. The gateway is patrolled by a lone soldier carrying a bayonet.

The entire middleground is filled with rubble, bordered by the buildings that escaped destruction. Among them is the synagogue, which had been built in 1711, after another fire had burned down the entire ghetto. Its distinctive western facade, with two pairs of arched windows on the upper story and four small square windows on the ground floor, is easily recognizable (see no. 49).

Schweyer was born in Nuremberg in 1754 and by 1782 had become court painter in Zweibrücken. He arrived in Frankfurt around 1790 and remained there for the rest of his life. He worked as a painter and engraver, specializing in portraits, society and farm scenes, and *vedute*, of which this view of the ghetto is an example. The publisher's name is visible at the lower left.

1. *Geschichte des Bombardments der Stadt* (Frankfurt: 1796), quoted in Historical Museum Frankfurt, *Documentation Guide*, p. 296.

REFERENCES: P. F. Gwinner, *Zusätze und Berichtigungen zu Kunst und Künstler in Frankfurt am Main vom dreizehnten Jahrhundert bis zur Eröffnung des Städel'schen Kunstinstituts* (Frankfurt: 1867), p. 81, no. 30; Rubens, *Iconography*, 1981, no. 1311. Rubens identifies this engraving as "View of Ghetto After the Fire in 1711."

E. D. B.

99. Return of the Jewish Volunteer from the Wars of Liberation to His Family Still Living in Accordance with Old Customs (*Rückkehr des Freiwilligen aus dem Befreiungskriege zu den nach alte Sitte lebendem Seinen*)

Frankfurt, 1833–1834
Moritz Daniel Oppenheim (1800–1882)
Oil on canvas
34 × 36 in., 86.3 × 91.4 cm.
Collection of Mr. Edgar Rebner

This painting is the first in which Oppenheim represented a specifically Jewish subject. A wounded Jewish soldier in a Hussar's uniform has returned from fighting for Germany in the Napoleonic wars, arriving in the middle of a Sabbath afternoon. His mother and elder sister are concerned with his well-being; his younger siblings gaze in rapt admiration at the medal he has received for bravery, while another brother is distracted by the hero's splendid helmet and sword. The father turns from a Hebrew text to regard the Iron Cross, incorporating a Christian symbol, displayed on his son's chest with a mixture of pride and suspicion.

The episode is set in a cozy bourgeois interior filled with objects of both Jewish and German significance: a brass hanging Sabbath lamp (for a more elaborate silver example (see no. 116), a *kiddush* cup (see no. 114) on the table, a *mizrach* (see no. 4) hanging next to the bookcase, and a tower-shaped spicebox (see no. 122) on the bottom of the corner cabinet, above and to the left of which hangs an equestrian portrait of Frederick the Great of Prussia. The remnants of a long *ḥallah* lie on the table. Twenty years after completing this work, "Return of the Jewish Volunteer," Oppenheim would again turn to scenes of Jewish domestic life in his famous series

99

Bilder aus dem altjüdischen Familienleben (*Pictures of Traditional Jewish Family Life;* see no. 130 in this exhibition).

This painting was presented to Oppenheim's friend Gabriel Riesser by a group of Jews from Baden in gratitude for his efforts to help them secure full civil rights, and it may have been commissioned by them. Indeed, its theme, which touches on so many issues relating to the emancipation, was particularly appropriate in a gift for Riesser, a leader in the struggle for full Jewish enfranchisement. Opponents of this movement questioned the patriotism and loyalty to Germany of the Jewish population, though hundreds of Prussian Jews had taken part in the War of Liberation against the French in 1813. Many of these volunteers died in battle, and a large number were awarded the Iron Cross for their heroism. The painting can thus be understood as a refutation of these doubts and a plea for full Jewish rights.

On the other hand, it also highlights some of the conflicts that arose as a result of emancipation, particularly between the generations. Greater freedom and increased contacts with the world outside the ghetto brought greater possibilities for assimilation and the weakening of traditional Jewish values and practices. The young volunteer has violated the injunction against traveling on the Sabbath and has brought the alien symbol of the cross into the midst of his family's holy day observance. Although the father and younger sons wear *yarmulkes,* the soldier's head is uncovered.

Riesser commented on this aspect of the painting's meaning in his letter of thanks to the Baden Jews:

> Foolish the father who wishes to wrap his son in the garments of antiquity . . . but the son ashamed of his father, the generation ashamed of its past is without honor.[1]

1. Gabriel Riesser, "Ein Wort des Dankes an die israelitischen Bürger Badens, 1835," *Gesammelte Schriften,* IV (Frankfurt and Leipzig: 1868), pp. 720–721.

REFERENCES: *Erinnerungen,* pp. 109–110, 113; Heilbrunn, p. 299; Roth, *Jewish Art,* p. 197; Hoelterhoff, n.p.; Werner, p. 54; Cohen, *Bulletin des Leo Baeck Instituts,* pp. 63–64; Jewish Museum, *Oppenheim,* n.p.

E. D. B.

100. Portrait of Gabriel Riesser and Moritz Oppenheim Painting a Self-Portrait

Frankfurt, 1840
Philipp Veit (1793–1877) and Moritz Daniel Oppenheim (1800–1882)
Pencil on paper
10 × 14-1/2 in., 25.5 × 36.2 cm.
Leo Baeck Institute, New York, 78.455

This sheet was included in an album presented to Gabriel Riesser (1806–1863) in 1840, when he left Frankfurt to return to his native Hamburg. It contains a portrait of Riesser, the champion of Jewish emancipation, on the right side of the page and a representation of his friend, the painter Moritz Oppenheim, seated at his easel painting a self-portrait. The sheet has been executed by two distinct hands and bears two signatures. Beneath the bust of Riesser are inscribed *Zur Erinnerung an vergnügte Stunden* ("In remembrance of happy hours") and the signature "Moritz Oppenheim." Below and to the left of these lines appears "Veit f. 21-2-40."

The portrait of Riesser, rendered with soft, feathery strokes, is by Veit; the representation of Oppenheim painting his self-portrait, executed in a firmer and more linear style, is the work of Oppenheim himself, and his monogram appears in the upper right-hand corner of the canvas propped on the easel.[1] A Hebrew inscription to the right of the easel is an ironic comment on the artist's depiction of himself in the act of painting a self-portrait:

Hebrew Inscription

Charm is deceitful and beauty is vain (Prov. 31:30)

This phrase underscores the disparity between the two likenesses of Oppenheim; the image on the easel is the more flattering of the two. In particular, the treatment of the hair differs in the two representations. In the portrait on the easel it is executed with a softer touch, and the side of the pencil has been used to achieve a fuzzy texture, whereas in the other portrait parallel strokes create a harder effect. Oppenheim, who derived much of his livelihood from painting portraits of leading social and intellectual figures of his day, thus commented on the gap between reality and art, particularly in portraiture.

Veit was the maternal grandson of Moses Mendelssohn, the leading philosopher of the Jewish Enlightenment. Veit's mother had left her husband for the philosopher Friedrich Schlegel and subsequently converted to Roman Catholicism, as did Philipp and his brother Johann, also an artist. Philipp joined the Nazarene brotherhood of artists in Rome in 1815, where he remained until 1830; he then moved to Frankfurt to become director of the Städelsches Kunstinstitut. Oppenheim and Veit first met in Rome (see no. 102) and, despite their differing attitudes toward Judaism, resumed their friendship in Frankfurt.[2]

For the relationship between Oppenheim and Riesser, see no. 99.

1. Cf. an earlier self-portrait drawing in the Israel Museum, Cohen, *Israel Museum News*, fig. 1.
2. See *Erinnerungen*, pp. 85–86, 88–90.

REFERENCE: Hoelterhoff, n. p.

E. D. B.

101. Portrait of Leopold Sonnemann (1832–1909)

Frankfurt, *c.* 1870
Photograph
9-7/16 × 7-1/16 in., 23.4 × 18.0 cm.
Verlaghaus Frankfurter Societäts-Druckerei

102. Sketchbook

Italy, Austria, Germany, 1825
Moritz Daniel Oppenheim (1800–1882)
Pencil and brown ink on paper
4-3/4 × 6-3/4 in., 12.1 × 17.1 cm.
The Jewish Museum, New York, gift of Georges E. Seligmann, JM 68-59

Moritz Oppenheim filled the thirty-eight sheets of this sketchbook with drawings and notes recording the scenery, people, and works of art that he encountered on his trip from Rome to Frankfurt in 1825, after a four-year sojourn in Italy. In a minute and often illegible pencil scrawl, which covers a little more than six sides at the back of the sketchbook, Oppenheim kept a day-by-day account (March 20–May 19, 1825) of the places he stayed and the sites and people he visited. Although the telegraphic style suggests that the notes served the artist more as *aide-mémoire* than as an actual diary, these pages afford useful insights into this transitional period in

Oppenheim's life, a period to which he devoted less than two pages in his memoirs.[1] In particular, they show that he combined a strong sense of Jewish identity with a worldly sophistication appropriate to the social and artistic circles in which he moved. Throughout his travels he was received by aristocrats and art collectors, and in Munich he visited the Crown Prince, later King Ludwig I.

On March 30 he remarked on having found a Jewish inn in Bologna and wrote of spending Passover with friends in Venice. "Passover" appears in Hebrew, as does every instance of the word "Sabbath." Oppenheim also noted that on the Sabbath, April 14, he visited a synagogue in Stuttgart and was called up to the Torah reading. Most of his activities on Jewish holy days, however, suggest that he was not strictly observant.

The written portions of the sketchbook, as well as the drawings after works that Oppenheim studied on his travels, reveal a preference for the art of the Italian Renaissance, particularly the works of Raphael and his school, and for early German and

102

Netherlandish painting, which he saw at Schleissheim Castle (April 27) and in the collection of the Boisserée brothers in Stuttgart (May 10–16). Furthermore, with the exception of two sketches of farm animals after a painting by Paul Potter,[2] all the drawings after other artists are of Christian subjects; not a single sheet illustrates a theme from the Hebrew Bible.

The order of the drawings can be correlated with Oppenheim's progress north and with his notations in the back of the sketchbook. A landscape outside Terni is the subject of the first drawing, followed by a waterfall near that town; the entry for March 20 reads, "auf Terni gefahren . . . Wasserfall gezeichnet" ("went to Terni . . . made drawing of waterfall"). The next few pages are filled with similar Italian views, as well as a compositional sketch for "A Father Telling a Parable to His Children" (no. 105), which is the only drawing in this sketchbook executed in ink. Only two drawings are after Italian paintings: the Mary Magdalene of Timoteo Viti,[3] which Oppenheim saw in Bologna, and the central mandolin-playing angel from Giovanni Bellini's San Giobbe altarpiece in the Galleria dell'Accademia, Venice.[4] With the exception of these two and the drawings after Potter, all the sketches after paintings are of works by early Netherlandish and German masters that Oppenheim was able to study in the famous collection assembled by Sulpiz and Melchior Boisserée.[5]

An admiration for late medieval art was characteristic of German Romanticism, and the brothers Boisserée contributed to this movement through their collection and their writings on the art and architecture of the German past. The German painters in Rome, known as the Nazarenes, were not only influenced by stylistic features of German medieval art but also sought to emulate its religious content. They even modeled their artistic brotherhood on the medieval guild system.[6] Viewing the Boisserée collection was clearly a highlight of Oppenheim's trip, and his response to it reflects the extent to which he had been influenced by his contact with the Nazarenes during his stay in Italy.

Judging by the number of sketches devoted to it, Oppenheim seems to have been most impressed by the Columba Altar (at the time thought to be by Jan Van Eyck, though today attributed to Rogier van der Weyden),[7] from which he copied the figure of Joseph,

illustrated here. The style of the drawing, executed in a fine pencil line that emphasizes the contours of the forms, is reminiscent of Nazarene draftsmanship. Oppenheim paid close attention to the profusion of detail in the rich costumes and sumptuous vessels in Rogier's depiction of the Three Magi and included color notations in his observations.

Perhaps Oppenheim's special interest in the Columba Altar was stimulated by Goethe's pronouncement after studying the painting: "I have written many poems in my life, among which are a few good ones and many which are mediocre; and here is Van Eyck who paints *one* such picture which is worth more than all my work put together."[8]

1. *Erinnerungen*, pp. 70–71.
2. Alte Pinakothek München, *Katalog* III. *Holländische Malerei des 17. Jahrhunderts* (Munich: 1967), pp. 53–54, pl. 49.
3. A. Emiliani, *La Pinacoteca Nazionale di Bologna* (Bologna: 1967), no. 116.
4. R. Giotto, *L'opera completa di Giovanni Bellini detto Giambellino* (Milan: 1969), no. 101.
5. See E. Firmenich-Richartz, *Die Brüder Boisserée,* I. *Sulpiz und Melchior Boisserée als Kunstsammler: Ein Beitrag zur Geschichte der Romantik* (Jena: 1916). This collection was acquired by King Ludwig I of Bavaria in 1827 and is now in the Alte Pinakothek in Munich.
6. See Andrews, *Nazarenes.*
7. M. J. Friedländer, *Early Netherlandish Painting,* II. *Rogier van der Weyden and the Master of Flémalle* (New York and Washington, D.C.: 1967), no. 49, pls. 70–71.
8. F. Biedermann and W. Herwig, eds., *Goethes Gespräche,* II (Zurich and Stuttgart: 1969), p. 1102, no. 4257. See also W.D. Robson-Scott, *The Literary Background of the Gothic Revival in Germany* (Oxford: 1965), pp. 190–191, 200.

REFERENCES: Cohen, *Israel Museum News,* p. 89; Jewish Museum, *Oppenheim,* n.p.

E. D. B.

103. Theater Program for Die Jüdin

Frankfurt, July 24, 1867
Printed on paper
11-3/4 × 7-3/8 in., 29.8 × 18.7 cm.
Leo Baeck Institute, New York

Die Jüdin, the German version of *La Juive* (The Jewess), is a romantic opera in five acts composed by Jacques Halévy in 1835. It tells the story of a renaissance prince who falls in love with a Jewish woman.

E. D. B.

Economic Activity

Many of the occupations pursued by Frankfurt Jews in the years between 1750 and 1870 were traditional ones: trading, manual labor, pawnbroking, and moneylending. But in response to economic pressures the range of occupational training had become broader than in the past. One society founded in 1825 trained bakers, bookbinders, lathe turners, glaziers, tanners, and so forth. After emancipation Jews entered the professions in greater numbers and also pursued careers in literature and the arts.

The economic strength of the community was vested in its financiers. Foremost among them were the Rothschilds, whose name was derived from *roth Schild* (red shield), referring to the sign affixed to the dwelling of Isaac Elḥanan (d. 1585). The family first attained wealth and prominence through the efforts of Mayer Amschel (1744–1812), who began his career as a dealer in antiquities and antique coins. His relationship with Wilhelm, later Landgrave of Hesse-Kassel and an enthusiastic coin collector, led to Mayer Amschel's appointment as court agent. Mayer had five sons, each established in a different European capital. Usually acting in concert, the family amassed an immense fortune and became donors to many philanthropic endeavors.

104. Rothschild Postcard

Frankfurt, twentieth century
Published by Verlag L. Klement
Printed on paper
3-5/8 × 5-1/16 in., 9.2 × 12.8 cm.
Leo Baeck Institute, New York

The message on the card is *Gruss aus Frankfurt a. M.,* ("Greetings from Frankfurt o[n the] M[ain]." The pictures are a view of the Rothschild house and a portrait labeled *Maier Amschel Rothschild Begründer des Welthauses,* ". . . founder of the world house." This legend suggests the degree to which the Rothschilds were associated with the city, where their residence had become a landmark frequented by tourists (see no. 2).   E. D. B.

105

105. A Father Telling a Parable to his Children

Germany (?), *c.* 1825
Moritz Daniel Oppenheim (1800–1882)
Oil on paper, inscription in pencil
4-7/8 × 5-1/2 in., 12.3 × 14.0 cm.
The Jewish Museum, New York, gift of Mr. Georges E. Seligmann, 1981-299

The inscription beneath this oil sketch reads:

> Ein Vater vermahnt seine Kinder zur
> Ewigkeit und gibt ihnen ein Gleichnis.
> A father admonishes his children about
> eternity and tells them a parable.

The subject is based on a story told by Plutarch in the *Apophthegms of Kings and Great Commanders,* in which Scilurus, on his death bed, asks each of his four sons to break a bundle of darts. When they are unable to do so, he draws the darts out one by one and breaks each without difficulty, thus showing his sons that, if they remain united, they will be strong but that, if they fight among themselves, they will become weak. Aesop's fable "The Bundle of Sticks" has the same theme and moral. Oppenheim has used a classical setting for his sketch, with a statue of Athena atop a column near the right edge of the composition. Five sons are represented, however, instead of the four mentioned by Plutarch. According to Georges E. Seligmann, the artist's great-great-grandson and the donor of this painting, the five sons correspond to the five male children of Mayer Amschel Rothschild and his wife Gudule, and the work was intended as an allegory on the unity and strength of that important family. Indeed, the enormous wealth and power of the Rothschilds was owing in part to their adherence to the credo espoused in the ancient parable. Oppenheim enjoyed the Rothschilds' artistic patronage and financial support throughout his career. He traveled from Paris to Rome in 1821 courtesy of a friend in the Rothschilds' employ. Later that same year he met Baron Carl Mayer, who had opened a branch of the family business in Naples, and sold him three paintings. When Oppenheim returned to Germany and settled in Frankfurt, he began a fruitful relationship with the Frankfurt branch of the family and entered its service, executing commissions, giving lessons, and advising on acquisitions for the family collection. In his memoirs Oppenheim proudly recalled that he was known as "the painter of the Rothschilds and the Rothschild of painters."[1]

This oil sketch can be dated c. 1825 on the basis of a compositional sketch for it that appears in a sketchbook belonging to The Jewish Museum (see no. 102). It is close in style to other oil sketches executed around the same time, like "Farewell of the Young Tobias," c. 1825–1826.[2] Furthermore, it is still related to works of Oppenheim's Italian period (1821–1825) and reflects the strong influence of the Nazarenes on the artist at that time (see no. 102). The emphasis on outline, broad areas of color, the rather static symmetrical composition, and the treatment of landscape seen through the archway are indebted to the Nazarenes, particularly to the frescos of scenes from the story of Joseph in the Casa Bartholdy in Rome (1816–1817) by Peter von Cornelius, Johann Friedrich Overbeck, Wilhelm von Schadow, and Philipp Veit.[3]

Like his Nazarene colleagues, Oppenheim looked to Italian Renaissance masters for inspiration. The pose and placement of the figure at the right, who is trying to break the sticks over his knee, are based on those of the disappointed suitor breaking his staff in Raphael's "Marriage of the Virgin."[4]

A comparison between this oil and the prepara-tory sketch reveals only minor changes in the disposition of the figures. In the original conception, however, the son standing at the left has his hands at his sides, and is not shown in the act of breaking the single stick. By conflating the two major moments in the story, the initial attempt to break the bundle of sticks and the breaking of the single stick, Oppenheim increased the didactic impact of the oil sketch.

1. *Erinnerungen*, p. 75.
2. See *Erinnerungen*, pp. 101–103 and ill. following p. 64.
3. Andrews, pp. 33–37, pls. 4, 5, 25, 26.
4. Michele Prisco and Pierluigi de Vecchi, *L'opera completa di Raffaello* (Milan: 1966), no. 28, pl. II.

REFERENCE: Jewish Museum, *Oppenheim*, n.p.

E. D. B.

106. List of Coin Values and Rates of Exchange Belonging to Moses Rothschild

Frankfurt, 1760
Ink on paper
7-1/4 × 3-3/8 in., 18.5 × 8.1 cm.
Leo Baeck Institute, New York

107. Wanderbuch of Philipp Goldschmidt

Germany, 1827–1831
Ink on paper
6-1/4 × 3-15/16 × 3/8 in., 15.9 × 10.0 × 1.0 cm.
The Library of the Jewish Theological Seminary of America, New York, gift of Mrs. Henry Moses

This book is a sort of passport of the type required of an apprentice (in this instance a tanner's apprentice) before he could learn his trade in Germany in the early nineteenth century. At each place in which the apprentice worked, he was required to register with the police and to obtain from his master a record of his progress. Philipp Goldschmidt "wandered" through Frankfurt, Urdingen, Düsseldorf, Bruchsal, Mainz, and Karlsruhe between 1827 and 1831. His book contains sixty-four pages, not all of which are written on.

M. S. C.

108. Buying Fish for the Sabbath in Frankfurt am Main

Frankfurt, before 1887
Hermann Junker (1838–1899)
Oil on canvas
21-1/4 × 17-7/8 in., 54.0 × 45.3 cm.
The Jewish Museum, New York, Jewish Cultural
Reconstruction, JM 23-58

Since Talmudic times it has been customary to eat fish on the Sabbath: "Wherewith does one show his delight therein? . . . With a dish of beets, large fish, and cloves of garlic."[1] Not only is this practice supposed to enhance the joy of the holiday, but the association of fish with fertility also makes it appropriate Sabbath fare.[2] The purchase of fish is thus part of the preparation for the Sabbath.

Junker has depicted the fish market held on Fridays and Saturdays in one of Frankfurt's most historic squares, the Römerberg. The Church of St. Nikolai can be seen in the background, and in the right middle ground stands the Fountain of Justice (*Justitiabrunnen*). The original fountain, erected in 1611, was fashioned of sandstone, but in 1887 it was replaced by a bronze version. The statue of Justice depicted by Junker is the stone original, providing a *terminus ante quem* for the painting.

Under his arm the central figure carries a bag with an indecipherable Hebrew inscription. His dress—knee breeches, buckled shoes, and pointed hat—is of the eighteenth century. Like Moritz Oppenheim's views of Frankfurt Jewish life (see no. 130), Junker's painting is also set in an idealized past. The stalls, figures, and costumes are similar to those depicted in a painting of the same fish market by Christian Georg Schütz, the Elder, "*Der Römerberg*" of 1754.[3]

Junker's signature appears on a wooden plank in the roof of the stall at the right. Beneath it stands a man, isolated from the activity in the market and looking out at the spectator. Perhaps this image is a self-portrait of the artist as observer.

Junker was born in Frankfurt and studied at the Städelschen Institut with Jacob Becker and Edward von Steinle. In 1863 he went to Paris, where he came under the influence of Gustave Courbet. After further travels in Flanders and the Netherlands, he returned to his native city, where he worked as a genre and history painter and as an illustrator for *Kleine Presse*, a Frankfurt newspaper. Weizsäcker and Des-

108

soff mention that Junker executed "four pictures of traditional Jewish family life."[4]

1. Babylonian Talmud, *Shabbat*, 118 b.
2. Pollack, *Jewish Folkways*, p. 58.
3. Städelschen Kunstinstitut Frankfurt, Inv. no. 14; see *Bilder zur Frankfurter Geschichte*, no. 186.
4. II, p. 69.

E. D. B.

109. Legal Brief on Rights of Jews to Open Stores Outside the Ghetto

Frankfurt, 1771
Printed on paper
13-3/4 × 8-5/8 × 5/8 in., 35.0 × 22.0 × 1.5 cm.
Leo Baeck Institute, New York

110. Pinqas Frankfurt

Frankfurt, 1700–1773
Ink on paper
14-5/16 × 9-1/4 × 3/4 in., 36.4 × 23.5 × 1.9 cm.
The Library of the Jewish Theological Seminary
of America, New York, 3967

This notebook (pinqas) contains forty-seven communal documents of various sizes written, for the most part, in Judeo-German, though some are in Hebrew. Of special note is folio 5a, a draft letter in German (written in Hebrew characters) to the "Emperor of Rome" (the Holy Roman Emperor). The letter was obviously intended to be copied out in German script before being sent; the text is a pledge of loyalty to the Emperor.

M. S. C.

Jewish Home in Frankfurt

There is both documentary and pictorial evidence for the appearance of the typical Jewish home in Frankfurt in the years 1750–1870. Literary sources referring to living conditions and lists of household possessions are supplemented by the paintings of Hermann Junker (1838–1899) and Moritz Oppenheim (1800–1882), who depicted Frankfurt Jewish life, and by the graphics of their contemporaries.

In the fall, during the holiday of Sukkot, many household possessions were transferred to the sukkah (booth), where the family ate its meals and where members studied and entertained. Their "dwelling" in such temporary shelters was an annual reminder of the experiences of their Israelite forefathers, who had wandered for forty years in the wilderness of Sinai.

The major spring holiday, Passover, was celebrated within the home. Special dishes and utensils were reserved for this festival in accordance with the strict dietary laws entailed in its observance. The home thus took on a special aspect during the Passover season and contributed to enjoyment of the holiday.

This reconstruction of a Frankfurt home is focused on these two holidays and includes

works from the collection of The Jewish Museum that were made in Frankfurt and other German cities.

111. Tablecloth

Fürth, c. 1800
Linen damask
163 × 82 in., 407.5 × 205.0 cm.
The Jewish Museum, New York, gift of Dr. Harry
G. Friedman, F 3010

This elaborate damask cloth is woven with a series of subjects in superimposed zones. At the bottom are walled cities labeled "Pharan" and a scene of Moses kneeling before the Tabernacle. At the top of the Tabernacle God emerges from a cloud bank as a bearded man with aureole, His hands raised in blessing. Behind the clouds are small tents representing the Israelite encampment. This entire episode is labeled "Numeri XIII." Above are two spies bearing a bunch of grapes with the label "Calep / Iosue" ("Caleb / Joshua"). In the next zone large men dressed as warriors and bearing spears labeled "Nehel" alternate with grape vines; they are presumably the Nephilim, the giants who inhabited the land (Num. 13:33). This sequence of subjects is repeated twice in its entirety, and the beginnings of a third repetition are visible at top.

As the tituli indicate, the subjects were chosen from Numbers 13, in which is recorded the story of Moses' sending spies to scout the land while the Israelites camped in the wilderness of Paran. Of the twelve spies sent only Caleb and Joshua urged conquest; the remaining scouts despaired at the obstacles facing them: the fortified cities and their gigantic inhabitants. It is presumably for this reason that Caleb and Joshua are emphasized in the composition.

This tablecloth was purchased from a descendant of the Weichselbaum family of Fürth, who reported in 1952 that the cloth had been used for the seder by at least five generations of the family. Despite this ceremonial use in a Jewish home, it is unlikely that the cloth was woven specifically for Jews. First, the labels are in Latin, and, second, anthropomorphic depictions of God are rare, though not unknown, on works commissioned by Jews.[1]

1. See E. Saltman "The 'Forbidden Image' in Jewish Art," Journal of Jewish Art, VIII (1981), pp. 42–59.

V. B. M.

112. Ḥallah Cover

Germany, 1762–1763
Silk, embroidered with polychrome silk, metallic
threads, and beads
20-7/8 × 20-7/8 in., 53.0 × 53.0 cm.
The Jewish Museum, New York, gift of Dr. Harry
G. Friedman, F 511

Two finely modeled heraldic lions hold a shield embroidered with the monogram of the owner. Both
shield and lions rest on a flowering vine, which
serves as a ground line. The floral motif is echoed
in the crown atop the shield, the points of which
sprout as if they were miniature bushes. The blessing over bread is arranged in an arc surrounding the
pictorial elements.

ברוך אתה ה' אלהינו מלך העולם המוציא
לחם מן הארץ

Blessed art thou O Lord our God, King of the Universe, who brings forth bread out of the earth.

The Hebrew date appears below: תקכג, [5]523
[1762–1763].

Rampant lions are common on German Judaica.
Their interpretation as lions of Judah or as the protective beings of Solomon's throne facilitated their
adoption from general German art, in which such
lions were popular as early as the Middle Ages.

REFERENCE: *Fabric of Jewish Life*, no. 181.

V. B. M.

113. Kiddush Goblet for Festivals

Frankfurt, 1737
Johann Peter Beyer I (1697–1774)
Marks: Scheffler 141, 276
Silver, cast, engraved, stippled, gilt, and repoussé
4-1/8 × 2-3/4 in. dm., 10.5 × 7.2 cm.
The Jewish Museum, New York, gift of Dr. Harry
G. Friedman, F 32

The gently flaring upper portion of this cup is joined
to a fluted bulbous lower section executed in repoussé. Similar fluting occurs on the circular base,
which is connected to the cup by a short stem. An
engraved inscription on the rim reads:

וידבר משה את מועדי ה' אל בני ישראל

So Moses declared to the Israelites the set
times of the Lord (Lev. 23:44).

Below are three equally spaced cartouches, which
bear further inscriptions referring to the three pilgrim festivals:

בסכות תשבו שבעת ימים

You shall live in booths seven days (Lev.
23:42).

שבעת שבועת [כך!ן] תספר לך

You shall count off seven weeks (Deut.
16:9).

שבעת ימים תאכלו מצות

The last inscription is a play on the scriptural verse
"You shall eat unleavened bread for seven days"
(Lev. 23:6). Each larger cartouche is surmounted by
confronted lions bearing a smaller cartouche. In one
of them the date is engraved: תצז"ל, [5]497 (1737).

Beyer made an identical *kiddush* cup now in the
collection of the Frankfurt Historical Museum (Inv.
no. 30 029b) and a bench-type Hanukkah lamp once
in the Jewish Museum, Frankfurt.[1]

1. Inv. no. N67; *Notizblatt*, XXXIV (1937), p. 13.
REFERENCE: Kayser-Schoenberger, no. 113.

V. B. M.

114. Kiddush Goblet for Festivals

Frankfurt, c. 1725–1750
Master: GFB
Marks: Scheffler 129 (R³2008), GFB
Silver, cast, engraved, stippled, and gilt
5-1/16 × 2-1/2 in. dm., 12.9 × 6.4 cm.
The Jewish Museum, New York, gift of Dr. Harry
G. Friedman, F 225

The stepped and domed base of this goblet harmonizes in form and decoration with the cup it supports. Rising above the lowest circular band are two
octagonal steps, the shape of which echoes that of
the cup. One of them is decorated with engraved
tulip flowers, a motif that also serves to separate the
words engraved on the cup:

וידבר משה את מועדי ה' אל בני ישראל

So Moses declared to the Israelites the set
times of the Lord (Lev. 23:44).

This sentence begins the *kiddush*, the sanctification

over wine that is recited on festivals after the morning prayers.

Tulips are also incorporated in the design of strapwork and flowers engraved on each face of the cup. An elaborate stem with bosses links the cup and the base.

Similar faceted cups with engraved decoration and inscriptions were fashioned by silversmiths in Augsburg, Fürth, and other German cities.

115. Portion of a Dinner Service

Waldenburg, after 1831
Krister Porzellanmanufaktur
Porcelain, glazed
Tureen: 7-7/8 × 10-1/4 in., 20.0 × 26.0 cm.
Platter: 13-15/16 × 9-1/8 in., 35.4 × 23.2 cm.
Soup plate: 9-9/16 in. dm., 24.3 cm.
Gravy boat: 5-3/4 × 7-5/8 in., 14.6 × 19.4 cm.
Ladle: 8-5/8 in., 21.4 cm.
The Jewish Museum, New York, gift of Mrs. Ernest A. Kolbert-Bukoper in memory of her mother, Else Wachsmann, JM 42-77, 3, 11, 28, 30, 31

These dishes are made of white porcelain highlighted by an orange glaze. Orange lines of different thicknesses accent the edges of the forms, and the handles are decorated with orange floral and scroll motifs.

In an effort to support the Prussian porcelain industry, Frederick the Great promulgated a law in 1769 requiring Jews to purchase china in exchange for the granting of such official papers as residence permits and marriage licenses. According to family tradition, this set was purchased by the donor's family in order to obtain a marriage license. Although Frankfurt did not become part of Prussia until 1866 and Frederick's law was not applicable in Frankfurt

115

until then, this china is included because it is representative of the type used in German households throughout the nineteenth century.

116. Hanging Lamp for Sabbath and Festivals (See color plate, p. 11)

Frankfurt, 1680–1720
Johann Valentin Schuler (1650–1720)
Marks: Scheffler 122, 245
Silver, cast and engraved
22¼ × 14½ in. dm., 56.5 × 36.8 cm.
The Jewish Museum, New York, Jewish Cultural Reconstruction, JM 37-52

This Sabbath lamp consists of an elaborate central shaft surmounted by a large cast lion with attachment ring, a ten-branched star as lamp holder, and a catch basin with strawberry finial. The lightly engraved decoration consists of graduated cylindrical forms on the branches and flowers, fruit, and foliage on the basin. At the bottom of the star is a cast lion's head forming the center of a hinged door for emptying oil. Through its mouth passes a suspension ring for the catch basin. Around the base of the central shaft is a series of male faces, grotesque masks, and nozzles. Above them is an open story of balustrades alternating with cast male figures bearing symbols of the following holy days: Passover (*matzah* and *matzah* iron), Sukkot (*lulav* and *etrog*), Shavuot (Tablets of the Law), eve of Yom Kippur (knife and chicken), Hanukkah (*menorah* and urn for oil), Purim (hammer and what may be scroll case), Rosh Hashanah (trumpet and book of life), and the Sabbath (flaming *havdalah* candle and Sabbath candle). As Schoenberger noted, these figures appear to have been cast from stock forms to which flat Jews' hats were added (see no. 123). Above each figure a bell is suspended from a plane on which rest pinnacles for the balustrades and a series of small cast animal figures (squirrel, pelican, deer, and eagle) twice repeated. Set between the balustrades is a truncated cone cut out in abstract shapes. It is surmounted by a balustrade of fleur-de-lis and the cast lion.

In 1903 the lamp was transformed into an eternal light and various additions were made; they have now been removed, except for two flags inscribed:

לכבוד זכרון נשמת בעלה /
מוהר"ר שמעון המכונה /
ווילהעלם פרייהערר /
פאן ראטהשילד זצ"ל /
ת"ר"ס"ג לפ"ק /
לזכר עולם יהיה צדיק /
נר תמיד זה נדבה האלמנה /
הגבירה מרת מאטילדע /
פרייפרוי פאן /
ראטהשילד

To the honor of the memory of the soul of
   her husband,
. . . Shimon, known as
Wilhelm Freiherr
von Rothschild . . .
[5]663 (1902–1903) . . .
A righteous man will be an eternal
   remembrance
This eternal light was donated by the
   widow
. . . Mathilda
Freifrau von
Rothschild.

According to Schoenberger, the nozzles and masks of the central shaft were derived from the forms of public fountains. In the *Lekhah Dodi*, a sixteenth-century hymn of welcome to the Sabbath, the holy day is called a "fountain of blessing." The inclusion of figures referring to other holy days is to be explained by the fact that the lamp was used on those occasions as well.

Three of the cast animal figures, as well as the fleur-de-lis ornament, can also be found on a Frankfurt *menorah*, a work of Schuler's contemporary Johann Adam Boller.[1] Other extant Judaica by Schuler include a *menorah* (Frankfurt Historical Museum, X25312), a Hanukkah lamp (The Jewish Museum, New York, JM 19-64), the central shaft of another hanging Sabbath lamp (The Jewish Museum, F 2707), and the base of a *havdalah* candle or spice holder and another hanging lamp, both in the Skirball Museum.[2]

Schoenberger was perplexed by the unusual form of the master's mark, an S within a V. Scheffler's research has, however, proved the existence of a brother with a nearly identical name, Johann Michael Schuler, master from 1684 until 1718. Johann

Valentin may thus have emphasized his middle initial in order to differentiate his mark from that of his brother. On Johann Michael's mark, the M is also larger and projects above the other letters.

1. For an illustration, see *Notizblatt*, XX (1928), 8, fig. 2.
2. Landsberger, "Ritual Implements for the Sabbath," in *Beauty in Holiness*, fig. h and pls. 2, 5.

REFERENCES: G. Schoenberger, "A Silver Sabbath Lamp from Frankfurt-on-the Main," *Essays in Honor of Georg Swarzenski* (Berlin: 1951), p. 190; *Notizblatt*, XXVIII (1931).

V. B. M.

117. Spoon

Germany, probably eighteenth century
Marks: ICP in oval, 12 with an arrow (?) above,
an illegible third mark
Silver, cast and engraved
8-3/4 × 1-3/4 in., 22.2 × 4.5 cm.
The Jewish Museum, New York, gift of Dr. Harry
G. Friedman, F 3406

The lower portion of the handle of this spoon curves outward, then inward to form an arrow; then it gradually widens to form a rectangle at the upper end. The owner's name is engraved on the rectangle:

יעקב דוב / ב"ר / גרשון ז"ל

Jacob Dov son of . . . Gershon, may his memory be for a blessing.

V. B. M.

118. Ladle

Augsburg, 1767–1769
Johann Jacob Biller (1715–1777)
Marks: R^{3}268, 583
Silver, cast, gilt, and engraved
14 × 3 in., 35.6 × 7.6 cm.
The Jewish Museum, New York,
U 7306

The handle of this ladle is gracefully curved. Its upper section is decorated with an uninscribed shield from which rise two grooves; above is a scalloped terminus. A series of teardrop shapes forms the juncture of the handle and the cup. The interior of the cup is gilt. The following undeciphered inscription is engraved on the back of the handle:

ה ב ש ק / ח

V. B. M.

119. Sêder Telfillah Derekh Yesharah

Frankfurt, 1677
Edited by R. Yehiel Michal b. Abraham Segal
Epstein
Ink on paper
7-9/16 × 6-1/16 × 2-1/8 in., 19.2 × 15.4 × 5.4 cm.
The Library of the Jewish Theological Seminary
of America, New York

This prayerbook contains an elaborate Yiddish commentary.

M. S. C.

120. Pair of Sconces

Germany, eighteenth–nineteenth century
Brass, repoussé
31-1/2 × 15 in., 80.0 × 38.0 cm.
The Jewish Museum, New York, gift of the
Danzig Jewish Community, D 97 a, b

Each of these oblong sconces is formed of two sections bearing convex oval cartouches framed by beading and gadrooning. Symmetrical designs of flowers executed in repoussé fill the remainder of the surface. A single socket is attached near the lower edge of each.

These sconces are similar to eighteenth-century examples from a synagogue in Eichsfeld.[1] Related examples are depicted in nineteenth-century paintings of Jewish life (see, for example, no. 99), and in a scene of morning worship in the synagogue now in the Danzig collection.[2]

1. Göttingen, Städtisches Museum, inv. no. J44a n.b.; *Monumenta Judaica*, no. E 408.
2. *Danzig 1939*, no. 116.

REFERENCES: Danzig, 1904, nos. 126 and 127; Danzig 1939, no. 114.

V. B. M.

121. Hanukkah Menorah

Frankfurt, 1706–1732
Johann Adam Boller (1679–1732)
Marks: Scheffler 128(R³2005), 265(R³2054)
Silver, cast, engraved, filigree, hammered, and
gilt, with enamel plaques
17 × 14-1/2 in., 42.5 × 36.3 cm.
The Jewish Museum, New York, gift of Mrs.
Felix Warburg, S 563

During the last third of the seventeenth century and the first third of the eighteenth, three Frankfurt silversmiths made a series of Hanukkah *menorot* closely related in form, proportions, and decoration. All of them consist of central shafts and branches decorated with knops and flowers recalling the biblical description of the Tabernacle menorah (Ex. 25:33). From the shafts rise cast figures of Judith with the head of Holofernes. Judith was an Apocryphal Jewish heroine, whose brave act against an enemy general, Holofernes, became part of Hanukkah lore during the Middle Ages. On one of the five known lamps, in the Cluny Museum,[1] two figures of soldiers flanking the central shaft may represent Hasmonean warriors; cast lions on all the *menorot* of this group perhaps allude to Judah, his tribe, or Judah the Maccabee. The remaining decorative motifs, including an archer (perhaps Sagittarius), cast animals and birds, fleur-de-lis, and floral ornaments, were all common in the eighteenth century. Boller made two of the *menorot* in the series: the one ex-

121

hibited here and another in a private collection.[2]

The Warburg *menorah* is distinguished from the rest of the group in several ways. The lamp rests on an octagonal base, whereas the other examples rest on rectangular bases supported by rampant lions. On the Warburg *menorah* the motif of the rampant lion holding a shield is enlarged and given greater prominence by its assimilation into the shaft. Finally, there is greater emphasis on coloristic effects. Aside from lavish gilding, small colored enamel florets have been included among the filigree flowers along the branches, and on the base there are four oval enamel plaques bearing scenes from Genesis: Jacob rolling the stone from the mouth of the well (39:3), Rebecca and Eliezer (34:18), Jacob's dream (38:12), and Jacob wrestling with the angel (32:24). Guido Schoenberger suggested that these plaques are the work of Peter Boy, a Frankfurt goldsmith and enamelist born in 1680.

Engraved on the shield held by the lion are a stag and a dove, perhaps referring to the names of the couple owning the *menorah*. Solder marks at the top and bottom of the shield, however, suggest that it may be a replacement.

1. Cl. 12241; Narkiss, fig. 30.

2. *Notizblatt*, XX (1928), p. 8, fig. 2, no. 92. The two other *menorot* of the group are: Frankfurt Historical Museum (Inv. Nr. 12241) and a *menorah* once in the collection of Max Frenkel, Jerusalem (Narkiss, no. 185).

REFERENCE: Kayser-Schoenberger, no. 142.

V. B. M.

122. Spice Box (See color plate, p. 9)

Frankfurt, 1748–1776
Rötger Herfurth (1722–1776)
Marks: Scheffler 148, 287
Silver, cast, ajouré, engraved, and stippled
12-3/8 × 3-1/2 in. dm., 31.5 × 9.0 cm.
The Jewish Museum, New York, gift of Dr. Harry G. Friedman, F 4391

A single turret and flag top the hexagonal body of this spice box. Five of the six sides are engraved with single large flowers set in ovals formed by pairs of interlocking scrolls. The interstices between flowers and scrolls are open to allow the aroma of spices to escape. On the sixth side, the flower motif has been replaced by a hinged door, but the upper portions of the scrolls remain. A scroll and flag sit at each cor-

ner of the body, further emphasizing its hexagonal shape. The turret is also adorned with scrolls and openwork, growing progressively smaller and more elongated as the turret rises, accentuating the perspective effect and enhancing the sense of height. The entire box rests on a lobed stem and a stepped base; the indented, circular form of the latter harmonizes with the engraved decoration on the box itself.

Extensive openwork was characteristic of Frankfurt Judaica in the eighteenth century, as was the use of projecting scrolls as a border element (see nos. 65 and 69). As a result, the basic form of the object become obscured by the complex play between solid and void, between object and surrounding space. This is a characteristic of Baroque art in general.

Most of Rötger Herfurth's known works were made for Jewish clients, and he is credited with having created the characteristic Frankfurt form of Hanukkah lamp (see no. 27 and Scheffler no. 444).

V. B. M.

123. Havdalah Candle and Spice Holder (See color plate, p. 9)

Frankfurt, before 1731
Jeremias Zobel (1670–1741)
Marks: Scheffler 128 (R³2005), 257
Silver, cast, ajouré, and hammered
13 in., 33.0 cm.
The Jewish Museum, New York, gift of Dr. Harry G. Friedman, F 3661

From a circular base edged with scallops and decorated with bands of beadwork and acanthus leaves combined with strapwork, all in repoussé, rises a thick stem encircled halfway up by plain moldings. The stem supports a compartmented drawer, the cast sides of which are decorated with quatrefoil rosettes in openwork. An openwork balustrade of fleur-de-lis tops the drawer. At the corners of this balustrade four figures with symbols anchor four long poles terminating in pineapple finials, which serve as a candleholder. Prewar photographs show that a movable platform with a similar balustrade of fleur-de-lis was once part of this piece. It was used to push the candle upward.

This object serves as a container for two of the items necessary for the *havdalah* ceremony. This ritual, which marks the close of the Sabbath and its

121

separation from the working week, incorporates blessings over light (the candle) and spices (stored in the drawer) and over a valued liquid such as wine or juice. As blessings over wine are recited on many Jewish ceremonial occasions, goblets or beakers were generally not created specifically for *havdalah.* Among Ashkenazim, however, the use of spices and twisted candles was specific to the ceremony concluding the Sabbath, and special containers were created for it. That this piece was also used for the *havdalah* ceremony concluding festivals (though no blessing for light is recited then) is suggested by the small cast figures atop the spice drawer. One, symbolizing Passover, holds a *matzah* and a tool for scoring the unbaked dough; the second holds a knife and a fowl symbolizing *kapparah,* a ceremony performed on the eve of Yom Kippur; the third holds a flaming candle and a full goblet representing *havdalah;* and the fourth holds a hammer (*shulklapper*)[1] and a Torah finial, apparently symbolizing the synagogue. Such figures are found on various types of Judaica fashioned by Frankfurt goldsmiths around 1700: spice boxes, *menorot,* and Sabbath lamps, for example. In some instances, like one example in the Cluny collection dated to the seventeenth or eighteenth century, the attributes do not appear to have Jewish significance. Furthermore, many of these figures appear to have been formed through modification of stock workshop figures (*cf.* no. 116). For these reasons, Hallo suggested that the figures were originally incorporated as decorative elements. Mature examples of the eighteenth century like this candle and spice holder reflect a desire to invest the figures with symbolic significance.

Zobel also created the Frankfurt *rimmonim* in this exhibition (no. 69) and a related pair in the Frankfurt Historical Museum, as well as a beaker for the Pious Brotherhood of the Hanau community, once in the collection of the Hessischen Landesmuseum, Kassel. The exhibited object was once also in the Kassel museum, to which it had come from the Rothfels collection in that city.

1. In European Jewish communities, the beadle would call men to prayer by banging on their homes with a *shulklapper.*

REFERENCES: Hallo, no. 77, fig. 206; Hallo, "Jüdische Kult- und Kunstdenkmaler im Hessischen Landesmuseum Kassel," *Die Morgen,* IV (1928), p. 144, pl. III; *Notizblatt,* XXIII (1929), p. 7; and XXIV (1929), p. 6.

V. B. M.

124. Etrog Box

Germany, *c.* 1850–1860
Mark: 12
Silver, cast, repoussé, and engraved
5-1/4 × 4-7/8 in., 13.3 × 12.4 cm.
The Jewish Museum, New York, gift of Dr. Harry Friedenwald, JM 105-47

This lobed ovoid box with hinged cover rests on a short base with scalloped edge. Four ribs in repoussé run from bottom to top, dividing the box into four quadrants and at the same time unifying the box and its lid. Two confronted scrolls frame each quadrant. Arrangements of scrolls and flowers decorate the centers of the front and back quadrants, and a cast flower serves as handle. The inscription engraved on the front quadrant of the lid reads:

פרי עץ הדר / יוחנן בר חיים הלוי ז"ל

The fruit of the *hadar* tree (Lev. 23:40)
Yoḥanan son of Ḥayyim Halevi z.l.

Boxes like this one were generally used to hold sugar and spices, precious commodities that were locked up for safekeeping.[1] Because their form and size were suitable, Jews often used sugar boxes to hold *etrogim.* This one was owned by the donor's grandfather.

1. Scheffler, *Berlin,* figs. 54–65.

V. B. M.

125. Sêder Haggadah

Frankfurt, 1724
Published by Zalmen b. David Aptrud and Moses b. Jonah Gamburg
Ink on paper
7 × 4-3/8 × 3/8 in., 17.8 × 11.1 × 1.0 cm.
The Library of the Jewish Theological Seminary of America, New York

This edition of the *Haggadah* features seven woodcuts based on the signs of the zodiac: Aquarius, Gemini, Scorpio, Libra, Leo, Pisces, and Aquarius (a second time).

M. S. C.

126. Ewer and Basin for Passover

Germany, late eighteenth century
Mark: (on ewer only) figure of Justice holding
scales, animal running to left, below letters
Block . . .
Pewter, cast and engraved
Ewer: 9-1/2 × 7-7/8 in., 24.2 × 20.0 cm.
Basin: 10-1/2 × 2-9/16 in., 27.4 × 6.6 cm.
The Jewish Museum, New York, gift of Dr. Harry
G. Friedman, F 29a, b

The cylindrical form of the ewer tapers only slightly
from bottom to top. Raised moldings set off the rim
and base, and the ends of the long handle are rendered as shells. The spout has a strong sculptural
form with shell-like undulations. Below the rim are
engraved the words ורחץ/ורחצה ("and wash/
and washing"), the names of the two laving ceremonies at the *seder* on Passover.

Although the ewer and basin came to The Jewish
Museum as a set, the basin appears to have been
made by a different craftsman. The pewter is slightly
different in color and texture, and the basin lacks
the fine detailing of the ewer, for example, the raised
moldings. The initials מ ב ("M. B.") are engraved
on the rim.

V. B. M.

127. Seder Plate

Frankfurt, 1791
Johann Georg Klingling
Mark: figure of Justice holding scales; deer at its
right
Pewter, cast and engraved
15-3/16 in. dm., 38.4 cm.
The Jewish Museum, New York, gift of Dr. Harry
G. Friedman, F 2256

The plate is very simple in form, circular and surrounded by a plain border with raised rim. In the
middle is engraved a thirteen-pointed star, in the
center of which is a vase of fruit. The order of the
seder service is engraved on the rim, beginning with
קדש (the sanctification over wine) and ending with
שלחן עורך (the meal), followed by the letters
צפון ברך הלל נרצה, which are abbrevia-
tions for the last parts of the *seder: zafon* (eating of
afikomen), *bareh* (blessing after meals), *hallel* (re-
citing psalms), and *nirzah* (conclusion). In the remaining space are two confronted fish; two trees; a
crown over the Hebrew letter ט (*tet*), engraved on

126

a reworked area[1] and the date 1791.

Subsequent to its manufacture the plate was decorated by someone with a good knowledge of Hebrew but with a somewhat naïve artistic sense: The
designs in the center and on the border are not
aligned, not enough space was allotted for the inscription, and the points of the star are irregularly
shaped. To resolve the conflict between the odd
number of star points and the decorative scheme of
alternating shaded and plain forms, the artist simply
bisected the thirteenth point.

The collection of The Jewish Museum includes
four other pewter plates made in Klingling's workshop: F 5090, JM 48-51 (see no. 23), F 2838, and
F 4288.

1. On another *seder* plate by Klingling in The Jewish
Museum (F 5090), the owner's initials are engraved over
the letters IGK, the monogram of the craftsman.

V. B. M.

127

128. Matzah Bag

Germany, nineteenth century
Linen mesh, embroidered with wool, silk, and
beads; silk backing; linen dividers
19-5/8 × 16-7/8 in., 49.8 × 42.9 cm.
The Jewish Museum, New York, gift of Dr. Harry
G. Friedman, F 1315

In the center two confronted rampant lions grasp the
top of a Star of David enclosing the Tablets of the
Law. The lions and shield rest on a foreshortened
plane. Above is a quotation from Leviticus 23:6:

שבעת ימים מצות תאכלו

Seven days you shall eat unleavened bread.

A beadwork scroll design fills the four corners, and
a braided silk rope is sewn to the edges. The pouches
are formed of linen; the back of the bag is of silk.

Both stylistic and iconographic elements suggest
a nineteenth-century date. The naturalistic rendering of the lions' bodies, spatial relations, and even
cast shadows are typical of nineteenth-century German Judaica. Also, the Ten Commandments were a
popular motif later in the century. A related work
is a *hallah* cover in the collection of The Jewish
Museum (F 933).

REFERENCE: *Fabric of Jewish Life*, no. 175.

V. B. M.

129. Passover Towel

Southern Germany, c. 1800
Linen embroidered with silk, crocheted
61-3/4 × 15-3/4 in., 154.4 × 39.4 cm.
The Jewish Museum, New York, S 1430

Near the top of the towel is a frieze formed of two
interlocking wavy lines filled with decorative motifs
set into a field of small squares. Two somewhat similar friezes frame a decorated field at the center of
the towel; the decoration consists of a large rose
with flowering branches between bands of interlocking triangles. Between the top and the center is
a crowned cartouche flanked by birds bearing the
initials ‏ב א‎ (A B). The most elaborately embroidered
area is below the center of the towel. Between similar frames are two confronted rampant stags flanking a flowering standard. Flowering branches fill the
spaces around the stags. A border of crocheted linen
and fringes is attached to the lower edge of the towel.

Towels like this were made especially for the two
ablution ceremonies incorporated into the Passover
seder. A similar example in the collection of The
Jewish Museum (S 1279) came with a matching pil-
low cover.[1] Two others are in the Feuchtwanger Collection, the Israel Museum.[2]

1. *Fabric of Jewish Life*, no. 222.
2. Nos. 158/29 and 158/30; Shachar, *Jewish Tradition
in Art*, nos. 481 and 482.

REFERENCE: *Fabric of Jewish Life*, no. 220.

V. B. M.

An Ashkenazi Wedding

For the Jews of Frankfurt a wedding was not
only a happy personal event; it was also one
of communal significance, ensuring
continuity and the perpetuation of common
ideals. Many of the customs that grew up
around the basic religious requirements of
the marriage ceremony were designed to
strengthen the bonds between the bride and
groom, on one hand, and the larger
community, on the other. After his betrothal
a groom was required to donate to the local
school a sum determined by the amount of
the dowry. The community regulated the
date of festivities held in conjunction with
the wedding, the guest lists, and even the
dress worn by the families of the bride and
groom. One festivity was the *spinholts*, held
on the Sabbath before the wedding. In the
Talmudic period this ceremony had been a
public demonstration of the bride's ability to
spin yarn. By the eighteenth century it had
come to comprise receptions for the bride and
groom in their homes on Friday night and
Saturday afternoon, as well as processions to
the communal wedding hall, where further
festivities took place. The community also
assisted individuals by providing halls for
personal celebrations and even dowries for
indigent brides.

Festive meals were also held at the
exchange of *sivlonot* (gifts) between the bride
and groom and after the marriage ceremony.
The giving of *sivlonot* is mentioned in
German Jewish sources as early as the
twelfth century. Although a variety of gifts is

known, the most common were belts that were then worn at the marriage ceremony itself.

Before the wedding the families of the bride and groom wrote prenuptial agreements largely concerned with property. They could be written in any language, but Jewish law required that the *ketubbah* (marriage contract) itself be written in Aramaic, according to a standard formula that specified the groom's obligations to his bride. At the marriage the groom presented the contract and a ring to his bride, blessings were recited, and two cups of wine were shared by the couple. Weddings were joyous occasions, enhanced by music, dancing, and professional entertaining.

130. The Wedding

Frankfurt, 1866
Moritz Daniel Oppenheim (1800–1882)
Oil on canvas
26 × 21-1/4 in., 66.0 × 54.0 cm.
Oscar Gruss collection

"The Wedding" is one of a group of *grisailles* (paintings executed in shades of gray) that Oppenheim painted for his series *Bilder aus dem altjüdischen Familienleben (Pictures of Traditional Jewish Family Life)*. He started working on these genre scenes in color in the 1850s, including events from the Jewish life cycle, as well as Sabbath and festival observances. When the Frankfurt publisher, Heinrich Keller, wanted to issue a series of photographs after the original six color paintings, Oppenheim copied them as *grisailles* in order to facilitate their reproduction. "The Wedding" was one of the original series of six that Keller published in 1866. Oppenheim kept adding paintings to the group; twelve more appeared in 1868 and eighteen in 1874. Ultimately the series grew to include twenty paintings and was published in book form in Germany in 1881, with an introduction by Rabbi Leopold Stein (see pp.   and nos. 82, 83 and 84).

These works speak to the values of the conservative German Jewish bourgeoisie for whom they were intended. Religious piety, family devotion, and domestic harmony are glorified, not only here, but also in paintings of the Biedermeier period in general. Biedermeier is the name given to the period c. 1815–1848 in German-speaking countries. Art associated with it commonly expresses appreciation for comfort and the simple pleasures of life, often with sentimental or humorous overtones. Oppenheim's paintings of traditional Jewish family life are imbued with nostalgia for "the good old days." He did not depict Jewish life in the nineteenth-century Frankfurt he knew; rather, he set the scenes in the old Frankfurt ghetto and peopled them with figures in eighteenth-century dress. Instead of recording the persecutions and humiliations that were part of pre-emancipation Jewish life, however, he focused on the cohesiveness of the family and the community at a time before the inevitable pressures and conflicts that attended the greater freedom of the post-ghetto period. The same theme is expressed in "Return of the Jewish Volunteer" (see no. 99), a version of which Oppenheim eventually incorporated as the twentieth and final image in the 1881 edition of the series. Despite their sentimentality, however, these painting have a certain critical edge. In his declining years Oppenheim used depictions of the past as comments upon the state of Jewish observance in his own time. The comments are only undertones, however, and most of Oppenheim's public seems to have enjoyed his pictures for their nostalgic view of their grandparent's world, and were unaware of any deeper significance.

There are certain compositional differences between this *grisaille* of 1866 and the color painting "The Wedding," dated 1861, which is in the Israel Museum.[1] Mostly they involve background architecture, the placement of secondary figures, and the absence of a *ḥuppah* (marriage canopy) in the 1861 version. In this version, the wedding is viewed through an archway, and the figures are set more deeply within the picture, devices that serve to distance the viewer from the scene. In the *grisaille* and consequently in the widely disseminated photographic reproductions, the action takes place in the foreground, and all the details of costume and religious accessories are precisely rendered.

The wedding takes place in the square of the old Frankfurt synagogue built in 1711 (see no. 49),[2] and the figures wear eighteenth-century dress. Bride and groom stand beneath the *ḥuppah*, their heads covered by a single *tallit* (see no. 77). The rabbi faces the couple, wearing a large *tallit* and the Polish *streimel* (fur hat). After he recites the blessings, the groom will slip a gold ring on the first finger of the bride's left hand, saying, "With this ring you are consecrated unto me according to the laws of Moses and Israel." At the conclusion of the service, the groom will throw the glass of wine at the tablet with the Star of David (*Traustein*) mounted on the wall behind the *ḥuppah*. This act is interpreted as a sign of mourning for the destruction of the Temple in Jerusalem, but it may have originated as a practice for warding off evil spirits. Both bride and groom wear marriage belts made of metallic roundels, called *Sivlonotgürtel*. It was customary among German Jews for the bride and groom to exchange belts decorated with gold (see no. 131). The rabbi holds a document that appears to be a *ketubbah*, or marriage contract. The couple is surrounded by parents and guests; a fiddler and a man in harlequin dress will provide entertainment after the ceremony.

Oppenheim was extremely fond of this subject. A

131

126

third canvas entitled "The Wedding" was finished just two weeks before his death in February 1882.[3]

1. M 1149-3-56; ill. Cohen, *Israel Museum News*, p. 93 fig. 8.

2. Cohen, *Bulletin des Leo Baeck Instituts*, p. 72 and n. 56.

3. *Erinnerungen*, p. 117.

REFERENCES: *Erinnerungen*, pp. 114 ff., p. 119, I, 6; Heilbrunn, pp. 299 ff.; Hoelterhoff, n.p.; Werner, pp. 50, 54 ff.; Cohen, *Bulletin des Leo Baeck Instituts*, pp. 70 ff.; Cohen, *Israel Museum News*, 92–93; Jewish Museum, *Oppenheim*, n.p.

E. D. B.

131. Bridal Belt and Pouch

Germany, eighteenth or nineteenth century
Weave-patterned silk with gold metallic appliqués and buckle, silk lining
Belt: 4 × 26-1/4 in., 10.0 × 66.7 cm.; Pouch: 7-1/2 × 9-1/4 in., 19.0 × 23.5 cm.
The Jewish Museum, New York, gift of the Danzig Jewish Community, D 268

Both belt and pouch are made of rose, grey, and white silk woven with a pattern of green and white flowers and white fronds. The pouch is edged in metallic braid. Metallic appliqués are sewn on both objects. Each appliqué consists of a rosette with a series of hives with swarming bees (symbols of industriousness) around the circumference. Similar appliqués, joined together and attached to a frame, form the belt buckle.

An earlier fabric may have been used to make the belt and pouch, but it is impossible to determine from internal evidence when the cloth was adapted to its present form. These objects once belonged to L. Gieldzinski, who was informed by the director of the Städtisches Historisches Museum in Frankfurt, in a letter dated May 25, 1906, of the German-Jewish custom of having bride and groom exchange belts decorated with gold (*Sivlonotgürtel*). We may infer that the present example was acquired by Gieldzinski prior to the date of his inquiry to the Frankfurt Museum. Most extant German marriage belts, like those shown in the Oppenheim painting (see no. 130), are made entirely of metal; this silk example is rare.

REFERENCES: Danzig, 1933, no. 120, pl. 4; *Danzig 1939*, no. 8.

V. B. M.

132. Marriage Agreement

Frankfurt, November 6, 1819
Handwritten on paper
17-3/4 × 12-3/16 in., 45.0 × 31.0 cm.
Leo Baeck Institute, New York, Sinn collection,
AR-C, 404, 1161

This notarized document is the record of a civil contract between Lazard Lambert of Metz and his future bride, Gutel Horwitz, daughter of Hirsch Levy Horwitz, Chief Rabbi of Frankfurt from 1805 until his death in 1817. It records the conditions under which the couple is to marry, with the consent of the bride's mother and two guardians. The extent to which aspects of Jewish law were taken into consideration in this agreement is noteworthy.

In Article 1 it is stated that the bride and groom promise to marry and to love and be faithful to each other. The bride's determination to remain in her home town is safeguarded in Article 2: The only domicile of the future couple will be Frankfurt, and the groom agrees to do everything in his power to obtain a resident's permit. In Articles 3 and 4 the money and property that each party brings to the marriage are enumerated.

In Article 5 the groom promises to obtain the permission of his parents and a ḥaliẓah letter from his brother for his bride, free of charge, thus ensuring that she will be released from the obligation of a levirate marriage.[1]

In Article 6 specifies the amount of damages to be paid should either party fail to fulfill any of the obligations set forth in the contract, and Article 7 the extent to which Jewish and Roman law apply to the property settlement between the two parties.

The agreement is written entirely in German, though the signature of the bride's mother is in Hebrew.

1. Levirate marriage is marriage between a widow whose husband has died childless and the brother of the deceased. Ḥaliẓah is the ceremony in which the widow is released from her obligation to marry her brother-in-law.

E. D. B.

133. Wedding Ring

Europe, nineteenth century
Marks: none
Silver, engraved
13/16 × 1-1/16 in. dm., 2.1 × 2.7 cm.
The Jewish Museum, New York, gift of the
Danzig Jewish Community, D 279

Two plain raised moldings mark the edges of this wedding band. The center is engraved with the words מזל טוב (*mazzal tov*) framed in a cartouche.

According to the 1933 Danzig catalogue, this ring had come to the synagogue museum from the Gieldzinski collection, together with the bridal belt and pouch (see no. 131) and a silver-covered prayer book, although it is not listed in the earlier 1904 catalogue.[1] As Gieldzinski died in 1910 and there is reason to date the belt and pouch to the nineteenth century or perhaps earlier, we may assume a similar date for the ring. Documentary evidence for the use of marriage rings inscribed *mazzal tov* occurs as early as the eighteenth century.[2]

1. *Danzig 1939*, nos.
2. See J. Gutmann, "Wedding Customs and Ceremonies in Art," *Beauty in Holiness*, pp. 323–324, no. 21.

REFERENCES: Danzig, 1933, no. 120, pl. 4; *Danzig 1939*, no. 11.

V. B. M.

134. Kiddush Cup

Nuremberg, 1637–1671
Oswalt Haussner (d. 1671)
Marks: R³3761, 4214
Silver, raised, repoussé, engraved, and stippled
2-13/16 × 2-1/2 in. dm., 7.2 × 6.3 cm.
The Jewish Museum, New York, gift of Herbert
H. Lehman, JM 70-60

The cup is a hollow cylinder that flares outward at the top to form a lobed upper body with scalloped rim. Two rows of shells executed in repoussé against a stippled ground encircle the cylinder, whereas lightly engraved leaves decorate the upper section. The names A. L. Lehman and Heffa Lehman are engraved on the bottom. A portion of the rim is missing.

A. L. and Heffa Lehman, grandparents of Herbert and Irving Lehman, were married in Bavaria around 1799. This cup was used at their wedding for one of the two glasses of wine shared by a Jewish bride and groom as part of the wedding ceremony and was inscribed at that time. It was made, however, more than a century earlier by Haussner, a Nuremberg silversmith. Shell forms figure prominently among the decorative motifs on Haussner's known works listed by Rosenberg.[1]

1. M. Rosenberg, *Der Goldschmiede Merkzeichen*, III, Frankfurt a. M., 1925, no. 4214

V. B. M.

135. Woman's Cap

Frankfurt, 1845–1850
Net and lace
8-1/4 × 22-7/8 in., 21.0 × 58.0 cm.
The Jewish Museum, New York, gift of Mrs. Marina Nitrini, JM 1982-44

The cap proper is formed of five sections of netting attached to a band of double netting. Two triangular earpieces are suspended from the band. A single lace border design joins the sections of netting and edges the earpieces. This design consists of a scalloped line from which hang two pairs of leafy branches. Above the scallops are compartments of openwork lace.

According to the donor, this cap was worn by her great-grandmother, a native of Frankfurt, after her marriage, between 1840 and 1850.

V. B. M.

136. Cooking Pot

Frankfurt, 1580
Brass, cast, chased, and hammered
8-3/16 × 9 in. dm., 20.8 × 22.9 cm.
The Jewish Museum, New York, gift of Mr. and Mrs. Ben Heller, JM 23-64

On this cylindrical pot two rectangular handles have been placed below the molded rim. A chased and hammered inscription runs between and below the handles:

Hebrew Inscription

Hirtz Popert's w[ife], daughter of Moses zur Leiter, in [the year 5]340 [1580]

To the left of the word *Leiter* ("ladder") is a schematic drawing of a ladder. It is supposed that the penultimate word of the inscription, the chronogram, is a corruption of *cholent*, a dish usually containing meat, potatoes, and beans, that is made Friday before the Sabbath and cooked overnight. Lighting a fire and cooking are both types of work forbidden on the Sabbath, the day of rest; it is therefore necessary to prepare all Sabbath food beforehand. *Cholent* is eaten after morning services at the second of the three Sabbath meals; the dish is mentioned in sources as early as the fifteenth century.[1]

The inscription is also noteworthy for the manner in which it refers to its owner, not by her own name, but only as the wife of Hirtz Popert and the daughter of Moses zur Leiter. Hirtz Popert died in Frankfurt in 1625.[2] The family zur Leiter took its name from the sign, a ladder, on its house, built in 1533.[3] The wording of the inscription underscores the fact that marriage in the sixteenth century, as in later centuries, was less a union of individuals than an alliance of families.

The pot is a rare early example of cooking ware definitely made and used by Jews; it is also one of the few surviving objects that can be associated with the Frankfurt ghetto of the sixteenth century. It was formerly in the collections of Albert Figdor and Michael Zagayski.

1. Zunz, *Die Gottesdienstlichen Vorträge der Juden* (Frankfurt: 1892), p. 456.
2. M. Horovitz, *Die Inschriften des alten Friedhofs . . . Frankfurt-am-Main* (Frankfurt: 1901), no. 537.
3. Dietz, *Stammbuch*, p. 182; I. Kracauer, *Die Geschichte der Judengasse* (Frankfurt: 1906), p. 182.

REFERENCES: *Der Sammlung Albert Figdor Wien*, sales catalogue, P. Cassirer, Berlin, June 11–13, 1930, part 1, vol. 5, no. 420; The Jewish Museum, *Loan Exhibit of Antique Ceremonial Objects and Paintings from the Collection of Mr. M. Zagayski* (New York: 1951), no. 124; The Jewish Museum, *The Silver and Judaica Collection of Mr. and Mrs. Michael M. Zagayski* (New York: 1963), no. 51; *The Michael M. Zagayski Collection of Rare Judaica*, sales catalogue, Parke-Bernet Galleries, New York, March 18–19, 1964, no. 235.

Istanbul: A Sephardi Community

The Establishment of a Sephardi Community: Istanbul Until 1750

In 330 C.E. Constantine the Great, Emperor of Rome, established a capital on the site of the small Greek fishing town Byzantium, and renamed it Constantinople. Even before that date Jews had lived in the town; the first mention of a synagogue there occurred in 318. In general Byzantine rule over the Jews of Constantinople was harsh, and many repressive measures were enacted by the emperors. On two occasions, in 721–722 and in 1042, the Jews were banished from the city.

The conquest of Constantinople by the Ottoman Turks in 1453 destroyed the city. In order to repopulate his capital after the defeat of the Byzantine Greeks, Meḥmed II the Conqueror forced Jews, Christians, and Muslims from all over the Empire to settle in Constantinople (known from then on as Istanbul), where they were encouraged to pursue economic and government activities.

At the time of the conquest there were three groups within the Ottoman Jewish community: the Romaniotes (Greek Jews whose history dates back to the early Byzantine period); and Genoese and Venetian Jews, who lived in separate quarters under the jurisdiction of their cities of origin. The numbers of these groups who remained and the character of the community changed decisively during the reign of Sultan Bāyezīd II (1481–1512), however. In 1492 King Ferdinand and Queen Isabella of Spain expelled all the Jews of their kingdom who refused to convert to Christianity. Many sought refuge in Portugal, from which they were driven five years later. Thus ended a thousand years of Jewish life on the Iberian peninsula, a period of greatness known ever since as the Golden Age.

Bāyezīd instructed his governors to welcome Sephardi refugees; as a result, Jews from Spain and Portugal settled throughout the Ottoman Empire. The Jewish population of Istanbul increased from 8,000 to 30,000 in the 1520's. The Sephardim brought with them scientific and linguistic skills, commercial acumen, and knowledge of textile manufacturing, the making of firearms, and book printing. As a result of their abilities, the Sephardim soon became the dominant element among the Jewish population. They were soon joined by Marrano countrymen, Jews of Spain and Portugal who had publicly converted to Christianity but who had continued to practice Judaism secretly.

Under the tolerant rule of the Ottoman sultans, the Jewish community of Istanbul achieved great heights of culture, wealth, and power in the sixteenth and seventeenth centuries, in effect creating a new Golden Age.

137. Coin of Justinian

Constantinople, c. 550
Bronze, struck
15.9 grams
The Jewish Museum, New York, gift of the Samuel and Daniel M. Friedenberg Collection, 79–28

The head of Justinian I (483–565), Byzantine Emperor from 527 to 565, is depicted on the obverse, with his name and titles in Latin. On the reverse is the letter "M," which is the Greek denomination for forty units.

Under the reign of Justinian I there was an increase in the persecution of the Jews in the Empire. Justinian's *Corpus Juris Civilis* and his *novellae* (imperial instruction on specific subjects) included legislation restricting Jewish freedom and interfering with Jews' religious practices. For example, *novella* 146, issued in 553, included a prohibition on the use of the *Mishnah* for exegesis of the Torah, arguing that it was not a divinely inspired text.

The status of the Jews in the Empire under legislation initiated by Justinian did not change significantly for the following 700 years.

REFERENCE: *Coins Reveal*, no. 119.

E. D. B.

138. Travelogue of Benjamin of Tudela

Istanbul, 1543.
Published by Eliezer b. Gershom Soncino
Ink on paper
5-3/4 × 4 × 1/2 in., 14.6 × 10 1 × 1.2 cm.
The Library of the Jewish Theological Seminary of America, New York, Very Rare Collection, Mic. 5721, Yaari 135

Rabbi Benjamin of Tudela, Spain, is famous for a journey that he took from Spain through the Near East in the mid-twelfth century C. E. He described his visit to Istanbul:

> . . . It is a bustling city, with business coming to her from all foreign lands on land and on sea. There is no other city like her except Baghdad. There are the Church of Sophia (*bamah shel Tosfia*) and the Pope of the Greeks . . . and as many churches as there are days in the year, and in them incalculable wealth . . . more than in all the churches of the rest of the world [together]. . . . And there is a . . . hippodrome where the king organizes great games on the birthday of Jesus of Nazereth, and in that place are drawn pictures of all the kinds of men in the world before the king and queen with all types of sorcery. . . .[1]

This copy of the first edition of Benjamin's book is very rare.

1. ff. 66-72.

M. S. C.

139. Sippur Malkhei Ottomanlis

Istanbul, 1767
Joseph Sambari
Published by Reuven and Nissim Ashkenazi
Ink on paper
6-1/16 × 8 in., 15.4 × 20.0 cm.
The Library of the Jewish Theological Seminary of America, New York, * 0

Sippur Malkhei Ottomanlis (The Story of the Ottoman Sultans) is a Ladino translation of part of a larger work, *Divrei Yosef (The Words of Joseph)*, which was written in the Hebrew language in Egypt at the end of the seventeenth century. Such historical writings were meant both to inform and to entertain the reader.

J. H.

140. Bible

Toledo and Istanbul, 1492–1497
Ink on vellum
10-1/4 × 8-1/16 in., 26.0 × 20.5 cm.
The Library of the Jewish Theological Seminary of America, New York, Lutzki no. 6, ENA 310

In this Bible the personal history of its owner, parallel to that of all Spanish Jewry in the last decade of the fifteenth century, is recorded. The scribe, Hayim ibn Hayim, wrote:

> This volume, which contains the twenty-four sacred books, was written by the learned rabbi Abraham Calif in the city of Toledo, which is in Spain. It was finished in Nisan 5252 A.M. [1492] for the very learned R. Jacob Aboab, the son of the esteemed gentleman, R. Samuel. May the Almighty find him and his descendants worthy of meditating on it forever. On the seventh of Av of that same year, the exiles of Jerusalem who were in Spain went forth dismayed and banished by the royal edict. May they come back in joy, bearing their sheaves. And I, Hayim ibn Hayim have copied the Massorah and the textual variants in 5257 A.M. [1497] in the city of Istanbul. May salvation be at hand!

This volume is of exceptional beauty and has been widely exhibited.

M. S. C.

The Jewish Role in Turkey, 1453–1750

Early in the seventeenth century an English traveler wrote that "the whole commerce of all commodities in Turkey is in the hands of Jews and Christians," which was doubtless an exaggeration. This commerce was conducted on several levels. Most Jews were peddlers and petty merchants. Others were agents and brokers for European Christians. Jewish women sold goods in the sultans' harem; many achieved great political influence. Most powerful of all were the international merchants and financiers whose knowledge of European languages and whose banking connections in other cities were assets in the development of Turkey's international trade. Among this last group was Gracia Nasi (c. 1510–1569), a Portuguese Marrano who had left her native country and openly returned to Judaism. When she arrived in Istanbul in 1543, she brought with her large amounts of capital. In addition to her banking and economic activities, Gracia Nasi founded *yeshivot* (religious schools) and synagogues and continued her efforts on behalf of persecuted Marranos and Jews. Her nephew Joseph Nasi (c. 1524–1579) arrived in Istanbul in 1545, married Gracia's daughter, and launched a career as one of the most influential figures in the Ottoman Empire.

Physicians attached to the court constituted another group within the Jewish community that attained significant political power. Moses Hamon (c. 1490–1554), whose grandfather had been physician to the king of Granada, succeeded his father as one of the physicians to the Ottoman Sultan Selīm I (1512–1520) and later served Suleymān II the Magnificent (1520–1566). As a result of his influence at court, Hamon was able to aid the community by obtaining a *firman* (royal decree) protecting Jews from blood libels. His role as diplomat and intercessor on behalf of the Jewish community was later filled by other physicians. In 1712–1713 Joseph, a doctor at court, labored unsuccessfully to prevent the killing of the Ashkenazi Jews of Jersualem, who were oppressed by their debts to Muslim moneylenders.

The Sephardim who came to Istanbul in the late fifteenth and sixteenth centuries expanded industries previously little known: for example, the manufacture of textiles and firearms, and book printing. Jews also continued in occupations like tanning, in which they had been active under the Byzantines. There were also artisans, as well as boatmen, musicians, and wine merchants.

141. Marchant Juif (Jewish Merchant)

France, seventeenth-century (?) copy of a sixteenth-century original
Engraving on paper
10-1/2 × 6-11/16 in., 26.7 × 17.0 cm.
The Library of the Jewish Theological Seminary of America, New York

141

Like the representation of a Jewish doctor (see no. 146) this representation of a Jewish merchant in Turkey originally appeared in Nicolas de Nicolay's *Les quartres premiers livres des navigations et peregrinations orientales* (Lyons: 1568) and was subsequently copied for use in many publications on Oriental costume and the Levant.[1]

In contrast to the tall hat worn by the doctor, a form of headgear favored by Sephardi Jews, this merchant wears the turban of a native Turkish Jew. Nicolay observed that Jews wore yellow turbans to distinguish them from their Muslim neighbors.[2]

1. Rubens, *Iconography*, 1981, nos. 2353, 2359.
2. See Rubens, *Jewish Costume*, p. 36.

E. D. B.

142

Feme Juife Courtiere, qui porte ces marchandises aux jeunes Dames turques qui ne peuvent sortir.
Türckische Juden oder Macklerin welche denen Jungen Türckischen Frauen die nicht aus gehen darffen Wahren zutragt.

142. Feme Juife Courtiere

Augsburg, first half of the eighteenth century
After a design by Philippe Simonneau (1685–after 1753)
Published by Jeremias Wolff (1663 [1673?]–1724)
Hand-colored etching on paper
Page: 13-3/8 × 8-1/2 in., 34.0 × 21.6 cm.
Plate: 11 3/4 × 7-1/2 in., 29.8 × 19.0 cm.
The Library of the Jewish Theological Seminary of America, New York

This copy of the *Femme Juive Courtière* (*Jewish Woman Broker*), which originally appeared in *Recueil de cent estampes représentant differentes Nations due Levant* with text by the Marquis de Ferriol, was published in Paris in 1714 (see no. 143).[1] In the version published in Augsburg the legend appears in both French and German:

> Feme Juife Courtiere, qui porte ces marchandises aux jeunes Dames turques qui ne peuvent sortir.
> Türckische Jüden oder Macklerin, welche denen Jungen Türckischen Frauen die nicht aus gehen darffen Wahgen zutragt.

> Turkish Jewess or broker, who brings merchandise to the young Turkish women who are not permitted to go out.

Jewish women in Istanbul sold goods to members of the Imperial harem and thus served as almost the only contacts the sultans' women had with the outside world. Despite their confinement, however, the rulers' favorites, and particularly their mothers, wielded considerable power. These women frequently employed Jewish saleswomen as their agents in political and financial transactions. The most famous of these brokers was Esther Kyra, the widow of Rabbi Elijah Handali, who lived in the sixteenth century during the reigns of Suleymān II the Magnificent (1520–1566), Selīm II (1566 to 1574), and Murād III (1574–1595). She had free access to the royal harem, where she sold jewels, cosmetics, and rich fabrics and generally made herself indispensable to the ladies. She won the favor of Sultan Murād III's mother, Nūr Banū, and of his preferred concubine, the Venetian Ṣāfya Baffo, both of whom had enormous influence. Through them Esther, in turn, exercised considerable influence in Imperial appointments and became involved in political affairs. Her power and wealth aroused jealousy, and she was

143

Femme Juive,
en habit de cérémonie

tails of the costume shown in this print, particularly the purple cloak and the headdress incorporating a flat metal plate:

> The elder mabble their heads in linen, with the knots hanging down behind. Others do wear high caps of plate, whereof some I have seen of beaten gold. They wear long quilted waistcoats with breeches underneath, in winter of cloth, in summer of linen; and over all when they stir abroad, loose gowns of purple flowing from the shoulders.[4]

1. Rubens, *Iconography*, 1981, no. 2374.
2. See Galanté, pp. 14–15, and Cecil Roth, *The House of Nasi: The Duke of Naxos* (Philadelphia: 1948), pp. 200–202.
3. R. Withers, "The Grand Signiors Seraglio," in *Purchas His Pilgrimes*, IX (Glasgow: 1905), pp. 346–347; quoted in A. Cohen, *An Anglo-Jewish Scrapbook 1600–1840: The Jew Through English Eyes* (London: 1943), p. 122.
4. R. Sandys, "A Relation of a Journey Begun in 1610, A.D.," in *Purchas His Pilgrimes*, VIII, p. 175; quoted in Cohen, pp. 121–122.

E. D. B.

eventually murdered by her enemies *c.* 1593; her fortune was confiscated.[2]

Robert Withers, an English traveler in Istanbul at the time, commented upon the activity of Jewish saleswomen in the royal harem:

> The Sultanas have leave of the king that certain Jewes women may at any time come into the seraglio unto them . . . and coming in under colour of teaching them some fine needlework, or show them secrets in making waters, oils and painting stuffs for their faces (having once made friendship with the eunuchs which keep the doors, by often bribing them), do make themselves by their crafty insinuation, so familiar with the king's women, that they rule them as they please, and do carry out anything to sell for them, or buy and bring in whatsoever the Sultanas shall have a will to. And hence it is, that all such Jewes women as frequent the seraglio do become very rich.[3]

An approximately contemporary description of a Turkish Jewish woman in Istanbul corroborates de-

143. Femme Juive, en Habit de Cérémonie (Jewish Woman in Ceremonial Dress)

Paris, 1714
Gérard Jean-Baptiste Scotin (1671–1716)
Hand-colored etching and engraving on paper
Plate: 14 × 9-3/4 in., 34.5 × 24.7 cm.
Sheet: 19-1/4 × 12-5/8 in., 48.9 × 32.0 cm.
The Jewish Museum, New York, JM 165-67

This print was first published as plate 64 in *Recueil de cent estampes représentant différentes Nations due Levant . . .* by M. de Ferriol, which appeared in Paris in 1714. A version of the image published in 1768 bears an inscription stating that the festive garb was specifically for the girl's marriage ceremony.[1] Her headdress, incorporating a copper plate, is similar to one depicted in a contemporary Dutch engraving (1719) of a Jewish woman in Smyrna (Izmir).[2]

Charles Marquis de Ferriol (1652?–1722) served King Louis XIV as ambassador to the Ottoman court

144

in Istanbul from 1699 to 1709.

1. Rubens, *Iconography*, 1981, no. 2378.
2. Rubens, *Jewish Costume*, fig. 46, after M. Guerdeville, *Atlas historique* (Amsterdam: 1719).

REFERENCE: Rubens, *Iconography*, 1981, no. 2372.

E. D. B.

144. Medal of Gracia Nasi the Younger

Ferrara, 1558
Pastorino di Giovan Michele de' Pastorini
(*c.* 1508–1592)
Bronze, cast
2-19/32 in. dm., 6.6 cm.
The Jewish Museum, New York, gift of the
Samuel and Daniel M. Friedenberg Collection,
FB 77

The legend on this uniface medal, enclosing the portrait of a young woman, reads נרציה נשיא ("Gracia Nasi") A.AE. XVIII (eighteen years of age). It is the first instance of a Hebrew inscription on a medal known to have been made for a Jewish patron. Gracia is seen in profile facing left, wearing a high-collared Renaissance dress with jewels adorning her throat and coiffure. She was the wife of Samuel (Moses) Nasi (d. 1569), brother of Joseph Nasi, Duke of Naxos. This medal may have been cast in honor of their marriage.

The image on the medal is occasionally mistakenly identified as a portrait of the sitter's famous aunt, Gracia Mendes Nasi (*c.* 1510–1569),[1] the Marrano heiress and businesswoman, patron of Jewish learning, and champion of her Jewish coreligionists. But this Gracia would no longer have been a young woman in 1558.

1. For example, *Encyclopaedia Judaica*, XII, col. 836. For the Mendes/Nasi family tree, see col. 838.

REFERENCES: Cecil Roth, *The House of Nasi: Doña Gracia* (Philadelphia: 1947), pp. 72, 200, n. 8; Daniel M. Friedenberg, *Jewish Medals From the Renaissance to the Fall of Napoleon (1503–1815)* (New York: 1970), pp. 44–46, 128–129.

E. D. B.

145. Sêfer Takkanot U-Shetarot

Belgrade, Venice, or Istanbul, late seventeenth or early eighteenth century
Copied by Moses b. Michael Hakohen
Ink on paper
8-1/16 × 6 × 1/2 in., 20.5 × 15.2 × 1.2 cm.
Collection of Dr. Joseph Hacker

This manuscript contains regulations, by-laws, and deeds of Jewish societies and guilds (of boatmen, musicians, merchants, and other professions). In the late seventeenth century the scribe Moses Hakohen served the community of Belgrade; at the beginning of the eighteenth century he was active in Venice. At some time during those periods, he copied communal and legal documents of Istanbul Jews into this volume as models for his work in Belgrade and Venice; he may have done so on a visit to the capital.

The documents reveal that as early as the seventeenth century Istanbul Jews were organized into guilds according to their professions. One regulation required all guild members to close their businesses and to attend the celebrations and funerals of other members. Moses also copied the by-laws of communal societies such as Benevolent Societies, Burial Societies and Societies for the Care of the Sick.

J. H.

146. Médecin Juif (Jewish Physician)

France, nineteenth century, after a sixteenth-century original
Lithograph on paper
12-1/2 × 8 in., 31.8 × 20.3 cm.
The Library of the Jewish Theological Seminary of America, New York

This widely reproduced image is based on a portrait of Moses Hamon (*c.* 1490–*c.* 1554),[1] physician to Sultan Suleymān the Magnificent (1520–1566), which was published in *Les quatres premiers livres des navigations . . . orientales* (Lyons: 1568) by Nicolas de Nicolay, a geographer who accompanied one of companied one of Henri II's embassies to Istanbul in 1551. The portraits appeared again in later editions of Nicolay's book and was included in several costume books issued in the following centuries.[2]

Moses Hamon was born into a distinguished Spanish family of physicians. Following expulsion from Spain in 1492, Moses' father, Joseph, along with some other Spanish Jews, accepted the invitation of Sultan Bāyezīd II (1481–1512) to settle in Turkey[3] and became a doctor at court. His son Moses in turn became physician to Sultan Suleymān and also exerted considerable influence on the politics of the Ottoman court.[4] He accompanied the Sultan on military campaigns. When he returned to Istanbul from the Persian campaign of 1534–1535, Hamon brought back with him the Jewish scholar Jacob b. Joseph Taovs, who translated the Pentateuch into Persian. In 1546 Hamon published Taovs' work as part of a polyglot Bible that also included an Aramaic translation by Onqelos and an Arabic translation by Saadia Gaon, as well as the Hebrew and Persian texts.

Medecin Juif

Among Hamon's other philanthropies in the area of Jewish learning was the establishment and maintenance of a *yeshivah* in Istanbul.

Hamon used his influence with the Sultan to intercede on behalf of fellow Jews. After charges of ritual murder had resulted in the execution of innocent Jews in Amasya, Hamon prevailed upon Sultan Suleymān to issue a *firman* (decree) late in 1553 or early in 1554,[5] in which it was commanded that, whenever a Jew in the Ottoman Empire was accused of murdering a Christian, the case was not to be tried by local authorities but was to be brought before the imperial court. Thanks to Hamon's influence, the Sultan also intervened on behalf of Doña Gracia Mendes (see no. 144) in her struggle to force the Venetian government to allow her to emigrate to Turkey with her considerable wealth intact.

Moses' son Joseph Hamon followed in his father's footsteps both as court physician and as champion of Jewish rights and scholarship. The Hamon family is an outstanding example of the Jewish contribution to medicine in Turkey and the important role such learned men played in Ottoman political and cultural life.

1. Uriel Heyd, "Moses Hamon, Chief Jewish Physician to Sultan Suleyman the Magnificent," *Oriens*, XVI (1963), pp. 164–165.
2. See, for example, Rubens, *Jewish Costume*, p. 36, fig. 33; and Rubens, *Iconography*, 1981, nos. 2352, 2356, 2357, 2358, and 2366.
3. See Galanté, p. 7.
4. See Heyd, pp. 153, 158 ff.
5. Ibid., p. 161.

E. D. B.

147. Exchange of Letters: Joseph the Physician and R. Samson Wertheimer

Istanbul and Jerusalem, 1712–1713
Ink on paper
8-3/4 × 13-1/8 in., 22.3 × 33.5 cm.
The Library of the Jewish Theological Seminary
of America, New York, 77890

These two leaves contain an exchange of letters dated 1712–1713 between R. Samson Wertheimer and Joseph, a royal physician at the Ottoman court. Wertheimer was a leading financier and banker under Leopold I, his son Joseph I, and Charles VI. According to contemporary accounts, Wertheimer was called the *Judenkaiser* (Jewish Emperor) and had ten imperial soldiers posted as sentinels in front of his home. This exchange concerns Joseph's efforts to procure funds for the Ashkenazi community of Jerusalem threatened by its heavy indebtedness to Muslim moneylenders. As part of his campaign on behalf of his Jerusalem coreligionists, Joseph appealed to Ottoman officials, asking them to act on behalf of the Jews and to effect a renegotiation of their debt. These efforts failed and the Ashkenazi community of Jerusalem was subsequently destroyed by local mobs.

J. H.

Religious and Intellectual Life Before 1750

The Jews of Istanbul, like other non-Muslims in Islamic lands, had an autonomous central organization, whose leaders directed internal affairs according to Jewish law and served as intercessors at the sultan's court. The larger Istanbul Jewish community consisted of numerous congregations organized according to the countries or cities of origin of their founding members. Through the sixteenth century the divisions among the main groups, the Romaniotes, Ashkenazim, and Sephardim, remained clear, as the continued printing of polyglot Bibles demonstrates. Gradually, however, these groups became assimilated to one another, and the Sephardim became the dominant force. There was also an influential community of Karaites, a group formed in the eighth century that rejected rabbinic Judaism and accepted a literal interpretation of the Bible.

Jewish life in many parts of the Near East and Europe was disrupted in 1665–1666 by widespread messianic expectations aroused by Shabbetai Zevi of Izmir (1626–1676). Drawing upon traditional apocalyptic tendencies in Judaism and upon kabbalistic mysticism, Shabbetai Zevi declared himself the Messiah and attracted many followers. The Ottoman authorities, alarmed by the revolutionary implications of the movement arrested him and persuaded him to forsake Judaism and to become a Muslim, which he did in 1666. Despite the apostasy of its

leader, Shabbatean messianism remained a viable movement, influencing Jewish life and literature until the end of the eighteenth century. In Istanbul, however, it was never as strong as in Salonika and Izmir.

Religious poetry flourished among the Sephardim, who enjoyed a rich heritage of Spanish Hebrew poetry dating from the ninth through the fifteenth centuries. The Sephardim had also developed a tradition of secular poetry, especially love poetry, which was not considered antithetical to religious values.

148. Polyglot Bible

Istanbul, 1547
Published by Eliezer ben Gershom Soncino
Ink on paper
21 × 11-5/8 in., 53.3 × 29.5 cm.
The Library of the Jewish Theological Seminary of America, New York

Each page of this Bible contains the Hebrew text flanked by translations into Greek and Ladino, which are referred to on the frontispiece as the languages most used by the Jews of Turkey. It also includes the Aramaic translation of Onqelos and the commentary of Rashi.

Greek was spoken by the Romaniot community, which was established under Byzantine rule. The Sephardim who immigrated in the fifteenth century spoke Ladino, Spanish with an admixture of words from Hebrew and other languages.

J. H.

149. Tiqqun Qeri'ah Lekol Lailah Veyom

Amsterdam, 1666
Pubished by Isaac b. David de Castro Taztes
Ink on paper
5 × 3 × 1 in., 12.7 × 7.6 × 2.5 cm.
The Library of the Jewish Theological Seminary of America, New York

This book of Shabbatean religious readings is remark-

able for a number of features. Published in the heyday of Shabbetai Ẓevi and his followers, the exhibited pages include a frontispiece in which Shabbetai Ẓevi himself is seated on a messianic throne adored by angels and guarded by lions. The year 5426 (1666) is rendered as a chronogram on the title page; it can be found in the verse "Behold I shall redeem my people" (Zach. 8:7). The date on the colophon is shocking: the year of the Redeemer (*moshia* [5426]), year one.

150. Sêfer Ḥemdat Yamim

Istanbul, 1735
Published by Jonah b. Jacob, 1735
Ink on paper
9-1/16 × 6-13/16 × 1-7/8 in., 23.0 × 17.3 × 4.7 cm.
The Library of the Jewish Theological Seminary of America, New York

This book, by an unknown author, though often misattributed to Nathan of Gaza, describes the Sabbath and festivals in light of kabbalistic practice. It has been called "one of the most beautiful and affecting works of Jewish literature" by the late Professor Gerschom Scholem. It follows the entire liturgical calendar, beginning with the Passover holliday.

M. S. C.

151. Pizmonim Uvaqqashot

Istanbul, c. 1642
Joseph b. Moses Ganso
Ink on paper
5-9/16 × 3-13/16 × 1-7/16 in., 14.1 × 9.7 × 3.6 cm.
The Library of the Jewish Theological Seminary of America, New York, Very Rare Collection
5750, Yaari 246

This copy of the poetic anthology *Pizmonim Uvaqqashot* is the only one known to have survived. Unfortunately, it lacks about twenty-one pages, which have been replaced by a section of manuscript. The anthology contains poems in praise of God, each one an acrostic based on the author's name. Ganso wrote the poems as prayers for his own and others' use. He was a rabbi in Bursa and the head of a *yeshivah* attended by prominent scholars.

M. S. C. & J. H.

A Jewish Home in Istanbul

Despite its generally tolerant attitude, the Ottoman government nevertheless imposed special taxes and restrictions on non-Muslims. in accordance with practices established between the seventh and ninth centuries. Among the restrictions were regulations on the forms and colors of clothing and the appearance of synagogues and houses. Jewish homes were often drab and shabby outwardly, while inside the rooms were comfortable, even luxurious, as can be learned from this description written in 1836:

> . . . nor did the appearance of the house itself, as we crossed a miserable yard into which it opened, tend to give us a very favourable idea of the establishment. The window-shutters were swinging in the wind upon their rusty hinges . . . the path to the house was choked with rubbish; and the timber of which it was built was blackened both by time and fire. The first flight of stairs that we ascended, together with the rooms on the ground-floor, were quite in keeping with the exterior of the dwelling; but when we reached the foot of the second, we appeared to have been suddenly acted upon by magic; the steps were neatly matted, the walls were dazzlingly white, and at the entrance of the vast *salle* into which the several apartments opened, lay a handsome Persian carpet. . . . The courtesy and hospitality of the whole family was extreme.[1]

The reference to fire-blackened timbers underscores a real and constant danger facing the Jewish community. Fires were often deliberately set and economically motivated. As a result of frequent fires, the original neighborhoods settlements based on separate countries and cities of origin began to break down, and the Jews of Istanbul eventually became a more homogenous community.

1. S. Pardue, *The City of the Sultan and Domestic Manners of the Turks in 1836*, II, 1837, pp. 368f.

152. Two Cushion Covers

Probably Bursa, eighteenth or nineteenth century
Silk, embroidered with gilt metallic threads
20 × 16-7/8 in., 50.9 × 42.9 cm.
The Jewish Museum, New York, on permanent loan from the Leonard Stern collection

An overall pattern of large carnations flanked by buds is executed in dense gold embroidery on these rose-colored covers. The flowers are arranged in three staggered rows; at each end of the middle row only half the carnation motif was embroidered, as is clear from the space remaining at left between the half flower and the gold band that borders the embroidered field. The resulting composition reflects the preference in Muslim textile design for an infinite pattern, rather than a self-contained one, and the interlocking ogival forms of the flowers also appear on Ottoman silks from the sixteenth century onwards.

The quality and density of the embroidery are characteristic of textiles produced in Istanbul and Bursa for the sultan's court. From these centers textiles like this one were shipped to other Ottoman cities like Izmir and Ionnina.[1] These cushion covers once belonged to the same family as those numbered 153 in the exhibition.

1. *Cf.* Juhasz, no. 32.

V. B. M.

153. Three Cushion Covers

Turkey, nineteenth century
Velvet, embroidered with gilt metallic thread
a, b: 16-1/2 × 21-1/2 in., 42.0 × 54.6 cm.; c: 16-1/2 × 37-3/4 in., 42.0 × 95.9 cm.
The Jewish Museum, New York, on permanent loan from the Leonard Stern collection

153

These three matching cushion covers are all of purple velvet embroidered in gold with identical motifs: a large central medallion surrounded by symmetrical sprays of flowers and leaves and a running border of flowering vines. Isolated sprigs of flowers float in the spaces between the medallion and the border.

The homes of Turkish Jews were quite similar to those of their Muslim and Christian neighbors. A common feature was the long couch (*meldar* in Ladino (furnished with cushions in embroidered covers (*yastik* in Turkish). The couch was the focus of receptions and the setting for important events in the life of the Ottoman Jewish family, like the *meldado*, the annual service in memory of a deceased father.

The owner's family came from Ioannina, a city in western Greece that belonged to Turkey in the nineteenth century. Some members of the family served as local representatives of the sultan. These covers may be of local work, or they may have been imported from the Turkish mainland.

V. B. M.

154. Spoon Holder

Turkey, late nineteenth century
Marks: illegible *ṭughrā*s
Silver, cast, repoussé, ajouré
5-1/16 × 4-7/8 in. dm., 12.8 × 12.4 cm.
Collection of Mr. and Mrs. Ivan Schick

The holder is in the form of a fluted urn supported by a short stem and a base consisting of a series of lobes and scrolls in openwork. A row of cast palmettes masks this base, and two scroll handles are affixed to its sides.

For the use of the holder, see no. 155.

V. B. M.

155. Dish for Sweets, with Six Spoons

Turkey, 1876–1909
Mark: *ṭughrā*s, probably of ʿAbd al-Ḥamīd II (1876–1909)
Silver, spun and stamped
Dish, 1 × 6-5/8 in., 2.5 × 16.8 cm.
Spoons, 6-3/8 × 1-1/8 in., 16.2 × 2.8 cm.
Collection of Mr. and Mrs. Joseph Kattan

155

The dish is shallow, with a highly polished surface. Along the exterior, just below a beaded rim, is a band of stamped zigzags enclosing palmettes. The center of the interior is decorated with concentric circles and wavy lines similar to those on a *rimmon* (no. 204) dating from the same period.

The shaft of each spoon handle is stamped with wavy lines and lozenges. Near the scalloped end is a circular band of small zigzags framing a space for the monogram of the owner; these spoons, however, have not been engraved.

The offering of sweets to guests was a prominent feature of Jewish and Christian hospitality in Turkey. A complete service included a tray (*tavla de dulsi* or *tavla d'adulsar* in Ladino) with dishes for the sweets, a holder with spoons (see no. 154) and glasses for water.[1] The neoclassical ornament on the exterior of the dish exhibited was not confined to domestic silver but occurred also on objects for liturgical use (see no. 211).

1. For related examples from Izmir, see E.S. Juhasz, "The Custom of Serving Sweets Among the Jews of Izmir," *Israel Museum News*, XV (1979), 72–79.

V. B. M.

156. Coffee Pot and Brazier

Istanbul, nineteenth century
Christos Jean Hoshossis
Brass, cast; copper, tin, and wood
Pot: 4-1/4 × 3-1/2 in. (handle 8 in.), 10.7 × 8.9 cm. (handle 20.2 cm.)
Brazier: 5 × 5-1/8 in. (handle 4-1/2 in.), 12.7 × 13.0 cm. (handle 10.7 cm.)
Collection of Mr. and Mrs. Ivan Schick

The body of the brazier is a cylinder set on a stepped base; a cap at the top allows for the insertion of fuel. Another cylinder on a stepped base, set in the center, holds the wick. From the top of the fuel container three poles, topped by flat, arrow-shaped planes, rise to form a stand for the pot. Between two of the poles is stamped "Christos Jean Hoshossis/Bosphore (Arnaout-Keuy)." The coffee pot is a cylindrical form, the base of which flares outward; the lip is extended on one side to form a spout. Four lightly incised lines encircle the midsection of the pot, and the interior is tinned. The long, thin handle is held in place by three studs.

V. B. M.

157. Coffee Grinder

Turkey, 1922 or later
Brass, cast, stamped, and engraved; steel
12 × 2 in., 30.5 × 5.1 cm.
Collection of Mr. and Mrs. Ivan Schick

This brass grinder is made in sections that are turned by a handle, which fits over a steel rod running the length of the cylindrical form. Bands of stamped motifs and engraved lines around the circumference of the grinder are its only decoration. A stamp (a star and crescent inscribed "5 recep/garantı 5") appears on one side. 5 Recep is a date, fifth of the month of Rajab. Turkish was first written in Latin characters in 1922, which indicates that the grinder dates from that year or later.

V. B. M.

158. Two Coffee Cups with Holders

Turkey, late nineteenth century
Mark: illegible ṭughrās
Silver, spun and stamped; porcelain
Cup: 1-5/16 × 2-3/16 in., 4.0 × 5.5 cm.
Holders: 2-1/4 × 1-7/8 in., 5.6 × 4.7 cm.
Collection of Mr. and Mrs. Ivan Schick

The silver cup holders are conical in shape and supported by stems with flaring bases. Rows of beading decorate the rim and the edge of the base. A band of lozenges enclosing circles is stamped below the border. The porcelain cups are decorated on the interiors with single continuous flowering vines in red, blue, green, and orange placed just below the gilt rims.

V. B. M.

159. Eyeglasses and Case

Istanbul, nineteenth century
Copper; glass; leather
Glasses: 1-5/8 × 4 in., 4.1 × 10.2 cm.
Case: 2 × 4-3/8 in., 5.1 × 11.1 cm.
Collection of Mr. and Mrs. Ivan Schick

The leather case for the glasses is stamped:

Gr. Anestides/Opticien/Pera–Stamboul.

A Jew wearing such glasses is depicted in "Jewish Cemetery in Istanbul," no. 39.

V. B. M.

160. Spice Container

Turkey, nineteenth century
Marks: illegible ṭughrās
Silver: cast, ajouré, engraved, parcel-gilt
5-1/4 × 5-5/16 × 4-15/16 in., 13.3 × 13.5 × 12.6 cm.
The Jewish Museum, New York, gift of Dr. Harry G. Friedman, F 4072

Two containers in the shape of pine cones, rising from stems attached to a leafy base, held aromatic spices. The upper half of each fruit is hinged, so that it may be opened to allow the aroma of the spices to escape.

The workmanship of this object shows a concern

160

for naturalism: The fruits tilt as if blown by the wind, and their surfaces and those of the leaves are textured to resemble natural forms. The naturalistic depiction of fruits and flowers was one characteristic of Turkish art; it can also be seen in embroideries, where the color and form of the flora are so specific as to make possible the identification of individual species (see nos. 196 and 199). Turkish weavers working in Poland during the eighteenth century introduced such forms to Polish art.[1] A parallel influence from Turkish metalwork may explain the reproduction of similar spice boxes in Eastern Europe during the nineteenth century.[2] However the similarity between the forms of this container and works of known Turkish provenance (for example, the finial of no. 206), as well as the *tughrā* stamps, suggests that this spice box was made in the Ottoman Empire. A similar container is in the Hechal Shlomo Museum, Jerusalem.[3]

1. See *Danzig, 1939*, no. 57, and *Fabric of Jewish Life*, no. 48, for Jewish textiles produced in Poland that show Turkish influence in their naturalistic floral motifs.
2. Cf. Kayser-Schoenberger, nos. 92–93.
3. Bialer, *Jewish Life*, p. 132, where it is dated to the sixteenth or seventeenth century.

161. Ewer and Basin Used on Passover (See color plate, p. 16)

Istanbul, early nineteenth century
Copper, gilt, repoussé, punched, and engraved
Ewer: 12-3/4 × 8-1/2 in., 32.4 × 21.6 cm.
Basin: 14-1/2 in. dm. × 4 7/8 in., 36.8 × 12.3 cm.
The Jewish Museum, New York, the H. Ephraim and Mordecai Benguiat Family Collection, S 77a-c

The body of the ewer is bulbous in form, tapering to a narrow neck. The curve of the body is echoed in that of the spout. The scroll-shaped handle is soldered on opposite the spout; to it is hinged the dome-shaped cover with acorn finial. The body, the lid, and most of the spout are engraved with a diagonal repeat design of serpentine trees growing on a hillock edged at the top with scrolls. These smooth, highly polished forms stand out from a stippled ground. The same design covers the upper surface and drain of the basin. Punched holes in the minor tree branches of the drain allow for the flow of water.

The basin itself is deep, with a wide, almost horizontal rim. The drain, which rests on a projecting ledge on the interior below the rim, is convex; a small dish with scalloped edges is affixed to its apex. The following inscription is engraved in Ottoman characters, once on the ewer handle, once on the upper surface of the basin:

Aḥmad Pāshā Karīm ibn Sharīf Zuleyha [?], A.H., [1]266 [1850]

This set is an excellent example of *tombak* ware, gilt copper vessels that were popular among Ottomans in the sixteenth and seventeenth centuries. The closest published parallel is an ewer of that period that is decorated with contemporaneous textile design, similarly polished and set on a stippled ground.[1] Thus the set may have been made earlier than the date of the inscriptions, which must be regarded as marks of ownership, since its form resembles that of earlier nineteenth-century ewers. Sometime after 1850 the set came into the possession of the Benguiat family, who used it at the Passover *seder*.

1. Y. Petsopoulos, ed., *Tulips, Arabesques and Turbans* (London: 1982), no. 34.

REFERENCES: Adler and Casanowicz, 1901, p. 555, no. 29, pl. 16; 1908, pp. 719–720, no. 77, pl. 83.

162. Towel

Turkey, 1700–1750
Linen, embroidered with polychrome silk and metallic threads
78-1/2 × 9-1/2 in., 199.3 × 24.1 cm.
The Jewish Museum, New York, JM 44-73

At each end of the towel is a narrow border strip of metallic threads. The main decoration is a symmetrical representation of a vase containing flowers and budding branches that curve outward to the full width of the cloth. The colors used are silver, pink (or red, now faded), blue, green, and beige.

In embroidery technique and style, this towel resembles early eighteenth-century examples in Swedish collections that are dated on the basis of documentary evidence. The serrated leaves and twill technique imitating darning can also be seen on a

141

flowers growing from thick stems constitute the major decoration of the lower field. Birds fill some of the spaces between them. The upper field is bordered on only three sides. A large Star of David enclosing a five-branched lampstand is in the center; two floral sprays fill the lower corners.

Similar compositions, consisting of three large floral elements in a compartment framed by a border of smaller flowers, occur on two Turkish saddle cloths (shabraks) presented to King Gustavus Adolphus of Sweden in 1626. (The silver portions of the saddle fittings bear Constantinopolitan marks.) Furthermore, the flowers on one of the shabraks are executed in the "checkerboard" stitch also found on the cushion cover.[1] The use of tinsel on the cushion cover, however, and the less densely embroidered composition suggest a somewhat later date than that of the saddle fittings. A striking feature of the cushion cover is the incorporation of a Star of David and the prominent place accorded to it in the decorative scheme. These factors suggest that it was originally made for a liturgical purpose, perhaps for carrying an infant to the synagogue for circumcision,[2] or for use at a Passover *seder*.[3]

1. Geijer, *Oriental Textiles*, nos. 104 and 105, pls. 44 and 5.
2. M. Angel, *The Jews of Rhodes*,(New York: 1978), p. 118.
3. L.A. Frankl, "Nach Jerusalem," *The Jews in the East I*, trans. P. Beaton (London: 1859), p. 122. I am indebted to N. and Y. Stillman for this reference.

V. B. M.

towel bearing the date 1788 and the monogram of Gustav Celsing, who lived in Istanbul *c.* 1745–1750.[1]

It was customary for young girls in Turkey to embroider household and personal linen for their trousseaus.

1. Geijer, *Oriental Textiles*, no. 69.

V. B. M.

163. Cushion Cover (See color plate, p. 15)

Istanbul, late seventeenth or early eighteenth century
Silk, embroidered with metallic threads; metallic braid
19 × 21-3/4 in., 48.2 × 55.2 cm.
The Jewish Museum, New York, gift of Dr. Harry G. Friedman, F 5465

The front surface of this rose silk cushion cover is divided into two horizontal fields bordered by bands filled with series of discrete flowers. Three large

164. Sêder Haggadah shel Pesah

Istanbul, 1823
Published by Judah Yerushalmi
Ink on paper
7 × 4-11/16 × 7/16 in., 17.8 × 11.9 × 1.1 cm.
The Library of the Jewish Theological Seminary of America, New York

The regular text of the *Haggadah* is supplemented in this edition by kabbalistic prayers and special poems composed for each section of the *seder*. A Ladino translation of the entire text is included.

M. S. C.

165. Curtains

Turkey, nineteenth century
Linen, embroidered; cotton, crocheted
35-1/4 × 25-1/2 in., 89.5 × 64.8 cm.
Collection of Mr. and Mrs. Ivan Schick

Each of the curtains is composed of two pieces of white linen decorated with eyelet embroidery. The pieces are joined together by a panel of crocheted ogival medallions enclosing flowers. Crocheted borders surround each whole curtain, and tassles have been added to the bottom border. The eyelet design on each panel consists of a branch with two flowers, repeated twice, and a stylized medallion.

V. B. M.

166. Portable Food Container

Turkey, nineteenth century
Copper and brass, lined with tin, cast, incised, and punched
15-3/16 × 7-1/8 in. dm., 38.5 × 18.1 cm.
Collection of Mr. and Mrs. Ivan Schick

This five-part container consists of a lower brass dish and four copper ones arranged one above the other. There is also a copper lid to which are soldered two hooks for suspending the bars that hold the parts together. At the lower end the bars are held by tongue-and-groove fasteners attached to the brass dish. A handle for carrying is affixed to the lid. The copper dishes are distinguished by different numbers of leaves engraved in single rows on one side. On the opposite side of each dish is a single engraved bud.

Such containers were used to carry food to the men of the household while they were at work.

V. B. M.

167. Walking Stick

Istanbul, c. 1870
Wood, inlaid with mother-of-pearl; brass
36-1/4 in., 92.1 cm.
Collection of Mr. and Mrs. Ivan Schick

An overall pattern of lozenge-shaped pieces of mother-of-pearl covers the wooden grip. Below it are rows of inlaid pendant leaves. The remainder of the stick is decorated with two criss-crossing bands of mother-of-pearl outlining reserved lozenges. The ferrule is of brass.

The use of mother-of-pearl inlays on wooden objects was common in Istanbul during the nineteenth century. In many synagogues rebuilt during that period, for example, the Ohrid synagogue, mother-of-pearl inlays were used to decorate the ark and the *bimah.* The nineteenth-century Sephardi custom of carrying walking sticks, even on the Sabbath when that type of work was forbidden, occasioned the criticism of Ashkenazim whose religious observance was more stringent[1]

1. N. Stillman, *The Jews of Arab Lands* (Philadelphia: 1979), p. 335.

Communal Organization 1750–1870

At the beginning of Ottoman rule, the Jewish population of Istanbul was organized into congregations according to their members' places of origin. Although a variety of factors, including intermarrriage and mobility among neighborhoods in the city, led to mixing of the groups, individuals still paid taxes according to their original congregations, which bore names like Córdoba, Portugal, Sicily, Ohrid, and Salonika. In complete contrast to the ghettoized Jewish populations of European cities like Frankfurt, the Jews of Istanbul lived among Muslim and Christian neighbors in many quarters scattered through the city and its suburbs.

The Jews in each quarter (*mahalle*) had their own communal institutions, for example, rabbinical courts and schools, and their own budget. In addition, there were centralized bodies, serving the entire Jewish population: a high court, a council (*maamad*), and committees like the *Va'ad Pekidei Kushta* (Istanbul Committee for Palestinian Jewry), which had far-reaching powers. In times of fiscal crisis, however, as in the second half of the eighteenth century, individual communities reasserted control over a variety of functions ordinarily handled by the centralized bodies. There was no *hakham bashi* (chief rabbi) until the appointment of Rabbi

143

Abraham Ha-Levi in 1835; from then on he and his successors served formally as chief intercessors with the government on behalf of the Jewish community.

168. Map of Istanbul

England, 1840
B.R. Davies, after a design by J. J. Hellert
Published by the Society for the Diffusion of Useful Knowledge
Etching and watercolor on paper
12-3/4 × 15-3/4 in., 32.3 × 40.0 cm.
Collection of Mr. and Mrs. Ivan Schick

169. Mishnat Rabbi Eliezer

Salonika, 1853
Published by Saadi Hallevi Ashkenazi
Ink on paper
12-3/4 × 7-15/16 × 1-1/4 in., 32.4 × 20.2 × 3.2 cm.
The Library of the Jewish Theological Seminary of America, New York

This volume of contemporary *responsa* reflects Jewish life in the Ottoman empire in the mid-nineteenth century and specifically life in Istanbul. The author was concerned about the prevalent laxity in maintaining ancient communal customs and standards. He wrote ". . . now that the customs are overturned, as shall be demonstrated, and because this is an absolutely urgent matter, I shall direct myself to collect and gather all the customs . . . into one tent," so that they may be preserved for future generations. The volume contains an extremely valuable list of all the Jewish communities of Istanbul.

M. S. C.

170. Documents of Istanbul Rabbinical Court

Istanbul, eighteenth century
Ink on paper
11-1/2 × 8-1/4 in., 29.2 × 20.9 cm.
The Library of the Jewish Theological Seminary of America, New York, Mic. 3149

This volume contains sample legal documents, all written at the rabbinical courts of Istanbul, many of them at the court of the Balat quarter. They touch on many aspects of everyday life, including social customs, business regulations, and the appearance of houses. These copies were made for use by a scribe and served him as models.

J. H.

171. Pinqas Pekidei Kushta

Istanbul, eighteenth century
Ink on paper
13-1/2 × 18-1/2 in., 33.5 × 20.7 cm.
The Library of the Jewish Theological Seminary of America, New York, 4008

This manuscript is concrete evidence of the powerful role played by Istanbul Jews in the government of the Palestinian community. It contains the texts of hundreds of letters written by or to the Istanbul Board of Governors of Palestinian Jewry, one of the most important organizatons among Istanbul Jews. The manuscript includes decisions and orders sent by the Board to Palestine from the second decade through the end of the eighteenth century. The Board was also responsible for the disbursal of funds in Palestine, for the appointment of community leaders there, for the regulation of Jewish visitors in Palestine, and for many other similar matters.

Most of the letters are written in Ladino, but a significant number are in Hebrew.

J. H.

Relations with the Ottoman Government

Until the mid-nineteenth century the legal position of the Jewish community under the Ottomans was that of a protected minority. Relations with the government were generally good, though Jews were subject to discriminatory legislation in various aspects of life, including dress, the building of homes and synagogues, and taxation. Because they lived in the capital, the Jews of Istanbul often served as agents and intercessors for Jews residing elsewhere in the Ottoman Empire.

The decline of the Imperial power in the seventeenth century resulted in a general worsening of social and economic conditions, accompanied by excessive taxation and administrative abuses. Many residents of Istanbul, including Jews, sought protection from foreign embassies. Not until 1839 was the legal status of Ottoman minorities improved, through the first of two important Imperial decrees; the second, issued in 1856, declared non-Muslims to be equal citizens.

172. Medal Commemorating Journey of Sir Moses Montefiore and Isaac Adolphe Crémieux to Stop Measures Against the Jews of Damascus

Berlin, 1840
Artist: GNR
Silver, cast
1-5/8 in. dm., 4.2 cm.
The Jewish Museum, New York, gift of the Samuel and Daniel M. Friedenberg Collection, FB 802

On the obverse Sir Moses Montefiore and Isaac Adolphe Crémieux are depicted in audience with Sultan 'Abd al-Majīd. A turbaned Ottoman official is also in attendance. The group stands on a tiled floor before a collonnade; the sultan's plush chair is at the left. The inscription reads:

Mos. Montefiore u. Ad. Crémieux in Damascus. 1840. ת"ר
Mos[es] Montefiore a[nd] Ad[olphe] Crémieux in Damascus. 1840. [5]600.

prisoners in Damascus. Muḥammad ʿAlī refused, however, to reopen the investigation or to exonerate the Jews officially. The delegation then proceeded to Istanbul and appealed to Sultan ʿAbd al-Majīd, who issued a *firman* (decree) denouncing blood libels and prohibiting the accusation of Jews of such "crimes" (see no. 173).

REFERENCES: *Encyclopaedia Judaica,* V, col. 1250; *Coins Reveal,* no. 128.

E. D. B.

The inscription on the reverse reads:

> Die Redlichen sehen es und freuen sich und alle Bosheit schliesst den Mund/ wer doch weise waere dass er dies merkte u. dass sie einsaehen die Huld des Ewigen/ Ps. 107 v. 42, 43.
> The upright see it and are glad, and all iniquity stoppeth her mouth/ Whoso is wise, let him observe these things, a[nd] let them consider the mercies of the Lord. Ps. 107 v. 42, 43.

The audience actually took place in Istanbul, but the purpose was to resolve the infamous blood libel known as the "Damascus affair." An Italian Capuchin friar and his Muslim servant disappeared in Damascus on February 5, 1840. The French consul in Damascus, Ratti-Mentan, turned the matter over to Muslim officials and suggested that the Jews had murdered the two men in order to use their blood for the coming Passover. A Jewish barber was arrested and tortured until he "confessed," implicating seven prominent members of the community. They, in turn, were arrested and tortured. Two of the Jews died, one converted to Islam, and the others "confessed." Meanwhile sixty-three Jewish children were taken hostage, and the Jewish community suffered further violence at the hands of a mob.

When news of these atrocities reached Europe and the United States, the incident became a *cause célèbre.* In August 1840 Sir Moses Montefiore and Crémieux headed a delegation that traveled to Alexandria to meet with Muḥammad ʿAlī, governor of Egypt and Syria, and to plead the cause of the Jews. With the support of all the foreign consuls in Alexandria, except the French, they secured the release of the

173. Firman

Istanbul, July 11, 1866
ʾAbd al-ʾAziz
Photograph of document
Courtesy of the Jewish Community of Istanbul

This *firman*, or official decree, was issued by the Ottoman Sultan ʾAbd al-ʾAziz on July 11, 1866 (27 Safar, 1283) at Istanbul. Written in ponderous official language, it renews earlier guarantees of protection against the violence that periodically erupted over the rumor that Jews mixed human blood into unleavened bread for the feast of Passover.

The Hahambaşi Qāymaqām of the Jewish community had requested the renewal, and the Sultan's response was framed in careful legal terms: ". . . In reference to the records, according to expert investigations of the religious books of the aforementioned community and to the customary legal inquiry into the findings, in this fashion the truth appeared: Not only is human blood totally forbidden to the aforesaid community but even use of the blood of other animals is prohibited. . . ."

The *firman* goes on to reaffirm that members of the Jewish community were to be considered full-fledged citizens of the Empire with exactly the same privileges and obligations as other citizens.

The minority communities of the Ottoman Empire in the nineteenth century, however, generally resisted government attempts to integrate them into the polity, for equality carried with it the obligation of military service.

Estelle Whelan

174. Document of Appointment

Istanbul, 1762
Ink on paper
17-15/16 × 13-1/8 in., 44.0 × 33.3 cm.
The Library of the Jewish Theological Seminary
of America, New York, acc. no. 77890

This printed document announces the appointment of the scholar, Rabbi Hayyim Modai, as an emissary of the Istanbul committee concerned with the affairs of Safed, Palestine. It recounts the suffering of the Jews of Safed and their need for outside assistance. Their troubles included unbearable taxation, disease, the earthquake of 1760, torrential rains, and forced deportation by the local authorities to Akka (Acre). The letter continues: ". . . Therefore, we have decided that this might be a propitious time to send emissaries to all our brethren residing in the Diaspora, that they might take mercy upon us and revive a great number of people. . . ." This letter was printed, and copies were sent out to members of the Jewish community in Istanbul; the name of each addressee was inserted at the top of the page in a prepared salutation. This copy was sent to Abraham de Zevulon Galicci, whose name and address also appear on the reverse, so that it would show on the outside when the page was folded.

M. S. C.

175. Shiviti

Istanbul, 1753
Moses Ganbash
Paint, ink, and collage elements on paper
34-1/4 × 42-3/16 in., 87.0 × 107.2 cm.
The Jewish Museum, New York, gift of Dr. Harry
G. Friedman, F 5855

This unusual shiviti is in the form of a panoramic map of Palestine. The viewer's orientation is from west to east, with the Mediterranean Sea in the foreground and the Dead Sea at the top right. All major cities and biblical sites are labeled in Hebrew, with most prominence given to Jersualem (at right center) and Safed (at left center). Only these two cities are designated "holy city," with their names and titles in large letters. Most of the center section is executed in paint and ink, but the ground lines are cut from textured paper. On the inner border around the map is a brief poetic enumeration of the sites depicted. Centered at the top of the outer border is the sentence:

שויתי ה' (אדני) לנגדי תמיד

I have set the Lord always before me.
(Ps. 16:8)

On either side a grape vine grows from a footed urn. The same motif is repeated in the side borders but arranged in a vertical format below a framed amuletic adjuration text that begins on the right border and continues on the left. Each of the two urns in the field rests on the central pillar of an elaborate fence. Below it is a diagram of Jericho inscribed:

ויריחו סגרת ומסגרת

Now Jericho was straightly shut
up. . . . (Josh. 6:1)

The artist's signature appears on an ornamental building in the lower right hand corner:

הכותב / הצעיר משה גאנבאש / היו /
ניכתב בקושטה יע"א

The scribe . . . Moses Ganbash . . . written in Istanbul.

The same building form in the lower left corner is inscribed with the date, written as a chronogram:

בשנת / קוה אל ה' חזק / ויאמץ לבך וקוה... לפ"ק

In the year wait for the Lord; be strong and

let thy heart take courage; yea wait. . . .
(Ps. 27:14)

The map depicted on this *shiviti* is an elaborate example of a type of panoramic map popular in the nineteenth century. The earliest known example dates from 1837 and is hand-drawn, as is the present example. Later in the nineteenth century similar maps were printed in Germany and Poland. All were intended to remind the viewer of important places and holy sites mentioned in the Bible. Ganbash's work is more elaborate than the three other published examples and the only one to have been incorporated into a *shiviti*.

REFERENCES: Jerusalem, Israel Museum, *Art and Handicraft in Eretz-Israel in the Nineteenth Century* (in Hebrew) (Jerusalem: 1979), pp. 146–150; Shachar, *Jewish Tradition in Art*, no. 494; Z. Vilnay, *The Hebrew Maps of the Holy Land* (in Hebrew) (Jerusalem: 1968), pp. 32–33.

Economic Activity 1750–1870

Most of the economic endeavors and occupations pursued by Jews in Istanbul were traditional ones in which they had been active for centuries. A small proportion were bankers, moneylenders, mercantile agents, and physicians. Most, however, were peddlers and artisans. Jews predominated in the crafts of tin smelting, refining, tailoring, and parchment making. Most of the pearl merchants were Jews, and there were many Jewish manufacturers of cloth. Jews were also boatmen, water carriers, jewelers, shopkeepers of various kinds, and tinkers. Only a few Istanbul Jews in this period were wealthy; most were quite poor.

176. Marchand Juif à Constantinople (Jewish Merchant in Constantinople)

Paris, 1842
Camille Rogier
Hand-colored lithograph on paper
17-7/8 × 12-7/8 in., 45.4 × 32.7 cm.
The Library of the Jewish Theological Seminary of America

This lithograph is one of the illustrations (plate 8) from the section on Ottoman costume in *Galerie royale de costumes*, published in Paris in 1842. The merchant wears a long robe (*entārī*) of striped silk covered by a dark green cloak (*jubba*) (see the rabbi's costume no. 188). A broad black sash is wrapped around his waist. His stockings (*mest*) and slippers (*pābūj*) were mentioned as traditional features of Jewish dress by Thévenot in the seventeenth century,[1] and similar ones can be seen in Hamdy-Bey's photograph of the Ḥakham (Chief Rabbi) of Smyrna (Izmir) in 1873.[2] The headdress, called a *kaveze*, resembles one worn by a Turkish Jew in Bursa photographed by Hamdy-Bey in 1873. The *kaveze* has been described as follows: "a high crown of cardboard covered with a black material around which is rolled a piece of light-colour cotton."[3]

Camille Rogier[4] was a painter, engraver, and lithographer who worked in Paris. Between 1833 and 1848 he exhibited at the Salon, showing several drawings, watercolors, and lithographs of scenes and costume studies from his trip to the Orient.

1. M. de Thévenot, *Voyages* (Amsterdam: 1727), p. 264, cited in Rubens, *Jewish Costume*, p. 33.
2. Rubens, *Jewish Costume*, fig. 48, from Hamdy-Bey and M. de Launay, *Les costumes populaires de la Turquie en 1873* (Constantinople, 1873).
3. Rubens, *Jewish Costume*, fig. 52.
4. Dates unknown.

REFERENCE: Rubens, *Iconography*, 1981, no. 2413.

E. D. B.

177. Jewish Merchant

New York, 1862
C. Parsons, after a drawing by H. J. Van Lennep
Color lithograph on paper
18 × 13 3/16 in., 45.7 × 33.5 cm.
The Jewish Museum, New York, gift of the Dr. Harry G. Friedman, F 4182

This plate is taken from the same book as "Jewish Marriage" (see no. 184).[1] The author, Reverend Henry J. Van Lennep, an American missionary, identified the subject as "a Jewish gentleman of considerable property, Mordecai by name . . . who was born in Persia, but has long been settled in Turkey."[2]

Mordecai smokes a water pipe. Behind him a servant stands with a coffee pot and cup similar to nos. 156 and 158.

The lithographer who executed Van Lennep's drawing may have been Charles Parsons (1821–1910), an English artist who worked for many years in New York.

1. H. J. Van Lennep, *The Oriental Album* (New York: 1862).
2. In Rubens, *Iconography*, 1981, no. 2424.

REFERENCE: Rubens, *Iconography*, 1981, no. 2424.

E. D. B.

178. Juif/Jew

Europe, nineteenth century
Hand-colored lithograph on paper
9-1/8 × 6 in., 23.2 × 15.3 cm.
The Jewish Museum, New York, gift of Dr. Harry G. Friedman, F 5877

The Jewish man depicted in this print was probably a scribe. He carries tucked into his sash a metal pencase and inkwell of the same type as an example included in this exhibition (see no. 179). In his hand he holds a *çubūq*, a pipe generally between four and five feet long. The greater part of the stem is covered in silk and the bowl is made of baked earth. The *çubūq* and the water pipe (see no. 177) were the two most common ways of taking tobacco in the Ottoman Empire.

E. D. B.

179

178

179. Pencase and Inkwell

Turkey, 1861–1877
Marks: *ṭughrā* of 'Abd al-'Azīz (1861–1877); *ṣaḥ*
Silver, cast and engraved
10 × 2-1/4 in., 25.4 × 5.2 cm.
The Jewish Museum, New York, gift of Dr. Harry G. Friedman, F 3413

The quill container is a rectangular box with beveled edges whose decoration is confined to the caps affixed to the two ends. They are engraved with bands of foliate motifs that make an effective contrast with the smoothly polished surface of the container. One cap is hinged in the center to provide an opening; there is also a ring by which the pencase could be suspended from the scribe's belt. The attached inkwell is in the form of a small, bulbous chest with beveled edges, which are decorated with similar

150

bands of foliage accentuating the form and covering the bottom. Inset into the top of the chest is a hinged lid. This object has been stamped several times with the ṭughrā of Sultan 'Abd al-Azīz.

Although no inscription links this container with a Jewish owner, documents like the print *Juif/Jew* (see no. 178) show that such apparatus was used by Jewish scribes. These scribes worked not only for the Jewish community but also for Muslim Turks. On some occasions in the sixteenth and seventeenth centuries, when Jews served the Ottoman government as diplomats, treaties negotiated between the Ottoman Empire and foreign powers were written in Hebrew.[1]

A similar pencase was recently sold in Paris.[2]

1. See Galanté, p. 12.
2. *Arts Islamic*, Sales Catalogue, Nouveau Drouot, Paris, June 23, 1982, no. A.

Jewish Education

In the late fifteenth and sixteenth centuries many famous rabbis lived in Istanbul, and the city boasted Hebrew presses that printed important works of Jewish scholarship. Scholarly rabbis and significant traditional schools were still characteristic of Istanbul through the nineteenth century. But by the eighteenth century knowledge of Hebrew and traditional learning had declined among the general Jewish population, most of whom spoke Ladino, a language based on Castilian but including many Hebrew and foreign loan words. To fill the need for a literature that could educate the masses about their Jewish heritage, Rabbi Moshe Culi (1685–1732) began the *Me'am Lo'ez*, a multivolume compendium of Jewish lore organized in accordance with the weekly Torah readings in the synagogues. Rabbi Culi died before completing the second volume, and his work was taken up by other scholars. *Me'am Lo'ez* became extremely popular, and readings from it were a feature of many family and religious celebrations. The continued vitality of Ladino coupled with the decline in knowledge of Hebrew also led to the development in the nineteenth century of a rich secular and romantic literature in Ladino and to the printing of many Ladino periodicals and newspapers, which circulated throughout the eastern Mediterranean.

Still, the Jewish schools of Istanbul remained traditional in their orientation until the mid-century when Abraham Camondo established the first modern Jewish school there. He was fiercely opposed by the rabbinate and conservative segments of the Jewish population, and his school was eventually closed. Later attempts to establish liberal Jewish education (in 1854 and 1868) were more successful, and in 1874 the Alliance Israélite Universelle opened its first school in Istanbul.

180. Sêfer Melekhet Shelomo

Salonika, 1862
Solomon b. Nissim Joseph David Kimḥi
Published by Saadi Hallevi
Ink on paper
12-3/16 × 8-1/4 × 1 in., 31.0 × 21.0 × 2.5 cm.
The Library of the Jewish Theological Seminary of America, New York

This book of *responsa*, Talmudi *novellae* and ser- of the community, a new tax that the sultan had practice to the Sephardi masses, many of whom The volume contains (on f. 8b) the author's interesting opinion that it was forbidden to teach the Oral Law to Karaites, who were to be considered non-Jews in this context. The Karaite community complained bitterly, and the Chief Rabbi of Istanbul, Yakir Gheron, responded by ordering all available copies of this book to be burnt. This volume is thus a rare survival. It contains the lengthy *responsum* (no. 15, ff. 36a–39b) by Rabbi Isaac Aqrish in which he concluded that it was the duty of the Jewish community in Istanbul to pay, on behalf of the scholars of the community, a new tax that the sultan had levied on all homes, whether lived in or rented out. There is no mention whether or not the community acted in accordance with Rabbi Aqrish's view.

M. S. C.

181. Sêfer Me'am Lo'ez, vol. 1

Istanbul, 1730
Jacob Culi
Published by Jonah b. Jacob
Ink on paper
11-1/2 × 8-1/16 × 1-7/8 in., 29.2 × 20.4 × 4.8 cm.
The Library of the Jewish Theological Seminary
of America, New York

The *Me'am Lo'ez* is perhaps the outstanding work of Ladino religious literature. The book was written in order to reintroduce standard Jewish theology and practice to the Sephardi masses, many of whom were ignorant of Hebrew. Each volume is based on a single book of the Bible. The text discusses all aspects of Jewish life: law, philosophy, biblical exegesis, and custom. Culi died in 1732, in the midst of publishing the second volume. Other scholars took up the work and eventually completed it.

M. S. C.

182. Sêfer Eldad Haddani

Istanbul, 1766
Published by Ḥayyim Elia Padro
Ink on paper
5-3/8 × 4-1/8 × 3/4 in., 13.7 × 10.5 × 1.9 cm.
The Library of the Jewish Theological Seminary
of America, New York, ʿO

On the title page the following Ladino inscription is written in Hebrew characters:

> Dando a entender la grandeza de los
> shevatim che estan in tierras lexanas e
> cuentos de las Indias.
> Given to understand the grandeur of the
> tribes that are in distant lands and stories of
> the Indies.

This book purports to tell the story of Eldad the Danite (of the tribe of Dan), a ninth-century traveler who claimed to have come from a kingdom in Africa founded and inhabited by the ten so-called "lost tribes" of the northern kingdom of Israel. This romantic tale, dismissed by most modern scholars as either heavily fictionalized history or outright fiction, must always have held a certain attraction for Jews living under the rule of others. That a Ladino translation like this one was printed as late as the eighteenth century is proof of the enduring charm and romance of this legend.

M. S. C.

183. Presentation to Abraham Camondo

Rhodes, 1865
Ink on paper
8-5/8 × 5-7/8 in., 22.0 × 15.0 cm.
Collection of Dr. Joseph Hacker

This tribute was written to Abraham Camondo of Istanbul in 1865 in order to thank him for his assistance in building a Jewish community center and school on the island of Rhodes.

Camondo (1785–1873) was one of the most outstanding Ottoman Jews of the nineteenth century. A very wealthy banker, financier, and philanthropist, he was known as "the Rothschild of the East." Camondo was one of six members of Istanbul's Commission for Regulation of the City of Istanbul. His efforts to establish a modern Jewish school in Istanbul met with fierce opposition from the rabbinate and led to his excommunication, but he was subsequently exonerated.

J. H.

184

152

A Sephardi Wedding

Jewish law, followed by both Ashkenazim and Sephardim, requires that a marriage ceremony include the giving of a ring and a contract by the bridegroom to his bride, the recitation of blessings, and a period of seclusion for bride and groom after the ceremony. Different local groups elaborated these basic elements in distinctive ways. The Sephardim of Italy and the Near East developed a tradition of illuminating the marriage contract (ketubbah). In Turkey great emphasis was placed on the public showing of the dowry (ašugar), which typically included many textiles for different occasions, some embroidered by the prospective bride, others purchased. The emphasis on embroidery reflects the high esteem in which this work was held by the general population of Turkey.

184. Jewish Marriage

New York, 1862
C. Parsons, after a drawing by H. J. Van Lennep
Color lithograph on paper
18 × 13-3/16 in., 45.7 × 33.5 cm.
The Jewish Museum, New York, gift of Dr. Harry G. Friedman, F 4183

Reverend Henry J. Van Lennep, an American missionary, witnessed a Jewish wedding in Turkey and recorded his observations in a sketch for an illustration published in *The Oriental Album* (see also no. 177). Before the ceremony he had the bride's dress brought to him, so that he could depict its colors and decorative details accurately. Van Lennep also described the ceremony itself.

> The bridegroom was twenty and the bride twelve. They stood up in their bridal garments under a tentlike structure supported by poles and made of cloths belonging to the bride's dowry, erected in the largest apartment in her parents' house. The remainder of the dowry, besides what she wore, was contained in two green chests which stood behind them and were used as seats by the pair. The bride's pasteboard horn was the same as the Armenian bride

with this difference, that no veil was thrown over it in the present case. Natural and artifical flowers and sprigs of wormwood adorned her head like a crown. Her veil was of gauze and perfectly transparent and her eyes remained closed during the whole ceremony. Two tall candlesticks stood before them on which tallow candles burned all the while. . . . The mothers of the parties stood by them closely veiled during the ceremony soon after the conclusion of which the bride's peculiar ornaments were removed from her and she was allowed freely to mingle with the company.[1]

The unusual cornucopia headdress also appears in a seventeenth-century French book of women's costumes in Turkey.[2] Candlesticks similar to those depicted by Van Lennep are included in the exhibition (no. 189).

1. Quoted in Rubens, *Jewish Costume*, p. 37.
2. Georges de la Chapelle, *Recuel* [sic] *de divers portraits des principales dames de la porte du grand Turc* (Paris: 1648), pl. 8.

REFERENCES: Rubens, *Jewish Costume*, pp. 36–37, 45; Rubens, *Iconography*, 1981, no. 2422.

E. D. B.

185. Marriage Canopy

Turkey, nineteenth century
Silk, embroidered with metallic threads and sequins
77-3/16 × 77-15/16 in., 196.0 × 198.0 cm.
The Jewish Museum, New York, gift of Mrs. Albert List, JM 22-66

A stylized flowering vine scroll frames this square of red cloth. The corners are filled with elaborate embroidered designs of palmettes, scrolls, and pendant flowers. Eight-petaled rosettes arranged in rows decorate the field and fill the triangular points of a Star of David embroidered in the center. Metallic fringe is sewn to all four sides.

The uniform execution of the gold-embroidered decoration and the incorporation of the Star of David motif suggest that this cloth was made for ritual use. The size, square format, and fringed edges imply that it was designed to serve as a marriage canopy (huppah). When the cloth came into the collection of The Jewish Museum, it bore two appliquéd lions

153

holding a crown and two Hebrew letters, the abbreviation for "Crown of Torah," indicating that the cloth had been reused as a Torah curtain. These additions were removed.

Smaller cloths with similar compositions were often used as tablecloths.[1]

1. Juhasz, ill. nos. 17, 19–23.

REFERENCE: *Fabric of Jewish Life*, no. 127.

an opaque cluster of grape vines and wheat sheaves growing from the earth, which occurs near the hem on both front and back. The vines rise to the bodice, where they meet the intertwined floral vines surrounding the neck opening. The sleeves are similarly decorated with grape vines and flowering vines. Finally, a series of scalloped scrolls alternating with floral sprigs encircles the hem. The embroidery is elaborately worked in gilt threads of varying widths, colors, and composition; the resulting variety of textures produces an effect of relief in many areas.

The underdress is made of the striped linen and silk cloth known as "Bursa cloth." A stylized vine executed in gold tinsel and arranged in a zigzag borders the neck opening. Along the edges of the sleeves is a band of crocheted lace with pendant leaf forms. Portions of the leaves are of purple silk, and a sequin is attached to each. A band of crocheted openwork joins the sleeves to the main part of the dress.

In elaboration and density of the embroidered motifs on the overdress, this costume resembles examples like a dress in the Kunstgewerbemuseum, Zurich, dated to the seventeenth or eighteenth century.[1] Published examples of the late nineteenth and early twentieth centuries are less densely embroidered, and the motifs are more stylized.[2] The Yeshiva University dress was made for a wedding held in Gallipoli between 1850–1860.

1. Inv. Nr. 13805; Kunstgewerbemuseum, Zurich, *Aüssereuropäische Textilien* (Zurich: n.d.), p. 182.
2. See "Exhibits of the Month," *Israel Museum News*, XIII (1977), p. 78; A. Müller-Lancet, "Jewish Ethnography at the Israel Museum," *Israel Museum News*, XV (1979), p. 55, fig. 7; and Juhasz, no. 47.

V. B. M.

186. Bridal Dress

Turkey, *c.* 1850–1860
Outer dress: velvet, embroidered with gilt metallic threads, and lined with cotton;
Underdress: linen and silk, embroidered with gilt tinsel and edged in lace with sequins and purple silk
57-15/16 × 58-3/8 in., 147.0 × 148.3 cm.
Yeshiva University Museum, New York, gift of Mr. and Mrs. Nahman Yohai, T126-77 A, B

The wine-colored velvet of the outer dress is heavily worked with gold embroidery. The major design is

187. Veil

Turkey, nineteenth century
Silk, embroidered with gold tinsel and metallic threads
45 × 37 in., 114.3 × 94.0 cm.
Yeshiva University Museum, New York, T-142-79

The fabric of this veil is a thin silk gauze, with a border crocheted in metallic threads. A single embroidered motif executed in gold tinsel is repeated on all four corners. It consists of a spray of leaves, flowers, and buds framed by a flowering vine. Scattered around the floral spray are dots and isolated blossoms.

According to information furnished by the donor, this veil was first used for the ceremony of *las favas* (the naming of a girl), during which it was placed over the heads of the mother and baby. The veil was then kept until the girl wore it at her wedding.

V.B.M.

188. Rabbi's Costume

Istanbul, nineteenth century
Shoemaker: T. Papazran
Hat: red wool, gray satin, black silk tassel, 10 in. dm., 25.4 cm.
Pants: blue wool felt, lined with cotton, 31-3/8 × 39-1/8 in., 79.7 × 99.3 cm.
Robe: silk striped in yellow, gray, and red and lined with cotton, 52-7/8 × 63-3/4 in., 134.3 × 161.9 cm.
Jacket: dark-green wool, 22-1/2 × 60-1/2 in., 57.2 × 153.6 cm.
Coat: dark-green wool, 56-15/16 × 66 in., 144.7 × 167.7 cm.
Shawl: polychrome wool, 126-1/2 × 52-1/2 in., 321.3 × 133.3 cm.
Shoes: black and brown leather, 11-3/4 in., 29.8 cm.
United States Museum of Natural History, Smithsonian Institution, Washington, D.C., 154761

This costume was not acquired until 1893, but depictions of Jewish men from Istanbul published in 1842 and 1873 suggest that it probably dates from the third quarter of the nineteenth century. The "Jewish Merchant" (see no. 177), published in 1842, wears a striped robe (*entārī*) covered by a dark-green cloak. Photographs dated 1873 show the Ḥakham of Smyrna (Izmir) wearing a cashmere scarf like this one around his waist, over a striped *entārī*. Similar garb is worn by the Ḥakham of Salonika, whose headdress is close to the one on exhibition.[1]

Muslim law dating from the seventh century required that Jews and Christians dress differently from Muslim believers.[2] These strictures were often interpreted to mean that different colors, rather than different garments, were to be worn.

1. Rubens, *Jewish Costume*, figs. 48, 49.
2. See N. Stillman, *The Jews of Arab Lands: A History and Source Book* (Philadelphia: 1979), pp. 25ff.

REFERENCE: Casanowicz, 1929, no. 64.

V. B. M.

189. Pair of Candlesticks

Turkey, nineteenth century
Brass, cast and engraved
25-1/2 × 9-1/8 in. dm., 64.7 × 23.2 cm.
The Jewish Museum, New York, the H. Ephraim and Mordecai Benguiat Family Collection, U7627 a,b

189

These tall candlesticks consist of stepped domed bases and stems in the form of balusters with truncated cones for upper sections. Engraved lines and beading mark the junctures.

Similar candlesticks are depicted in "Jewish Marriage" (see no. 184), published in 1862. Other examples are in the collection of the United States National Museum of Natural History (nos. 315251, 315252, and 315253).

REFERENCE: Adler and Casanowicz, 1908, no. 63.

V. B. M.

190. Dowry List

Region of Istanbul, 1836
Ink on paper
20-7/8 × 15-1/16 in., 53.0 × 38.2 cm.
The Library of the Jewish Theological Seminary
of America, New York, acc. no. 57869

Rachel b. Abraham Gabbai was married to Menahem b. Mentash Yaffet on Friday, 6 Elul (called Rahamim here), 1836, in a town near Istanbul. This dowry list includes nine items already delivered, for a total of 7,780 grushot, and twenty-seven still outstanding, valued at 5,235 grushot; the total is 13,015 grushot. Amounts are given in Ottoman script in the left-hand column, and the document has been signed by the groom and his father, as well as by four other witnesses.

M. S. C.

191. Towel

Ottoman Empire, eighteenth century
Cotton, embroidered with silk and metallic threads
52-1/2 × 19-1/2 in., 133.4 × 49.5 cm.
The Jewish Museum, New York, the H. Ephraim and Mordecai Benguiat Family Collection, S 96

The towel ends are decorated with bands of silver openwork embroidery creating a network dotted

191

with buds; these bands have been overlaid with strips of a modified meander incorporating trefoils. This meander design has been executed in aqua silk threads, which contrast strongly with the silver of the openwork.

Similar fine openwork can be seen on many eighteenth-century pieces, though the motifs are usually more naturalistic in character.[1] The abstract forms on this towel recall the geometric motifs of sixteenth-century pieces.[2] For the function of these towels, see the entry for no. 162.

1. *Cf.* Geijer, *Oriental Textiles*, no. 151.
2. See, for example, Gönül, *Turkish Embroideries*, pl. 20.

REFERENCE: Adler and Casanowicz, 1901, p. 557, no. 40, pl. 25.

V. B. M.

192. Bedspread for a Bride

Istanbul, *c.* 1850
Silk, embroidered with gold metallic threads and sequins
72-1/2 × 63 in., 184.2 × 160.0 cm.
Collection of Ruth Blumberg

The spread is composed of three pieces of silk sewn together. Each panel is embroidered separately with two zigzag lattices of scrolls and sprigs alternating with bouquets of flowers. A light and airy effect has been achieved through attenuation of the shapes, the rendering of scrolls and some leaves in outline, and the flatness of most of the stitches. In contrast, the large flowers stand out because of the density and thickness of their embroidery and the use of clustered sequins to render the stamens. The naturalism of all the forms and the contrasting textures suggest a date in the mid-nineteenth century.

Bedspreads like this one formed part of the dowry in Turkey and were embroidered by the prospective bride herself. Before the wedding the trousseau was exhibited in a ceremony known as the *ašugar*.

V. B. M.

193. Pair of Clogs for the Bath

Turkey, nineteenth century
Wood, inlaid with engraved mother-of-pearl
10-1/4 × 2-3/4 × 3-1/8 in., 26.0 × 7.0 × 8.0 cm.
The Jewish Museum, New York, on permanent loan from the Leonard Stern collection

The slipper-shaped upper surfaces of these clogs rest on tall wedges separated by an arch. Each upper surface is inlaid with two stylized arrangements of flowers and leaves set in containers, a rosette, and a bird, all of engraved mother-of-pearl. Additional rosettes and abstract motifs decorate the wedges.

Turkish women wore clogs like these in the bath. Jewish women also used them when they attended the *mikveh*, the ritual bath, and a pair of such clogs, along with towels (see no. 191), were a traditional gift to the bride from the groom's family. Immersion in the *mikveh* marks the end of the state of ritual impurity associated with menses and is required of a bride before her wedding and of a married woman each month thereafter. A similar pair of clogs from mainland Turkey is in the collection of the Ethnography Department of the Israel Museum. This pair belonged to a Jewish family from Iaonnina in Greece, formerly part of the Ottoman Empire.

V. B. M.

194. Ritual Bath Sheet

> Turkey, *c.* 1875
> Linen embroidered with polychrome and metallic threads; crocheted cotton
> 53-7/8 × 100 in., 136.8 × 253.9 cm.
> The Skirball Museum, Los Angeles, gift of Mathilda Horn in memory of her mother, Raina Levy Eskenazi, and her sister, Mary Eskenazi Caraco, 78.202 (38.165)

The sheet is decorated on two sides by a triple border: an outer one of crocheted cotton lace, the other two—a thin undulating vine and a series of floral sprays—delicately embroidered with polychrome and metallic threads. When the wearer wrapped this sheet around her body, the plain edges were tucked inward, and the border showed.

Raina Levy Eskenazi embroidered this sheet as part of her trousseau; it was worn over another towel when she visited the Turkish bath before immersion in the ritual bath, the *mikveh* (see no. 193 for an explanation of the *mikveh*).

V. B. M.

193

195. Prayer Shawl

> Istanbul, 1898
> Silk, embroidered with tinsel
> 28-5/16 × 83-5/8 in., 71.9 cm.' × 202.4
> Collection of Irwin Schick and Rezan Benatar

Along the upper edge of this prayer shawl (*tallit*) the following inscription is embroidered in metallic foil:

יברכך ה' וישמרך יאר ה' פניו אליך ויחנך
ישא ה' פניו אליך וישם לך שלום. בן פרת
יוסף בן פרת עלי עין. המלאך הגאל אותי
מכל רע יברך את הנערים ויקרא בהם שמי.
לישועתך קויתי ה'. כמיל לבד

The Lord Bless you and keep you! The Lord deal kindly and graciously with you! The Lord bestow His favor upon you and grant you peace! [Numbers 6:22–6] Joseph is a you peace! [Num. 6:22–6] Joseph is a fruitful bough by a spring. (Gen. 49:22) The angel who has redeemed me from all harm—Bless the lads. In them may my name be recalled. . . . (Gen. 48:16)   I wait for your deliverance, O Lord! (Gen. 49:18).

195

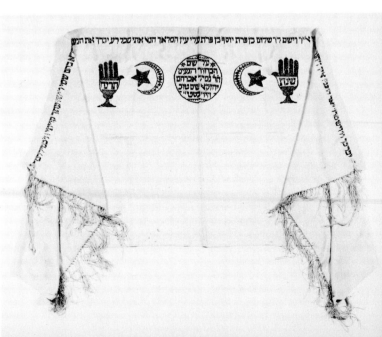

The last six letters are a mnemonic device for the following sentence from Psalms:

> For He will give His angels charge over thee, to keep thee in all thy ways. (Ps. 92:11).

Below is a symmetrical composition with a central circle flanked by a pair of star-and-crescent motifs, which are then flanked in turn by a pair of hands inscribed:

> the year [5]658 (1898).

The circle is inscribed:

עַל שֵׁם הבחור הנעים / הר גמיל אברהם /
יחזקאל שם טוב / היו בסי[ימן] ט[וב]

For . . . Jamil Abraham Ezekial Shem-Tov, may he live long with good luck.

The penciled lines that guided the embroiderer may still be seen beneath the threads of the designs.

In many Ashkenazi and Sephardi communities it is customary for a bride to present her groom with a prayer shawl. Turkish *tallitot* worn at weddings are often decorated with gold embroidery, which is also found on other liturgical textiles from the Ottoman Empire. This rich example integrates Ottoman embroidery techniques and motifs like the star and crescent with a Jewish motif (the blessing hands) and a complex Hebrew inscription.

V. B. M.

The Synagogue

Islamic law restricted the building of new synagogues. For this reason, established synagogues were often renovated or rebuilt on their original sites. For example, the synagogue of the Oḥrid community in Istanbul, on which the synagogue in this exhibition is loosely based, was in existence in the 1460s, when it was included in a list of Jewish congregations erected after the conquest of 1453. It was last renovated in the nineteenth century.

196. Torah Curtain (See color plate, p. 13)

Istanbul, c. 1735
Silk, embroidered with polychrome silks and metallic threads; metallic lace border
68-7/8 × 63 in., 175.0 × 160.0 cm.
The Jewish Museum, New York, the H. Ephraim and Mordecai Benguiat Family Collection, S 4

Four pieces of yellow silk have been sewn together to form the field of the curtain. A pair of undulating columns bearing urns with flowers is linked by two horizontal arrangements of scroll forms, one below the bases, the other at the level of the abaci. Garlands of pastel flowers form an arch between the columns, wind around their shafts, and intertwine with the scrolls. In the center is a mosque with distinctive Turkish "pencil" minarets at each corner of the building and framing the entrance, which is reached by a broad flight of steps. Two groups of three windows flank the entrance. The embroiderer took great care to articulate the masonry and separate parts of the building by varying the direction of the bands of metallic thread. An element of fancy has crept in with the leaves and flowers placed above the arched door. An inscription and a small *hamsa* (hand-shaped amuletic sign) are embroidered in the space between the upper scrolls and the mosque. The inscription reads:

בע"ה
בינימן [...] הי"ו... [...] למורינו הקדש לק"ק
תלמוד תורה מורינו נאברו ה"י ובנו הארום
וחשוב כה"ר שלמה נאבארו נ"ע

With the help of God, Benjamin . . . Modico dedicates to the h[oly] c[ongregation] Talmud Torah of our teacher Navarro and his . . . son Solomon Navarro . . .

The entire composition is framed by a series of undulating lines punctuated by flowers and leaves, and a second border, of metallic lace, surrounds the cloth. The Sultan Aḥmed Mosque (Blue Mosque), which was completed in 1617, was the first mosque in Istanbul to have six minarets, a design which stirred a lot of controversy.[1] Its entrance was approached by a flight of steps. From the care taken by the embroiderer to detail the features of the mosque depicted on the curtain, we may conclude it is a fanciful representation of the Blue Mosque and that this curtain was probably made in Istanbul. The dedicatory inscription and *hamsa* are cruder in workmanship and were evidently added by another embroiderer.

The curtain came to The Jewish Museum from the Benguiat Collection, together with a reader's desk cover that was obviously intended as a matching piece.[2] In material and the style of embroidery, both curtain and desk cover are similar to a dated Torah binder also in The Jewish Museum (see no. 199). Another Turkish Torah curtain in the collection of The Jewish Museum (JM 7-50) bears a similar composition: two undulating columns entwined with flowers. On this second curtain, however, the columns support a canopy from which hangs a lamp. A similar metallic lace border also appears on the amulet (no. 35) and need not be a later addition here.

1. I am grateful to Dr. Estelle Whelan for this information.

2. S 36; *Fabric of Jewish Life*, no. 55. A painted copy of the curtain is also in The Jewish Museum, JM 86-67, *Fabric of Jewish Life*, no. 57.

REFERENCES: Adler and Casanowicz, 1901, no. 7, pl. 5; *Fabric of Jewish Life*, no. 56.

V. B. M.

197. Reader's Desk Cover

Turkey, early nineteenth century
Wool and cotton, in Gördes knot
64-3/8 × 47-3/4 in., 161.0 × 119.0 cm.
The Jewish Museum, New York, gift of Dr. Harry G. Friedman, F 5182 A

This textile is modeled on a Muslim prayer rug with a prayer niche (*miḥrāb*) as the central motif and multiple borders of varying widths. On this example two pairs of stylized double columns support an entablature from which a lamp with a Hebrew inscription, the Tetragrammaton (YHVH), is suspended. Directly below, between the column bases, are two praying hands inscribed שדי , "Almighty." In large letters above the *miḥrāb* is woven:

זה השער לה' צדיקים יבואו בו

This is the gate of the Lord, the righteous shall enter into it. (Ps. 118:20)

Below the hands is another woven inscription:

שויתי ה' לנגדי תמיד

I have set the Lord always before me. (Ps. 16:8)

To the right of the latter the following verses begin:

כה אמר ה' אם לא בריתי יומם ולילה חקות שמים וארץ לא שמתי

Thus saith the Lord: if My covenant be not with day and night, if I have not appointed the ordinances of heaven and earth. (Jer. 33:25)

כה אמר ה' שמרו משפט ועשו צדקה כי קרובה ישועתי לבוא וצדקתי להגלות.

Thus saith the Lord: Keep ye justice and do righteousness; for My salvation is near to come, and My favor to be revealed. (Isa. 56:1)

ויהי דבר ה' אל שלמה לאמר: ושכנתי בתוך בני ישראל ולא אעזב את עמי ישראל.

And the word of the Lord came to Solomon saying: I will dwell among the children of Israel and will not forsake my people Israel. (I Kings 6:11,13)

A final inscription occupies the lower portion of the penultimate border strip:

הקדש של יהודה דאוילה לק"ק שיוויליא מנחת זכרון לנפש בתי גארסייה דאוילה שנת וי'י'ב'ר'כ'נ'י' ב'ג'ל'ל'ה'

A dedication of Judah d'Avila to the h[oly] c[ongregation] Seville, an offering of remembrance to the soul of my daughter Garcia d'Avila in the year "And the Lord has blessed me on her account" [a variation of Gen. 30:2, chronogram for [5]368(1607–1608)]

The remaining portion of this border strip is filled with stylized flowers and scrolls. Stylized flowers and geometric designs fill the other borders.

Although in some respects this rug is comparable to other Turkish examples, in many ways it is unusual. The placement of the hands at the bottom, instead of above the *miḥrāb*, is a departure from Muslim examples, in which the woven hands are placed where those of the prostrate worshiper would fall. Another unusual feature is the use of multiple Hebrew inscriptions. As several forms of God's name are incorporated into the weave, and as the name is venerated in Judaism, this rug was probably never placed on the floor. Furthermore, the wear and repairs visible in the central portion suggest that it was used not as a Torah curtain but as a reader's desk cover.

Although the inscribed date is early, this rug is probably a later copy of an earlier model. The stylization of architectural features, apparent in the columns, first became common in the eighteenth cen-

159

tury. Early in the nineteenth century the imitation of light-colored carpets first produced between 1580 and 1650 became popular; hence the early inscription on this rug and similar examples.[1] Two other nineteenth-century rugs in the collection of The Jewish Museum bear inscriptions indicating that they were used in synagogues (no. 198 and F 3409). An earlier example is in the Textile Museum, Washington, D.C. (R 16.4.4 and R 1.62).[2] Another is in the Hechal Shlomo Museum, Jerusalem.[3] It was common for Sephardim to name their synagogues after their cities of origin.[4]

1. I am indebted to Professor Walter Denny, University of Massachusetts, Amherst, for this information.
2. See Textile Museum, *Prayer Rugs* (Washington, D.C.: 1974), no. V.
3. Bialer, *Jewish Life*, p. 104.
4. See Galanté, *Les synagogues d'Istanbul*, pp. 5–15.

REFERENCE: *Fabric of Jewish Life*, no. 54.

V.B.M.

198. Reader's Desk Cover

Central Anatolia, nineteenth century
Wool, in Gördes knot
67 × 41-3/4 in., 170.0 × 106.0 cm.
The Jewish Museum, New York, gift of Dr. Harry
G. Friedman, F 3494

In the field a stepped niche encloses a six-branched lamp on a tall stem with stepped base. On either side of the stem are the initial words of the Ten Commandments. A Star of David is woven in each of the spandrels. Above and below the field are friezes of stylized crenellations. The inner border consists of stylized flowers. Other stylized flowers and leaves fill the wide central border; an outer border contains a series of stars. Signs of wear and replacement weaving can be seen in the lower section of the field.

The composition and colors (blue, red, yellow, beige, and brown) of this rug suggest an Anatolian origin. The knotting technique and the central border motifs are characteristic of rugs from western Anatolia. The crenellations above and below the field and single elements in the spandrels can also be seen on an Anatolian rug now in the Kunstgewerbemuseum, Zurich, dated *c.* 1800.[1] What is unusual about the rug in The Jewish Museum is the incorporation of a Hebrew inscription and of Jewish

198

iconographic elements, in place of motifs normally found on Anatolian rugs: the Star of David replaces ewers or octagons commonly found in the spandrels, and the standing lamp replaces the hanging mosque lamp that is frequently depicted in the central prayer niche (*miḥrāb*). Two factors argue against the use of this textile as a floor rug: the woven inscription, including the name of God, and the absence of appropriate signs of wear. In fact, the worn areas suggest that this rug served as a reader's desk cover. (For another rug used in a synagogue, see no. 197.)

1. Inv. Nr. 3726, Kunstgewerbemuseum, Zurich, *Äussereuropäische Textilien* (Zurich: n.d.), p. 181.

V. B. M.

199. Torah Binder

Turkey, 1735–1736
Mandolinah Bassan
Silk, embroidered with polychrome and metallic
threads; metallic lace border
6-1/8 × 133-1/16 in., 15.5 × 338.0 cm.
The Jewish Museum, New York, the H. Ephraim
and Mordecai Benguiat Family Collection, S 17

A continuous band of strapwork laid in a scalloped pattern runs the length of this yellow silk binder. Overlaid on it are sections of flowering vines executed in polychrome threads, alternating with large pine cones in both metallic and polychrome threads: Two repeating patterns of morning glories, carnations, and roses are paired with two different versions of the pine cones. A border of metallic lace is attached to one side. The left end of the binder, which was held against the scroll at the beginning of the wrapping, has a straight edge, but the other end is pointed. It is on the pointed section that the inscription is embroidered, within the spiral that begins the strapwork:

ויצא פרח ויצץ ציץ וינמול שקדים מעשה
ידי ריקמא [כך!] במלאכת הקדש מירית
מנדולינה באשאן ת[בורך] מ[נשים] א[הל]
בשנת תצו׳ לפ״ק

And [the staff of Aaron] put forth buds, bloomed blossoms and bore ripe almonds. (Num. 17:23).A work of embroidery done as a holy craft. Mandolinah Bassan, she shall be blessed above the women of the tent [a play on Judges 5:24] in the year [5]496 (1735–1736).

In many respects, this binder is similar to a Torah curtain and matching reader's desk cover (see no. 196 and *Fabric of Jewish Life*, nos. 55 and 56) in the incorporation of naturalistic flowers combined with metallic strap- and scrollwork and in the use of similar yellow silk and metallic lace borders. Two motifs of this binder are hallmarks of Ottoman Turkish art: the carnation and the large pine cone with patterned sections. The pine cones combined with spiral lines appear in embroideries as early as the sixteenth century,[1] and the cone itself appears in later metalwork (see no. 160).

1. See Gönül, *Turkish Embroideries*, pl. 4

REFERENCES: Adler and Casanowicz, 1901, p. 546, pl. 2 fig 1; Adler and Casanowicz, 1908, p. 707, pl. LXVI, fig. 1; *Fabric of Jewish Life*, no. 20.

V. B. M.

200. Torah Mantle

Istanbul, *c.* 1881
Velvet, embroidered with metallic and silk
threads
36-5/8 × 19-11/16 × 10-5/8 in. dm., 93.0 × 50.0 ×
27.0 cm.
The Jewish Museum, New York, the H. Ephraim
and Mordecai Benguiat Family Collection, S 19

The mantle is composed of Üsküdar velvet woven to form a symmetrical composition about the central vertical axis. The main motif at the bottom is a woven quatrefoil entwined with flowers, which frames a central medallion. Above it, along the vertical axis, are other medallions formed by the background fabric as it appears between cut velvet framing elements. Scattered flowers and leaves fill the remainder of the panel. Above are two bands: one of red and white floral bouquets and a second of arches and flowers. At the sides of the central panel are bands filled with bouquets of red flowers. The back of the mantle is a patchwork of woven decorative elements of the types already mentioned. The mantle is split the entire length of the back in the Sephardi manner. Green silk fringe lines both sides of the opening and the hem.

The following embroidered inscription has been appliquéd on the main panel:

למנוחת / מרת / רחל / נבת אשת /
אברהם / ז׳ גיאת / חיו סט

For the repose of Mrs. Rachel, may her soul rest in the Garden of Eden, the wife of Abraham [Be]nguiat, pure Sephardi.

Rachel and Abraham Benguiat were the parents of H. Ephraim, one of the donors. A photograph in the collection of The Jewish Museum shows Rachel's tombstone, engraved April 2, 1881.

Üsküdar is a suburb of Istanbul known for its velvets; mantles similar to this one can still be seen in the synagogue of Kuzguncuk just north of Üsküdar.

REFERENCE: *Fabric of Jewish Life*, no. 61.

V. B. M.

201. Torah Mantle (See color plate, p. 14)

Turkey, nineteenth century
Velvet, embroidered with gilt and metallic
threads, lined with silk and linen,
sequins; metallic braid
35-1/4 × 9 in. dm., 89.5 × 22.9 cm.
The Israel Museum, Jerusalem, 151/114

Two pieces of burgundy velvet form the sides of this mantle. Except for the inscription, the embroidered composition is symmetrical about a central foliate medallion. The field is bordered by a flowering vine. Stylized vases holding flowers and leaves fill the corners and establish diagonal axes that are aligned with the tips of four fleur-de-lis in the central medallion. Four small flower motifs lie on the vertical and horizontal axes. Around the upper section of the medallion is the following inscription:

הקדש למנוחה משה בנגיאת בן מרים
מ[נוחתו] ב[כבוד].

Dedicated for the repose of Moses Benguiat son of Miriam. May his repose be in honor.

Individual sequins are scattered on the background surrounding the inscription. This portion of the mantle is lined with silk. The top piece appears to be an older, reused section. It is a linen-lined velvet, very worn, of a somewhat different color, and embroidered in other techniques. The incomplete motifs on this portion (two large stylized flowers attached to vines) do not continue on the sides. A metallic braid is sewn to all the edges.

Centralized compositions on dark red velvets are characteristic of nineteenth-century embroidered Turkish textiles. Another example is the marriage canopy (no. 185), the border design of which is similar to that on this mantle. The form of the inscription, in which the name of the deceased is linked with that of his mother, rather than of his father, is a Sephardi usage.

V. B. M.

202. Torah Shield (See color plate, p. 14)

Turkey, 1863–1864
Mark: ṣaḥ
Silver, cast, repoussé, engraved, parcel-gilt, and nielloed
11-7/16 × 10 in., 29.0 × 25.4 cm.
Division of Community Life, National Museum of American History, Smithsonian Institution, Washington, D.C., 154.990

A braided border surrounds this rectangular shield with arcuated top. Two columns wrapped with garlands flank the central field, in which two crowned lions support an oval cartouche engraved with a bouquet of flowers and the following inscription:

זאת נדבה האשה פרידא ביילע בת אלקנה
ברוך בן משה הלוי

This was donated by the woman Frieda Beila, the daughter of Elkanah Barukh son of Moses Halevi

The cartouche and lions stand on a richly textured scroll. Similar scroll forms inhabited by birds rise from the top of the cartouche and surround the pair of crowned doors, on the exteriors of which are engraved the Ten Commandments. The doors open to reveal an aperture through which can be seen the names of holidays nielloed on a revolving disk that can be rotated from the back of the shield for different occasions. Beneath the aperture is engraved יום שבת קודש , "the day of the Holy Sabbath," and on the interior of the doors, the date שנת תרכד , "the year [5]624 (1863–1864).

In shape and composition this shield resembles Polish examples of the eighteenth and nineteenth centuries. In view of the Ashkenazi name of the doner, the use of Polish models is not surprising. Turkish artisans were active in Poland in the eighteenth century, which may also explain northern stylistic influences in the Ottoman Empire, as could the taste for European things among residents of Turkey in the nineteenth century. The execution of this shield is, however, not European, especially the treatment of individual forms and the emphasis on texture. Also, the shield was stamped ṣaḥ (registered in Turkish and has an Istanbul provenance.[1]

1. Adler and Casanowicz, 1908, pp. 709-710.

REFERENCES: Adler and Casanowicz, 1908, 709–710, pl. LXVIII; Casanowicz, 1929, p. 5, pl. 2.

V. B. M.

203. Rimmon (See color plate, p. 14)

Turkey, late nineteenth century
Mark: ṭughrā of ʼAbd al-Hamīd II (1876–1909)
Silver, raised, repoussé, ajouré, and engraved
15-5/16 × 4-3/8 in., 38.9 × 11.1 cm.

The Jewish Museum, New York, gift of Dr. Harry G. Friedman, F 3174

The tall, tapering shaft, with a ring molding at each end, rises from a concave base. At the top of the shaft fleshy leaves appear to support the body of the *rimmon*, which has a bulbous lower and a piriform upper section, with a crescent-and-star finial. In contrast to the simple, smooth silver of the base and shaft, the body is decorated with elaborate floral and scroll designs. On the lower part, three inscribed oval cartouches are separated by flowers flanked by leaves. The inscriptions read:

ה׳ר דוד / הכהן /
הי״ו ה׳ר אהרן הלוי / הי״ו
וה׳ר יעקב / אבן אדיב״ה / הי״ו

David Hacohen,
Aaron Halevi
and Jacob ibn Adibah

They are completed on the base:

המשתדלים בחברה קדושה יע״א
[יבנה עירנו אמן]

who are active in the Burial Society, may our city [Jerusalem] be rebuilt, Amen.

On the upper section of the body a series of flowers and curling leaves, partially executed in openwork, are capped by a row of engraved elongated leaves.

V. B. M.

204. Rimmon (See color plate, p. 14)

Turkey, late nineteenth century
Mark: illegible *ṭughrā*
Silver: raised, engraved, ajouré, and stamped
15-3/8 × 4-1/2 in., 39.0 × 11.5 cm.
The Jewish Museum, New York, gift of Dr. Harry G. Friedman, F 1956

This *rimmon* is basically in the shape of a chalice; a tall, tapering shaft rising from a concave base set on a circular foot and a cup-shaped lower body. The upper body is piriform with punched holes; it is capped by a naturalistic cluster of leaves and a crescent. Moldings separate the distinct forms: the upper and lower sections of the body, the body and shaft, the shaft and foot. The resulting effect is of component parts simply added together, rather than blended, yet the repetition of the moldings and of the engraved wavy lines on foot and body lend a sense of unity.

Similar decorative lines appear on no. 155, a sweets dish dated 1876–1909.

V. B. M.

205. Rimmonim

Turkey, 1861–1877
Marks: *ṭughrā*s of Maḥmūd II (1808–1839)
Silver, cast, engraved, and ajouré
14-13/16 × 3-15/16 in., 37.6 × 10.0 cm.
The Jewish Museum, New York, gift of Dr. Harry G. Friedman, F 3141 a, b

The slim, tapering shaft of each *rimmon* supports three baskets with undulating rims decorated with strawberry vines executed in repoussé, engraving, and openwork. A design of scallops follows each rim. The baskets diminish in size from bottom to top. The inverted cone that caps each *rimmon* just fits the upper basket. It, too, is engraved with ajouré strawberry vines and with the scalloped design around the rim. A wreath of acanthus leaves encircles the point, to which is affixed a finial in the form of a winged crown. An engraved inscription along the shaft of one *rimmon* reads:

של הארום הח[כם] הכי יצחק ברוך הכהן
י״צ ש פ״ז

[This] belongs to the betrothed Isaac son of Barukh the kohen. . . .

V. B. M.

205

206. Torah Crown with Rimmonim

Istanbul, 1845–1846, 1849–1850, 1879–1880
Silver, raised, repoussé, engraved, gilt, and
punched; wood
Crown: 9-1/2 × 8-5/8 in. dm., 24.2 × 21.8 cm.
Rimmonim: 13-3/16 × 4 in., 24.2 × 21.8 cm.
The Israel Museum, Jerusalem, 146/33, 147/213
A, B

From the inscriptions, the workmanship, and the color of the silver, it seems clear that the crown and *rimmonim* were not all made at the same time nor even by a single silversmith, though they were evidently used together.

The tiered crown consists of silver sheets attached to a wooden form, with two holes in the bottom for the staves of a Torah scroll. A second set of holes was cut into the upper part of the crown to receive a pair of *rimmonim*. The lower three tiers of the crown consist of series of arches and half-domes (?) executed in repoussé and decorated with engraved palmettes and other leaves. A parallel combination of stylized architectural motifs and natural forms is also found on the fourth level, a dome capping the whole. Its entire surface is engraved with imbrications framed in an arcade; single engraved leaves project above the columns into the spandrels of the arcade. A pine-cone finial rising from a bed of cast leaves is affixed to the apex of the dome. Punched beaded borders mark the lower edge of each tier, except for the very bottom, where there is a band of gadrooning instead. The following inscriptions (now fragmentary because of breaks) were engraved below the gadrooning:

שנת כתר תורה לפג [כך!]

. . . in the year Crown of Torah [chronogram for [5]606 (1845–1846)]

הקדישו ה"מ יעקב בארוקאס נ"ע ע"י
המשתדל מ"ע עטו"ר מו"ה.... ...רון נר"ו לק"ק
ג'ורלו יע"א בש[נת] התר'רטו לפ"ג [!]

Jacob Barokas the one who works . . . and [name lost] dedicated [this] to the h[oly] c[ongregation] Jorlo [?] . . . in the y[ear] 5615 (1854–1855).

The decorative motifs of the crown are repeated on the *rimmonim* but in varying sizes and orientations. The lower body of each is an inverted version of one of the lower three tiers of the crown; it is separated from the upper body by a plain band with engraved inscriptions. On one *rimmon* (I.M. 147/213 B) the inscription reads:

ק"ק מאייור י"ע'א' שנת אתן כפלח הרמון
רק'ת'ך ל'פ'ק'

H[oly] C[ongregation] Maior, in the year [chronogram for [5]610 (1849–1850)] "Thy temples are like a pomegranate split open" (Cant. 43:6)

The second *rimmon* (I.M. 147/213 A) bears a different inscription:

ק"ק מאיור יע'א'ושנת תריל לפ"ק

H[oly] Congregation Maior . . . the year [5]640 (1879–1880).

On the larger upper body of each *rimmon* are two similar tiers of decoration; on the earlier example the upper tier is considerably smaller than the lower, and the dome at the top is decorated with arcading and imbrications similar to those on the crown; the finial is in the form of an acorn. The workmanship and style of the second *rimmon* reflect its later date. The decorative motifs are more crudely executed, and the dome is decorated with a simple diaper pattern divided into four zones by a narrow border. Also, the silver of this finial is of a different color from that of the first.

It seems likely that the crown initially had no *rimmonim* but was modified to receive them, for the holes cut into the crown break the decoration and do not seem to have been planned initially. It was probably at that time that the second inscription was engraved on it. In 1879–1880 one of the original *rimmonim* was replaced. The Maior synagogue was in existence at the time of Meḥmed II the Conqueror.[1]

The combination of two types of Torah ornament in a single complex is usually found among Sephardim, rather than Ashkenazim, and is especially common among the Jews of Italy, with whom Turkish Jewish communities have always been in close contact.

1. See Galanté, *Les synagogues d'Istanbul*, p. 8

REFERENCE: "Selected Acquisitions," *Israel Museum News*, XV (1979), p. 38.

V. B. M.

164

207. Torah Pointer

Turkey, nineteenth century
Silver, cast and engraved
12-1/4 × 1-1/4 in., 31.1 × 3.2 cm.
The Israel Museum, Jerusalem, 149/214

The pointer is composed of two tapering shafts joined at the larger ends by a faceted knob, with a terminal knob at one narrow end and a flat open hand (ḥamsa) held by two scrolls at the other. All these parts are threaded on a rod. Narrow, cut-out borders, perhaps once inlaid, separate the parts. The shafts are divided into elongated panels, each engraved with a continuous vine. A rosette inscribed in a lozenge decorates the main facets of the central knop. The following inscription is engraved within a circular field on the palm of the ḥamsa:

קדש לה' / על שם / מלטאז בת / דוד

Holy to the Lord. (Ex. 28:36) In the name of . . . Maltaz daughter of David.

For the significance of the ḥamsa see no. 196. This motif generally occurs on Torah pointers made in Muslim countries, in contast to the hand with pointing finger commonly found on Western European Torah pointers.

V. B. M.

208. Lectern Cover of the Chief Rabbi of Izmir

Turkey, eighteenth century
Velvet, embroidered with metallic threads, seed pearls, and silk
36-9/16 in. dm., 92.9 cm.
Yeshiva University Museum, New York, gift of Victor Alhadiff, T134-77

The densely embroidered decoration of this lectern cover comprises three elements: a central hexagram, a triangular arrangement of flowering vines and tulips repeated six times to form a circle, and a border composed of floral sprays and clusters of tulips. These elements are worked in various metallic threads, creating different textures and levels of relief. The incorporation of seed pearls and of both silver and gilt threads also creates variations in color, which are used for naturalistic effect. The forms of the flowers are also quite naturalistic: such details

as the stamens are included, and the flowers themselves are foreshortened.

The density of the embroidery and the naturalism of the forms suggest an eighteenth-century date.[1] Other works known to be from Izmir are not particularly close to this piece.[2] Rather the dense gold embroidery suggests that the lectern cover was created in an atelier close to the court. The imperial style of the so-called Tulip Period also influenced later works like a bridal dress of c. 1850 worn by members of a Gallipoli family (no. 186), which shows coloristic and textural effects similar to those on the lectern cover, though its forms are more stylized.

1. Cf. Gönül, *Turkish Embroideries*, p. 16 (an eighteenth-century Qurān case); and Geijer, *Oriental Textiles*, no. 105, pl. 44 (a seventeenth-century saddle bag from Istanbul).
2. Cf., numerous pieces in Juhasz.

V. B. M.

209. Bêt Tefillah

Istanbul, 1739
Published by Jonah b. Jacob
Ink on paper
6-1/4 × 4-9/16 × 1-1/8 in., 15.9 × 11.6 × 2.8 cm.
The Library of the Jewish Theological Seminary of America, New York, *L acc. 9172

This prayerbook in Hebrew has a Ladino translation by Abraham Asa.

M. S. C.

210. Alms Box

Turkey, 1904
Marks: ṭughrā of 'Abd al-Hamīd II (1876–1909)
Silver, raised, hammered, and engraved
3-1/16 × 4-3/4 in., 7.7 × 12.1 cm.
The Jewish Museum, New York, S 1502

This alms box is in the shape of a barrel to which a lid and scroll handle have been attached. A slit in the lid received the coins. Scrolls, flowers, and strapwork engraved on a matte ground cover most of the box, except for three ovoid fields and a band at the top, which are reserved for inscriptions (portions of which are illegible):

רב א... חיים ן' עטר... הרר שמואל ב יצחק /
חברה קדושה [!] / קייסיויים (?) די /
חאסקיואי / אהרן אלבוחא (?) ידי שבתי
בכר / משה / גבאים / ישראל ב' מרדכי /
ה'ו יצחק אלאלו / הי"ו 5664

. . . Ḥayyim son of Attar . . . Samuel son of Isaac, the Burial Society of. . . .di Hasköy, Aaron Albuha [?], [by] the hands of Shabbetai son of Moses, the *Gabbaim* Israel son of Mordecai, Isaac Alalu, 5664 (1903–1904)

A nearly identical alms box in the collection of The Jewish Museum in London was used in a Sarajevo synagogue and is said to bear early nineteenth-century Turkish marks[1]. If that is true, then the box exhibited here is a late example of a form in use throughout the nineteenth century.

1. Barnett, no. 578.

V. B. M.

211. Eternal Light

Turkey, 1917
Silver, cast, stamped, engraved, and gilt
26-5/8 × 6-3/4 in. dm., 67.6 × 17.1 cm.
The Israel Museum, Jerusalem, 120/25

The lamp is suspended by three chains from a small canopy with suspension ring. Its body is of baluster form and is undecorated, except for a single gadrooned molding, a row of palmettes along the upper edge, and three symmetrical floral motifs applied between the scrolls by which the chains are attached. A boss and a stylized flower are affixed to the base. Below the gadrooned molding is an engraved inscription:

ה"ק[דש] לק"ק פורטוגאל יב"ץ לע"ן מ'
חנולה בת פירלה ובנו [?] יוסף קארירון בן
חנולה מ'ם' 20 שבט 5677

De[dicated] to the h[oly] c[ongregation] Portugal . . . Hannulah, daughter of Firlah and her son Joseph Cairiroun son of Hannulah 20 Shevat 5677 (February 12, 1917).

Similar applied silver ornaments also appear on Turkish domestic silver.[1]

1. See E. Juhasz, "The Custom of Serving Sweets Among the Jews of Izmir," *Israel Museum News*, XV (1979), p. 72, fig. 1; p. 77, fig. 11.

V. B. M.

210

Bibliography of Frequently Cited Sources

Adler and Casanowicz, 1901
Adler, C., and Casanowicz, I. M., *Descriptive Catalogue of a Collection of Objects of Jewish Ceremonial Deposited in the U.S. National Museum by Hadji Ephraim Benguiat* (Washington, D.C.: 1901).

Adler and Casanowicz, 1908
Adler, C., and Casanowicz, I. M., *The Collection of Jewish Ceremonial Objects in the United States National Museum* (Washington, D.C.: 1908).

Andrews, *Nazarenes*
Andrews, K., *The Nazarenes: A Brotherhood of German Painters in Rome* (Oxford: 1964).

Anglo-Jewish Historical Exhibition
Jacobs, J., and Wolf, L., *Catalogue of the Anglo-Jewish Historical Exhibition, Royal Albert Hall, London, 1887* (London: 1888).

Barnett
Barnett, R. D., ed., *Catalogue of the Permanent and Loan Collection of the Jewish Museum London* (London: 1974).

Beauty in Holiness
Gutmann, J., ed., *Beauty in Holiness: Studies in Jewish Customs and Ceremonial Art* (New York: 1970).

Bialer, *Jewish Life*
Bialer, Y. L., and Fink, E., *Jewish Life in Art and Tradition: Based on the Collection of the Sir Isaac and Lady Edith Wolfson Museum, Hechal Shlomo, Jerusalem* (New York: 1976).

Bilder zur Frankfurter Geschichte
Kramer, W., ed., *Bilder zur Frankfurter Geschichte* (Frankfurt: 1950).

Casanowicz, 1929
Casanowicz, I. M., *Collections of Objects of Religious Ceremonial in the United States National Museum* (Smithsonian Institution United States National Museum Bulletin, 148; Washington, D.C.: 1929).

Cohen, *Bulletin des Leo Baeck Instituts*
Cohen, E., "Moritz Daniel Oppenheim," *Bulletin des Leo Baeck Instituts*, 53–54 (1977–1978), pp. 42–74.

Cohen, *Israel Museum News*
Cohen, E., "Moritz Oppenheim 'The first Jewish Painter,' " *The Israel Museum News*, 14 (1978), pp. 86–93.

Coins Reveal
The Jewish Museum, New York, *Coins Reveal* (New York: in press).

Danzig, 1904
Katalog der alten jüdischen Kultusgegenstände Gieldzinski-Stiftung in der Neuen Synagoge zu Danzig (Danzig: 1904).

Danzig, 1933
Sammlung jüdischer Kunstgegenstände der Synagogen-Gemeinde zu Danzig (Danzig: 1933).

Danzig 1939
The Jewish Museum, New York, *Danzig 1939: Treasures of a Destroyed Community* (Detroit: 1980).

Dichtung und Wahrheit
Goethe, J. W. von, *Aus meinem Leben: Dichtung und Wahrheit (Goethes Werke)*, vol. 8 (Berlin and Weimar: 1966).

Dietz, *Stammbuch*
Dietz, A., *Stammbuch der Frankfurter Juden: Geschichtliche Mitteilungen über die frankfurter jüdischen Familien von 1349–1849* (Frankfurt: 1907).

Encyclopaedia Judaica
Encyclopaedia Judaica (16 vols.; Jerusalem: 1972).

Erinnerungen
Oppenheim, M. D., *Erinnerungen*, ed. by A. Oppenheim (Frankfurt: 1924).

Fabric of Jewish Life
The Jewish Museum, New York, *The Fabric of Jewish Life: Textiles from The Jewish Museum Collection* (New York: 1977).

Freimann and Kracauer
Freimann, A., and Kracauer, F., *Frankfort*, trans. by B. S. Levin (Philadelphia: 1929).

Galanté
Galanté, A., *Histoires des juifs d'Istanbul* (2 vols.; Istanbul: 1941).

Galanté, *Les synagogues d'Istanbul*
Galanté, A., *Les synagogues d'Istanbul* (Istanbul: 1937).

Geijer, *Oriental Textiles*
Geijer, A., *Oriental Textiles in Sweden* (Copenhagen: 1951).

Geschichte der Juden im Rheinland
Aus der Geschichte der Juden im Rheinland: Jüdische Kult- und Kunstdenkmäler (Rheinischer Verein für Denkmalpflege und Heimatschutz, I; Düsseldorf: 1931).

Gönül, *Turkish Embroideries*
Gönül, M., *Turkish Embroideries XVI–XIX Centuries* (Istanbul [?]: n.d.).

Hallo

Hallo, R., *Jüdische Kunst aus Hessen und Nassau* (Berlin: 1933).

Hallo, *Jüdische Kult- und Kunstdenkmäler*

Hallo, R., *Jüdische Kult- und Kunstdenkmäler im Hessischen Landes-Museum zu Kassel* (Kassel: n.d.).

Hammer-Schenk

Hammer-Schenk, H., *Synagogen in Deutschland: Geschichte einer Baugattung im 19. und 20. Jahrhundert (1780–1933)* (2 vols.; Hamburg: 1981).

Heilbrunn

Heilbrunn, R. M., "Leben und Werk des Malers Moritz Oppeheim," *Bulletin des Leo Baeck Instituts,* 33–36 (1966), pp. 285–301.

Historical Museum Frankfurt, *Documentation Guide*

Historical Museum of the City of Frankfurt, *Historical Documentation Guide: A Guide to the Permanent Exhibition of Frankfurt's History from the 9th Century Up Until the End of World War I* (Frankfurt: 1979).

Hoelterhoff

Hoelterhoff, M., *A Monograph on the Works and Life of Moritz Oppenheim (1800–1882)* (Washington, D.C.: 1974).

Jewish Encyclopedia

The Jewish Encyclopedia (12 vols.; New York: 1901).

Jewish Museum, *Oppenheim*

The Jewish Museum, New York, *The Paintings of Moritz Oppenheim: Jewish Life in 19th Century Germany,* exhibition brochure (New York: 1981–82).

Juhasz

Juhasz, E. S., *Golden Textiles in Their Use by Jews in Sephardi Communities in the Ottoman Empire* (in Hebrew; unpublished masters thesis).

Kayser-Schoenberger

Kayser, S., and Schoenberger, G., *Jewish Ceremonial Art* (2nd ed.; Philadelphia: 1959).

Mitteilungen

Mitteilungen der Gesellschaft zur Erforschung jüdischer Kunstdenkmäler zu Frankfurt a. M. (8 vols. in 7; Frankfurt: 1900–1915).

Monumenta Judaica

Kölnisches Stadtmuseum, *Monumenta Judaica: 2000 Jahre Geschichte und Kultur der Juden am Rhein* (Cologne: 1963).

Moses

Moses, E., "Jüdische Kult- und Kunstdenkmäler in den Rheinlanden," in *Aus der Geschichte der Juden im Rheinland: Jüdische Kult- und Kunstdenkmäler* (Düsseldorf: 1931).

Narkiss

Narkiss, M., *The Hanukkah Lamp* (in Hebrew; Jerusalem: 1939).

Notizblatt

Notizblatt der Gesellschaft zur Erforschung jüdischer Kunstdenkmäler (34 nos.; Frankfurt: 1902–1937).

Pollack, *Jewish Folkways*

Pollack, H., *Jewish Folkways in Germanic Lands (1648–1806): Studies in Aspects of Daily Life* (Cambridge, Mass.: 1971).

R

Rosenberg, M., *Der Goldschmiede Merkzeichen* (3rd ed.; 4 vols.; Frankfurt: 1922–1925, Berlin: 1928).

Roth, *Jewish Art*

Roth, C., ed., *Jewish Art—An Illustrated History* (rev. ed.; Greenwich: 1971).

Rubens, *Iconography,* 1981

Rubens, A., *A Jewish Iconography* (rev. ed.; London: 1981).

Rubens, *Jewish Costume*

Rubens, A., *A History of Jewish Costume* (rev. ed.; New York: 1973).

Scheffler

Scheffler, W., *Goldschmiede Hessens: Daten, Werke, Zeichen* (Berlin: 1976).

Scheffler, *Berlin*

Scheffler, W., *Berliner Goldschmiede: Daten, Werke, Zeichen* (Berlin: 1968).

Scheffler, *Niedersachsen*

Scheffler, W., *Goldschmiede Niedersachsens: Daten, Werke, Zeichen* (2 vols.; Berlin: 1965).

Schudt

Schudt, J. J., *Jüdische Merkwürdigkeiten* (4 vols.; Frankfurt and Leipzig: 1714–1718).

Shachar, *Jewish Tradition in Art*

Shachar, I., *Jewish Tradition in Art: The Feuchtwanger Collection of Judaica,* trans. by R. Grafman (Jerusalem: 1981).

Shachar, *Jewish Year*

Shachar, I., *The Jewish Year* (Leiden: 1975).

Synagoga

Historisches Museum Frankfurt am Main, *Synagoga, Jüdische Altertümer, Handschriften und Kultgeräte* (Frankfurt: 1961).

Towers of Spice

The Israel Museum, *Towers of Spice: The Tower-Shape Tradition in Havdalah Spice Boxes* (Jerusalem: 1982).

Weizsäcker-Dessoff

Weizsäcker, H., and Dessoff, A., *Kunst und Künstler in Frankfurt am Main im neunzehnten Jahrhundert* (2 vols.; Frankfurt: 1907–1909).

Werner

Werner, A., "Oppenheim: A Rediscovery," *Midstream,* June–July 1974, pp. 46–57.